S0-DLS-753

LIVES and LEGENDS of SAINT BRENDAN the VOYAGER.

LIVES and LEGENDS of SAINT BRENDAN the VOYAGER.

DENIS O'DONOGHUE

ON BACK OF WHALE.

First published at Dublin, 1893.
Facsimile reprint 1994 by
LLANERCH PUBLISHERS, Felinfach.

ISBN 1 897853 35 1.

PREFACE.

I HAVE compiled this volume of *Brendaniana*, or a miscellaneous collection of "matters and things" relating to St. Brendan, the patron of the dioceses of Clonfert and Ardfert, as well as of my church and parish of Ardfert-Brendan, from various sources. I have drawn largely upon the texts edited some years ago by Cardinal Moran and published in his *Acta Sti. Brendani*, the most valuable and the most accessible repertory we have of "matters Brendanian"—of the most important documents, bearing on the history of St. Brendan, whether in its authentic or in its legendary phases, and I have translated those texts from their mediæval Latin, as literally as I could, not always an easy task, into fairly readable English. I have put into a modern English dress, and prepared to present in a complete and separate form, before readers of English, the famous *Navigatio*, the Latin version of the voyage of St. Brendan, which is known as the Brendan Legend *par excellence*—the most widely popular "Tale of the Sea" in the middle ages, which had passed, in various shapes and versions, into almost every language and dialect of mediæval Europe. What had afforded entertainment, and edification also, to so many in those past ages, may surely be read nowadays with some interest, and perhaps instruction. To this primary legend of the saint I have added some minor ones from the luxuriant growth of legend that had clustered around his name from generation to generation in many countries of

Europe, and, as occasion served, I have suggested the plain and simple facts that may have been the germs of the extravagant growth of many of those fanciful legends.

The most important document I have translated from the *Acta Sti. Brendani* is, undoubtedly, the tract known as the *Vita Sti. Brendani*, or Latin Life of the saint, which records many interesting facts of his authentic history, after his famous voyages, as well as of the histories of many of his contemporary Irish saints, that cannot now be found elsewhere; and I have endeavoured to supplement the record of those facts by inserting whatever additional notices of the saint I could glean from other sources. Instead of the early chapters of this Latin Life, I have given the portion of the Irish Life from the *Book of Lismore*, from which those chapters had been evidently borrowed; and as I have accompanied this Irish text—a genuine specimen of ancient Gaelic—with a literal English translation, it will, I trust, prove interesting and useful to those readers, who, though not Gaelic scholars, may desire to form some acquaintance with the venerable language of the Gaodhal.

In this portion of the Irish Life of St. Brendan, and in the copious notes which I have appended to it, will be found some accounts of the topography and of the earliest ecclesiastical history of ancient Kerry, that ought to interest in a special manner my Kerry readers. In other parts of the volume also I have noticed some old associations and early traditions connected with St. Brendan, of which I could find any traces in Kerry; but which are, alas! very few and faint, and fast disappearing from amongst us. The historical sketch of the rise and ruin of the holy places of Ardfert-Brendan, which I have prefixed to the volume, will, I hope, be interesting to others besides local readers.

Those who may expect to find in those pages a complete

history of St. Brendan, and a finished portraiture of his holy life and character, will, I fear, be much disappointed. The materials for a history of the saint that have come down to us through the waste and wreck of ages are mere fragments, the *disjecta membra* of a great personality, often disguised or distorted by a parasitical growth of extravagant legend, which twined round the name and fame of St. Brendan in singular luxuriance. Those sparse fragments I have endeavoured to bind together, and to mould, as best I could, into life-like form; but I know well that my best efforts could only result in a poor and incomplete counterfeit of the grand original. I have made no attempt to pourtray the virtues of his holy life, and on that head I will only borrow the words of an ancient panegyrist of the saint, from a "Fragment" preserved in the *Codex Salmanticensis:* "Who can describe the virtues of St. Brendan—his humility and meekness; his charity and tender compassion; his patience and gentleness; his fasting and abstinence; his constant assiduity in prayer? Because he had perfectly fulfilled all the Commandments of Christ, and had faithfully practised all those virtues and many others of a like nature, the Blessed Brendan, in a good old age, among choirs of angels, with great joy and triumph, amid gleaming lights and choral psalmody, departed unto the Lord, to whom be all honour and glory for ever and ever! Amen."

DENIS O'DONOGHUE, P.P.

ST. BRENDAN'S, ARDFERT,
Feast of St. Brendan, 1893.

PREFACE TO THE SECOND EDITION.

IN publishing a Second Edition of my Book on St. Brendan, I wish to express my grateful appreciation of the very kindly and favourable manner in which the First Edition was received, as far as I have observed, by its readers, and of the many notices of it that have appeared in the Press, both in Ireland and America, which were uniformly kind and encouraging. Indeed, with respect to the criticism of my little volume, I may well say :—*Funes ceciderunt mihi in praeclaris*.—"The lines have fallen unto me in goodly places."

I beg to thank Mr. W. A. Cadbury, of Birmingham for copies of two ancient Maps he kindly sent to me, which show the Isle of St. Brendan and the Isle of Hy-Brazil, in the Western Ocean. I have had copies made on a reduced scale of one of these Maps, which was drawn in A.D. 1581, by the famous geographer, Abraham Ortelius, of Antwerp, and they will be found at page 304, where they may serve to illustrate the interesting Legends of the Isle of St. Brendan and of Hy-Brazil, which precede that page.

DENIS O'DONOGHUE, P.P., M.R.I.A.

ST. BRENDAN'S, ARDFERT,
May, 1895.

Since the publication of this volume the author has received, among many other complimentary letters and favourable notices of the Press, the following very kind and highly-valued letters :—

ARCHBISHOP'S HOUSE,
DUBLIN, *August*, 1893.

VERY REV. DEAR SIR,

I beg to return thanks for the copy of *Brendaniana*, which you have been pleased to forward. I have already read a considerable portion of your notes and illustrations, and I congratulate you most sincerely on the light which you have thrown on the life of your great patron, St. Brendan. It would be a great blessing for the Church of Ireland if a similar light were thrown on the life of each one of our Diocesan Patrons.

Now that you have completed this work, perhaps you would sketch the lives of St. Brendan's successors in the See of Kerry. As far as I have been able to judge, some of those lives would form a very interesting page of our ecclesiastical history.

Believe me to remain,

Very faithfully yours,

✠ PATRICK F. CARDINAL MORAN.

REV. D. O'DONOGHUE, P.P.,
St. Brendan's, Ardfert.

TRINITY COLLEGE,
DUBLIN, *9th August*, 1893.

DEAR FATHER O'DONOGHUE,

I received your *Brendaniana*, and read it with much interest, and I congratulate you on your publication.

It is clear to me from the "Icebergs," that St. Brendan had landed in America, for the icebergs hug the Labrador, Newfoundland, and the Canadian coasts, keeping near the shore by the rotation of the earth. I venture to think that the "great river E. and W." is the St. Lawrence and not the Ohio.

The story of Judas Iscariot, in the Old English Version, is very powerful.

Yours sincerely,

SAMUEL HAUGHTON.

REV. DENIS O'DONOGHUE, P.P.

CONTENTS.

THE IRISH LIFE OF ST. BRENDAN.

INTRODUCTION.

IN the following pages are given the text and translation, with some notes, of what may be called the biographical portion of the *Betha Brenainn* (Irish Life of Brendan) from the *Book of Lismore*, a MS. containing lives of some of the early Irish saints and many other ancient documents, written, as O'Curry tells us, "in Gaelic of great purity and antiquity." It is now the property of the Duke of Devonshire, and is kept in Lismore Castle, Co. Waterford, where it was discovered in 1814, by some workmen in a walled-up door or passage, concealed in a wooden box, along with a beautifully worked ancient crozier; hence its name, *Book of Lismore*. But it ought to be called rather the *Book of MacCarthy Reagh*, for it is now ascertained that it was compiled, in the latter half of the fifteenth century, from the lost *Book of Monasterboice* and from other ancient MSS. for Finghin MacCarthy Riabhach, and his wife Catharine, daughter of Thomas, eighth Earl of Desmond. It is also known that it had been seen and examined by Michael O'Clery, one of the Four Masters, in Timoleague Abbey, Co. Cork, on the 20th June, 1629. Thence it was carried to Lismore Castle, probably by one of the Franciscan friars of Timoleague Abbey, who sought refuge there when his convent was despoiled, and deposited for greater security with the ancient crozier of the Bishop of Lismore, and other precious relics, in that stronghold. This castle sustained several sieges during the wars of the Catholic Confederation, after 1641; and it was, very probably, during one of those sieges that the box containing the Book and the crozier was built into a doorway for concealment from the besieging enemies.

Soon after its discovery, in 1814, the Book was lent, as O'Curry informs us in his *Lectures on the MS. Materials*, to an Irish scribe in Cork, where it was sadly mutilated, and many of the "staves" purloined—about one-third of the whole, O'Curry believed. Among the parts thus removed was the "Betha Brenainn;" and it was many years afterwards when the stolen portions were traced, principally through the exertions of O'Curry himself, and copies of them made by him were added to the copies he had already most carefully made of the other portions for the Royal Irish Academy, that this "Betha Brenainn" was restored to its proper place in O'Curry's fine copies of the "Book" as we have them at present.

The Irish text I have printed from a copy of O'Curry's transcript in the Royal Irish Academy, made made many years ago by the late Mr. W. M. Hennessy, which he kindly lent to me for this purpose. I give the text, with his reading of the contractions, which I find to be almost identical with that lately published by Dr. Whitley Stokes, in his *Lives of Saints from the Book of Lismore*, in *Anecdota Oxoniensia.*

I had made the translation as literally as I could before I saw Dr. Stokes' publication; but when I read the work, I found his rendering of some passages that puzzled me more satisfactory than my own, and I took the liberty of adopting it—a liberty which I hope he will graciously pardon. I have also taken into my text some additions from the Paris and Egerton MS. copies of this *Betha Brenainn*, which Dr. Stokes had adopted and placed within brackets in his edition, and which I mark off in my text in a like manner.

The notes I append, in illustration of some historical and topographical references in the text, will, I trust, be found useful and interesting to those who may desire to know something about the places and persons that were associated in some way with the history of St. Brendan in his native Kerry.

The portion of the *Betha* that I print and translate forms about one-half of the whole text, as it is found in the *Book of Lismore*, or in any other copy that has been yet discovered. This gives, in a simple and archaic style, the outline of the life of Brendan up to and including his setting sail on his famous voyages in quest of the "Land of Promise of the Saints;" the remainder of the text consists almost entirely of the Irish version of those voyages in a fragmentary and imperfect form, but which is very interesting and valuable, as containing the earliest germs, the protoplasm, so to speak, of the later and more finished Latin versions of the Brendan legend. I will give a summary of this Irish version as an introduction to my translation of the most perfect and accurate text of the Latin version, namely, *The Navigatio Brendani*, edited some years ago by Cardinal Moran in his *Acta Sti. Brendani*.

BETHA BRENAIN, MAIC FHINNLOGHA.

"Beatus vir qui timet Dominum, in mandatis ejus volet nimis." (Ps. cxi. v. 1.)

Is fechtnach 7 as firen foirbhthe in fer forsa mbi ecla 7 imuaman an Coimded cumachtaigh 7 accobhras codermhair timna 7 forceatal De do comallad, amail, luaitter i canoin petarlaice 7 nuthiadnissi in t-aithiuscso.

Sochaidhi tra do uasalaithribh 7 d'faidibh 7 d'apstalaib 7 do deisciplaib in Choimdhedh, frisi ndebhradh i petarlaic 7 i nuithiadnissi in t-aitheasc-sa .i. a bheith fechtnach firen forbhthe forasta ar accobar 7 ar ailgius leo na timna 7 in forcetuil diadha do comhallad, 7 ar imecla in Coimdedh cofoirbhthe 'na cridibh 7 na menmannaibh cen scrutain aili acht mad sin (namá).

A oen iarum don luct-sin in nuifhiadnissi inti'dia ata lith 7 foraithmet ind ecmong na ree-sea 7 na haimsiri .i. hi xvii. kl. Iuin. .i. Brenain mac Finnlogha do shlict Ceir meic Fherghusa. Ceann creitme 7 crabhaidh ermhoir in domuin uili inti noem-Brenainn; .i. amail Abraham n'irisech. Sailmchetlaid primhfhathacdai amail Daibith mac Iese. Ecnaid derrscaightech amail Sholmain mac n Daibid. Rechtaidhi amail

LIFE OF BRENDAN, SON OF FINNLUG.

"Blessed is the man who feareth the Lord; he shall delight exceedingly in His commandments" (Ps. cxi. vs. 1.)

Blessed and righteous and perfect is the man who hath (*lit.*, "upon whom there are") the fear and awe of the Lord Almighty, and who desireth exceedingly to fulfil the commands and teachings of God, as is stated in the Canon of the Old and New Testament, by this declaration.

Multitudes there were of patriarchs and prophets and apostles and disciples of the Lord in the Old and New Testaments, to give testimony to this truth, who were truly blessed, faithful, perfect, and persevering in their desire and ardent longing to fulfil the Divine commands and teachings, and in the holy fear of the Lord, perfectly in their hearts and minds, without consideration of aught else save this alone.

One of that class under the New Testament was he whose festival and commemoration occurs at this time and season, the 17th of Calends of June (May 16th), namely, (1)* Brendan, son of Finnlug, of the race of Ciar, son of Fergus. A chief leader in faith and piety throughout most of the world was this holy Brendan; just was he, like unto Abraham; a prophetic psalmist, like unto David, the son of Jesse; an eminent sage,

* These numbers refer to the Notes appended to this Life.

Mhoysi Mac Amhra. Tintodhach tidhnactech amail Cirine faidh. Intliuchtach amhra amail Aguistin. Morleighnidh primhcoitcheann amail Origin. Ogh amail Eoin bruinnedalta in Coimdhed. Soiscelaigthe amail Matha. Foircetlaid amail Pol. [Primapstal dilguda amail Petar n-ardespal. Cend] ditreabhuch amail Eoin baitsi. Trachtaire amail Grigoir Roma. Techtaire treabaireac mara 7 tire amail Noei mac Laimech. Uair amail rothocaibh Noei in n-airc uas tonnghor na dilenn ind airdi, as amail sin toicebus Brenainn a mhanca 7 a mhuintera a n-airdi uas teinid bhratha, cuna riadé na ceo na crithir iat tre cumhachtaibh 7 caencrabud Brenainn meic Finnlogha.

A n-aimsir immorro Ængusa meic Nat-fraeich righ Muman, is ann rogenair inti noem-Brenain. Do Chiarraigi Luacra dho, .i. do Alltraigi Caille do shainred. Bá fer saer socheneoil craibhdech irisech a athair in meic-sin, .i. Finnlogh. Is amhlaid batur in lanamhain sin, i smact 7 i coibligi dlighthigh fo riagail Espuic Eirc. Atconnaic mathair Brenainn aislingi resiu rogenair Brenainn .i. lan a hochta dh'or glan do bheith aice 7 a ciche do taitnemh amail t-snechta. Iar n-indisi na haislingi d'espoc Eirc adubairt gu n-geinfeth uaithi gein chumhachtach bhudh lán do rath in Spirta Noibh .i. Brenainn.

Arailli fer Saidhbhir bai i n-aitreibh cofada o taigh Finnlogha, Airdi mac Fidhaig a ainm. Tainic primhfhaidh na h-Eirenn intansin co techAirrdhe meic Fidhaig like unto Solomon, son of David; a law giver, like unto Moyses, son of Amram; an inspired interpreter, like unto Saint Jerome; of surpassing intellect, like unto Augustine; of excellent general scholarship, like unto Origen; a virgin was he, like unto John, the bosom foster-child of the Lord; an evangelist, like Mathew; a preacher, like unto Paul; a chief missioner of forgiveness, like unto Peter, prince of the apostles; chief of hermits, like unto John of the Baptism; a commentator, like Gregory of Rome; a prudent guide over land and sea, like Noah, son of Lamech. And as Noah raised aloft his ark over the swelling waves of the Deluge, so will Brendan raise up his monks and his people above the fires of the Judgment, so that, through the power and true piety of Brendan, son of Finlugh, neither smoke, nor mists, nor sparks should touch them.

It was in the time of Ænguis, (2) son of Nathfraech, King of Munster, that this great St. Brendan was born; of Kerry-Luachra was he, within the district of Alltraighe-Cuile. His father, Finnlugh was a freeman, of noble birth, devout and righteous, who, with his lawful wife, lived in obedience and religious discipline under the rule of Bishop Erc. The mother of Brendan, (3) before he was born, saw in a vision, her bosom-full of pure gold, and her breasts glistening like the snow. When she told her vision to (4) Bishop Erc, he said: "There shall be born of thee a child of power, who will be full of the grace of the Holy Ghost," that is, Brendan.

There dwelt at some distance from the house of Finnlugh, a certain rich man, whose name was (5) Airde, son of Fidach. At this time there came to

.i. Beg Mac De. Rofiafraigh Airrdhe do Bec: "Cid ni is nesa dún innosa"? Adubhairt Bec: "Geinfidh do ri dilis dingbhála fein eadrat 7 muir inocht, 7 bidh sochaidhi do righaibh 7 do ruirechaibh aidheorus he, 7 berus leis docum nime." Isin adhaigh-sin gene Brenainn rucsat tricha bo tricha laegh ag Airrdhe Mac Fidhaig. Iarsin roeirig [comoch ar na barach] Airdhi, 7 boi oc iarrad in toighi a rucad in mac beag, 7 fuair tech Finnlogha, 7 in naidheu ann, 7 roshlecht coduthrachtach 'na fhiadhnusi, 7 ros-edbair in tricha loilgech cona læghaibh dhó, 7 ba si sin cedalmsa Brenainn. Rogabh iarsin an brugaid in mac ana laim, 7 adubairt: "Bidh dalta damsa in macso tre bithu na bethad," ol se.

A n-adaig immorro ghene Brenainn adconnaic espoc Eirc Alltraigi-cailli fo ænlasair dermhair amail na aices riamh roime, 7 timtirecht examuil na n-aingiul i n-edaighibh glegheala imon tir immacuairt. Eirghius espoc Eirc gu moch aramharach, 7 tainic gu tech Finnlogha, 7 roghabh in mac ina laim 7 adubairt fris: "A dhuine Dhé .i. duine fhoigenus do Dhia, gabh misi cucat amail mhanach ndilius; et cidh sochaidi is forbhfhælid friat ghein as forbhfailid mu cridi-si 7 mh'ainim," ol espoc Eirc. Iarsin roshlecht 'na fhiadhnusi 7 rochi codermhair i comurtha fhaeilti, 7 ron-baist iarsin 7 his mansion a chief prophet of Erin, whose name was (6) Becc MacDé; Airde inquired of Becc, "What unknown event was soon to happen there;" and Becc answered: "There will be born this night, between you and the sea, your true and worthy king, whom many kings and princes will devoutly honour, whom he will bear with him to heaven." On this night of Brendan's birth, thirty cows belonging to Airde MacFidaigh gave birth to thirty heifer calves. Next day Airde rose early, and went in quest of the house where the child was born, and found the dwelling of Finnlugh, and the young babe there; he eagerly knelt before the child, and presented to him the thirty newly-calved cows with their thirty calves. This was the first alms-offering made to Brendan. Then this great land-holder took the child in his arms, and said: "Let this child be my foster-son henceforth and for ever."

Now on the night that Brendan was born, Bishop Erc saw Alltraighe-Cuile in an extraordinary blaze of light, such as he never saw before, and various ministering of angels in snow-white robes through the district all around. In the morning he rose early, and proceeded to the house of Finnlugh; taking the child in his arms, he addressed him thus: "Oh, man of God" (that is, man who will serve God), "receive me as thy faithful votary, and many will greatly rejoice at thy birth, as my heart and soul now greatly rejoice thereat;" thus spoke Bishop Erc. Then he prostrated himself in his presence, and wept copiously through joy; he soon after baptized him, and the name, Mobhi, was given tugad Mobhi fair mar ainm artus oa thustidhibh, [ut dixit poeta :—

Mobhi a ainm-sium artus
Othustidhib, caomh a rus ;
Macaom sluaghach, sirtech, seng,
Ba cobair d'feraib Erenn.]

Iarsin rofherastar broen find .i. ciabhor fhinn, cu rolin in fhianann uili. As de sin Broenfinn a ainm sium. Finn immorro doradh fris, ar ba find o churp 7 o anmain, [ut dixit :—

Braonfind a ainm-sium iarsin
O curp ocus o anmain
On braon sin fuair slain
O epscop Eirc a aon rain.]

Is ann sin roscennset tri muilt corcra asin topur fiac baistigi Brenainn [ut :—

Tri muilt corcra, suairc in tred,
Fiacha baistigh Brenainn beg,
Rosgeinset, ba caom an cor
Asin topur an aonor.]

Rucsat a mhuinter leo he cu mboi bliadhan occa iarsin [ica altrum. I cind bliadne iarsin] ruc espoc Eirc lais he aramus a mhuime fein, .i. Ita, 7 bai coic bliadne oc Itta, 7 tuc in chaillech gradh ndermair do, áir itceth timterecht na n-aingel huasa 7 rath in Spirtu Noib fair cofollus, 7 do bhith Brenainn oc sirghaire frisin caillig cech tan atcidh hi. Araili la rofhiarfaig Ita dhe : "Cidh dogni faeilti dhuit, a næidhi noebh?" ol si. "Tusa," ol se, "atcim oc labra frim choidhchi 7 ogha to him at first from his parents' wish, as the poet said:—

> Mobhi his name at first
> Given by his parents; fair his face,
> A youth hostful, searchfull, lithe,
> He was a help to the men of Erin.

Afterwards a white drop (*broen finn*), that is, a white mist, fell there, which spread over all Fenit (7). Hence his name Broenfinn, *find*, "white," was truly said of him, for white he was in body and soul, as the poet said:—

> *Broenfind* his name after that,
> In body and in soul,
> From that mist he found the whole;
> From Bishop Erc one part of it.

It was then that there leaped forth out of the (8) fountain (of his baptism) three purple or dark-red wethers, the fee for Brendan's baptism as was said:—

> Three purple wethers, pleasant the flock;
> Baptismal fees for young Brendan;
> Sprang—a handsome treat,
> Out of the well alone.

His family then took him with them, that he may remain at nurse for one year; after which Bishop Erc took him away to his foster-mother (9), St. Ita, and he remained five years with Ita; and the nun gave him exceeding love, for she saw the ministering of the angels about him, and the grace of the Holy Ghost manifestly upon him, and Brendan was always joyfully crying aloud to the nun whenever he saw her. One day Ita asked him: "What is it that causes thee so much joy, my holy child?" said she. "Thou," said he, "whom I see speaking to me continually, and many virgins imdha [diairmithi] ele amail tusa, 7 siat acum comhaltram as cech laimh diachéle." Aingil immorro batar ann sin i ndealbhuibh na n-ogh :—

> [Aingil i ndealbhaibh ogh find
> Badar ic altram Brenainn,
> As cech laim inacheile
> Don naoidhin cin mormheile.]

Iarsin rolegh oc espoc Eirc a Shalma cogressach [i cinn. u. mbliadne], 7 ba fada la Ita beith 'na ecmais. Ni rabha immorro bó blicht oc espuc Eirc, air'ni gabhudh almsana acht becan o dhainibh riaghalda. Roboisiumh tra i n-araile la oc iarrad bainne for a aidi. "Is tualaing Dia ón, a mhic," ar espoc Eirc. Is iarsin ticedh ind agh allaid cech lai do Shleibh Luachra cona lægh le, co mblighthe dosum hi, 7 teighedh ahoenar isin sliab iarna bleagain.

Is annsin boi Brig inna farrad-sum .i. derbhshiur dho, 7 ba dermhair méd a grada lais, ar ba follus do timtirecht na n-aingel fuirre, 7 rofhegadh gnuis a aidi amail ruithen n-grene samhrata.

Araili la dochuaidh espoc Eirc do proicept. Luidseom lais isin carput, 7 ba hæsach deich mbliadne Brenainn intansin. Facabar-somh a ænar isin charputiar ndul don clerech don proicept. Suidhius Brenainn isin carput 7 se oc gabail a shalm a ænar. Is ann sin doriacht ingen min macachta mongbhuidhe, do cenel rigda, gusan carput cuici-siumh, 7 sillis fair, 7 feghaidh a ghnúis aluin edrocht, 7 fuabrais leim chuice isin carpat fochedoir 7 a cluiche do denamh ris. Is ann aspertsom fria : "Imthigh dod tigh 7 beir mhiscaidh cidh (without number) like you, and they are fondly nursing me from one to another;" angels were there in the guise of the virgins :—

> Angels in the guise of fair virgins,
> Were fostering Brendan,
> From one hand to another
> Without much hurt to the babe.

Afterwards, for five years, he read the psalms constantly under Bishop Erc, and Ita grieved much at his absence. Now, Bishop Erc had not a milch-cow, for he received but moderate alms-offerings from the faithful. On a certain day, therefore, he wanted milk for his foster-child, and he said: "God is able to provide it, my son." After this a (10) wild cow came every day with its calf from Slieve-luachra, to be milked for him, and returned alone to the mountains, after being milked.

At this time there lived with him Brig (11), who was an own sister of his, and great was his affection for her, for the service of the angels about her was visible to him, and he saw the countenance of his foster-father shining with the radiance of a summer sun.

One day Bishop Erc proceeded on a mission of preaching the Word of God, taking Brendan with him in the carriage, who was then ten years of age. While the clergy were engaged at their preaching, Brendan was left alone in the carriage, where he sat reading the psalms. Then a young maiden, gentle, modest, flaxen-haired, of a princely family, drew nigh to the carriage close to him, and she looked at him, and saw his face so beautiful and bright; all at once she makes a sportive bound into the carriage, in order to play her game with dod-fucc ille," 7 geibhidh-sium ialla in carpait, 7 gabhuidh fora sraeighled cucruaidh cu raibhi ic cai 7 occ diucairi, cu riacht gu hairm a raibe a mathair 7 a h'athair, .i. in ri 7 in rigon. Impoidius iarsin espoc Eirc, 7 gabuidh ica cairiughudh-sum cugér im bualad na noighi neimelnidhi. "Dogen-sa aitrighi inn," ar Brenainn, "7 abair-si hi." "Tair isin uamaidh-sea co maduin," ar espoc Eirc, " 7 bi at ænar innti cu torussa cugut imarach." Suidhis Brenainn isin uamaidh iarum, 7 gabhais a shalma 7 a immna molta don Coimdhid innti. Oirisidh espoc Eirc i bhfarrad na huamadh ic eistecht ra Brenainn cen fhis dó. Atclos tra foghur gotha Brenainn ag gabáil a shalm mile ceimeann for cech leth. Do cluinti foghur gotha Coluim-cille in comhfhad cetna intan robhith ic cantain a shalm 7 a immunn :—

[Foghar gotha Brenainn bhinn
Isin uama 'con fhiannaind
Mile ceimend in cech dinn
Atcluintea a ardguth alainn.]

Is ann sin adconnuic in clerech buidhne aingel suas cu nemh 7 anuas co talmain immon uamhaid co maduin. Osin imach immorro nir'chumhaing nech gnuis Brenainn d'faiscin ar imad na ruithned ndiadha, act Finan Cam a ænar, air ba lán do rath in Spirta Noib eisidhe.

Araile la batar oc imthecht foran sligid .i. Brenainn 7 espoc Eirc. Do rala oenóclach ina cuidechta him. Then he said to her: (12) "Go away home, and have ill will (or blame) to whoever left you here," and he seizes the reins of the carriage, and gives her with them a severe flogging, until she was crying and bawling, and ran away to the place where the king and queen, her parents, were biding. Soon after Bishop Erc returned, and gave him a severe rebuke for beating the guileless maiden. "I will do penance for it," said Brendan, "and do you pronounce what it shall be." "Go into that (13) cave there until morning," said Bishop Erc, "and remain there alone until I visit you to-morrow." Then Brendan sat down in the cave, and therein he began his psalms and his hymns of praise to the Lord. Bishop Erc watched beside the cave, listening to Brendan, without his knowing it. Now, the sound of Brendan's voice, chanting the psalms, was heard a thousand paces on every side. The sound of the voice of Colombcille was heard to the same distance when he was chanting his psalms and hymns:

> The sound of the voice of melodious Brendan,
> In the cave near Fenit,
> A thousand paces on every height
> His high fine voice was heard.

It was then that the clergy saw troops of angels up to heaven and down to earth, around the cave until morning. Thenceforth no one could fixedly gaze upon Brendan's countenance, because of the abundance of its divine radiance, save only (14) Finan Cam, who was himself full of the grace of the Holy Ghost.

On a certain day, Brendan and Bishop Erc were on a journey, when a young man joined their company on foran sligid. Teacmhuidh didiu namhait batur aigi dhó .i. moirsheser laech, 7 gabhais ecla mhor in t'oclach, 7 adubairt: "Muirbhfit sud mhisi innosa." "Eirg becan ar scath in chairthi cloichi ucut," ar Brenainn, "7 sin ara scath tú." Doghnisium tra amlaid sin, 7 tocbhuidh Brenainn a lama fria Dia, 7 doghni ernaighthi, co rosoeirtea in t'-oclach i rict coirthi cloichi. Teacait iarum a namhait-sium cosin coirthi, 7 benuid a cenn de ina richt-som, 7 gonait in coirthi 'na thoebh, 7 faccbhait in cloch 'arna dicennad, 7 berait in cenn leo a rict cinn a namhat. Et maraidh beos in cloch sin isin luc cetna [amail aderid na h'eolaig]. Conudh ann sin doroine Brenainn cloich don duine 7 duine don cloich. "Denaidh aithrigi," ar espoc Eirc, "uair ceann na cloiche fil occuibh, 7 ro imthig bur namhat imshlan uaibh." Dogniat iarum aithrigi ndicra fo riaguil espuic Eirc osin immach.

Iar bfogluim immorro canone petarlaice 7 nuifiadnaisse do Brenainn, dob ail dó riagla noem n-Eirenn do scribadh 7 d'fogluim. Cedaighis tra espoc Eirc dosum dul d'fogluim na riagla-sin, ár rofhitir gurup o Dhia robui dosomh in comairli-sin. Et adubairt espoc Eirc fris: "Tar doridhisi cucamsa, 7 na riagla-sin leat, cu roghabha tú gradha uaimsi." Iar ndul dosom d'agalluim a muime .i. Ita, is ed adubuirt in cedna fris, .i. riagla næmh n-Eirenn d'fogluim, 7 adubhairt ris: 'Na dena foghluim ag mnaibh na oc óguibh, cu nach derntar h'egnach. Imthigh," ar si, "7 teicemhaid læch the way. There chanced to meet him some enemies he had, seven fighting men, and a great fear seized him, and he said: "These men will murder me now." "Go on a little," said Brendan, "in the shadow of that pillar-stone there, and lie down in its shadow." So he acted in this manner, and Brendan raises his hands to God, and prayed that the young man may be saved in the appearance of the pillar-stone. Then his enemies come to the pillar-stone, and they cut off its head in shape of his, and they wounded the pillar-stone in the side, and leave the stone beheaded, and carry the head with them in the shape of the head of their enemy. And still that (15 stone remains in the same place, as intelligent people tell us. Thus Brendan made there a stone of the man, and a man of the stone. "Do penance," said Bishop Erc to them, "for the head of the stone that you have, and that your enemy passed away from you safe and sound. They afterwards did condign penance under the guidance of Bishop Erc thenceforward.

After Brendan had learned the Canonical Scriptures of the Old Testament and the New, he desired to write down and to learn the rules of the Saints of Erin. Bishop Erc then granted permission that he should go to learn those rules, for he knew well that such counsel came to him from God. And Bishop Erc said to him: "Come back again to me when you have got those rules, in order that you may receive (16) Holy Orders from me." When Brendan went to take counsel with his foster-mother Ita, she said the same to him: "Learn the rules of the Saints of Erin;" and she said also: "Do suaichnidh sochenelach dhuit ar an sligid." Ecmaing, dano, ba hé Mac Lenin 'in læch-sin. Iar n-imthecht immorro do Brenainn dorala Mac Lenin dó. Is ann doraidh Brenainn fris: "Dena aithrigi, ar itá Dia ocut toghairm, 7 ba at macdilius dó o sunn amach." Is ann sin rosoei Colman Mac Lenin cusan Coimdhi, 7 cumhduighter eclas lais focedair: *ut dixit Colman*:—

Brenuinn breo betha buadhaig.
Beim in æl airimh ænuigh
Siar cu hairhbire in ænuigh
Thiro tairngire tæbhuigh.

. . . .

Iarsin rosiact Brenainn crich Connacht fo clu araill fir craibdhigh bai ann .i. Iarlaithe mac Logha, meic Trena, meic Feic, meic Macta, meic Bresail, meic Sirachta, meic Fiachach Finn. Et ros-foglaim-sium .i. Brenainn, na huili riagla naom Eirenncha' aicisein. Et asbert fria Iarlaithi: "Ni hann so bias h'eiseirgi etir," ar se. "A meic noeib," ar Iarlaithi, "cid uma bhfolcai forainn ratha diadhai in Spirta Noibh filet innat cofollus 7 cumachta diarmhidi in Choimdhed cumachtaigh fil guhincleithe it menmain neimellnidi? Tusa tra doriacht cucamsa do fhoghlaim occum" ol Iarlaithi. "Misi immorro bias ogutsa osunn amach, acht geibh misi it mhanchaine tria bithu na bethad. Act cena," ar Iarlaithi, "abuir frim c'ait i mbia mo eiseirghi?" Atbert Brenainn fris: "Dentur carput nua leat," ar se, "ár is senoir thu, 7 eirg inn foran sligid. Ocus cipe inadh i mebsat dá fhertais an carpait, is ann bias h'esseirghi 7 eiseirghe shochuidhi immaile frit." Iarsin tra teit in not take this learning from women or virgins, lest you give occasion for reproach." "Go," said she, "and there will meet you on the way a charming nobly-born soldier;" and it happened that Mac Lenin was that warrior. After Brendan had proceeded on his travels, Mac Lenin met him. Then said Brendan to him: "Do penance, for God is calling upon thee, and be unto Him a dutiful son henceforth." Then was (17) Colman Mac Lenin converted to the Lord, and there was built for him a church very soon afterwards, as Colman said:

(18) Brendan flame of the victorious life.

. . . .

Afterwards Brendan entered the country of Connaught, because of the fame of a certain devout man who dwelt there named (19) Iarlath, son of Lug, son of Tren, son of Fiach, son of Imcadha (or Mochta), son of Bresal, son of Siract, son of Fiacha-finn; and Brendan learned from him all the rules of the saints of Erin. Then said Brendan to Iarlath: "Not here will be the place of thy resurrection." "My holy son," said Iarlath, "why do you conceal from us the divine graces of the Holy Spirit that are manifestly in you, and the countless powers of the Lord Almighty that lie secretly in thy spotless soul? You now come to learn from me," said Iarlath, "but it is I that will be yours henceforward, only take me as thy faithful votary for evermore; but tell me now where will be the place of my resurrection." Then Brendan said to him: "Let a new carriage be made for you as you are a bishop (or a senior), and you will travel in it on your journey.

Seanoir isin carput, 7 ni cian rainic intan romebsat da fhertais in carpait; 7 as e ainm an inaidh-sin, Tuaim da Ghualann. Is ann sin doronsat a n-dis in laidh-sea eturra, ic feghudh na reilgi uathaibh, 7 timtirecht na n-aingel co-follus di; 7 asbert Brenainn na .u. cetrainn di 7 asbert Iarlaithi iarsin :—

BRENAINN.

I.

Ard reileac na n-aingel n-an
Atcim tar mo shuil
Ni tadhbhaister ithfern uar
Anas tardtar ana h'uir.

II.

Comad oin iar tairceall cros
Doro in fotan glas
Niba h'aitreabh dheaman ndur
Taithfentar dhun ass.

III

Bidh airdceall cun-imut cliar
I m-biat senadh mor
Bidh lighi tren acus truagh
Bidh sligi do shlog.

IV.

Diultfait do manaig do cill,
Bid beir tabair treall,
Olc in comba ros-bia inn
Tadhall ithfrinn tall.

V.

Ticfat do braithre biaidh uair
Doroichset do chein,
Bidh tusa bhus fuighleoir dhoibh
Do genat do reir.

And at whatsoever place the two shafts of the carriage will break, there will be your resurrection, and the resurrection of a multitude along with thee." Soon after the bishop travelled in the carriage, and he had not proceeded far when the two shafts thereof broke, and the name of that place is Tuaim-da-ghualann. Thereupon the twain composed this poem between them, as they looked towards the burial-place from some distance, while the ministering of the angels about it was quite visible to them; Brendan spoke the first five verses of it, and Iarlath spoke the rest:—(20)

BRENDAN.

I.

Noble churchyard with angels radiant,
Bright is its splendour before my eyes;
Hell's torments shall not be endured
By those who are interred in its clay.

II.

'Twas the archangel who marked it around with crosses,
And consecrated its green sod;
It is not the abode of the hideous demon
That shall be shown to us therein.

III.

It shall be a noble church, with numerous clergy,
There great synods will be held;
It will be a refuge for great and lowly,
There will be place for multitudes.

IV.

Should your faithful forsake your church,
Their time will be a time of tribulation;
Evil the ruin that comes therefrom here,
The dooming to hell beyond (hereafter).

V.

When in future time your brethren shall come
Summoned to the judgment-seat,
It is you that will be their advocate,
If they follow your guidance now.

IARLAITHI.

I.

In airet donet mu riar
Mairet in da clar
Cuirfit a naimdhi i cein,
Lasfait amail grein.

II

In airet donet mu reir
Budh fir dhamh an rann
Betit a maic taraneis,
Ni biat i pian tall.

III.

Mogenar thoghfas in clar
Ard na n-iubur n-ur,
Ni ba hitfernach iar mbrath
Neach rosia 'na huir.

IV.

Ni budh bairnech a mheic Dhuach
Rot-fia limsa a luach,
Neam ocus tuile cen tlath,
Mo chuile cen crich.

V.

Buaidh righ is cleirech dod shil
I cein bed dom reir;
Nocha cirrfa nech do giall
Cindfet tar gach reir.

Iar bfacbail Iarluithe annsin do Brenainn gabais roime foramus Mhuighi h'Ai. Dorala immorro aingel dó for an sligid, 7 is ed asbert fris: "Scribh," ar se, "briatra in crabhaid uaimsi." Scribhais Brenainn annsin oconn aingel ind uili riagail n-eclusdai noemhda, 7 maraid bheous in riagol sin. Intan immorro batar oc imthecht in muighi conaicet in fuat, 7 duini marbh fair, 7 a charait icá chainuidh. "Tairisnigid isin

IARLATH.

I.

As long as they live obedient to me,
And while the cross remains,
They will banish their enemies afar;
They will shine like the sun.

II.

As long as they live obedient to me—
I speak the truth, it is no falsehood—
Their sons shall survive them;
They will not suffer pain hereafter.

III.

Happy he who takes the cross
On the hill of evergreen yews.
He will not be hell-doomed after judgment,
Whosoever shall lie in its clay.

IV.

Be not angry, O MacDuach!
I will give you its full price:
Heaven and abundance without stint,
And my berth* without end.

V.

Kings and clerics of thy seed will triumph
As long as they are obedient to me,
No man shall claim their hostages:
They will overcome every assailant.

When Brendan had left Iarlath he proceeded on his way towards the plain of Ai. There met him on the road an angel, who thus addressed him: "Write down from me the rules of the religious life (lit., *the words of piety*)." Thereupon Brendan wrote down from the angel all the holy ecclesiastical rules, and this (21) rule is still extant. When they were travelling in this plain they see a bier, and the corpse of a man upon it,

* My "corner," or place in heaven.

Coimdhid," ol Brenainn, "ocus bidh beo in duine fil ocuibh." Iar ndenum ernaighthi co Dia do Brenainn eirghes in t-oclaech acedoir, 7 berait a muinter leo he co bhfaeilti ndermhair. Iarsin tra geibhidh cach ica fhegad-somh cumor, 7 berait leo hé cu righ in mhuighi. Et tairgidh in ri feraim dó in bhaile in budh ail do isin maigh-sin, 7 nir' ghabh uadha, ár nir'b ail leis beith isin magh-soin.

Iar scribeann tra riaghla ind aingil 7 riaghla noemh n-Eirenn cona mbeasaibh 7 cona crabud do Brenainn, impais co h'espoc Eirc 7 gabais gradha uaidh. Is ann atcualaidh-siumh isin tsoscéla : *Qui reliquit patrem aut matrem aut sororem aut agross, centuplum in procenti accipiet et vitam eternam possidebit.* Is iarsin tra rofhás gradh in Coimdhéd codermhair ina cridhi-siumh, 7 ba h'ail dó a thir 7 a talam 7 a thustidhi 7 a athardha dh'facbail, 7 rothothlaigh coduthrachtach ar an Coimdhid cu tarda thalmain nderrit ndiamhair n-inill n-aluind n-etarscartha dhó o dhainib. Iar codlad immorro dosum in adaigh-sin cu cuala guth in aingil do nimh 7 atbert fris : "Eirigh, a Brenainn," ar se, "7 dorad Dia duit inni rocuinghis .i. tir tairngire." Eirghis Brenainn iarum, 7 ba maith lais a menma on aitheasc-sin, 7 teit a aenar i Sliabh n-Daidche, 7 feghais ind aicen ndermair ndosholachta uadh for cech leth, 7 is ann sin atconnuic-sium an innsi n-aluind n-airegda co timtirecht na n-aingel di. Iarsin tra anaidh-siumh tredhenus annsin, 7 codlais doridhisi. Tic aingel in Coimdhéd dia acallaim annsin, 7 atbert fris : "Biatsa," and his friends lamenting him. "Put your trust in the Lord," said Brendan, "and the dead man you have will be restored to life." After Brendan had prayed to God, the young man arose at once to life, and his family take him away with exceeding joy. After this all the people begin to gaze upon him very much, and they take him before the king of the plain. And the king offered him land in whatever district he chose in the plain, but Brendan accepted it not, for he did not wish to abide there.

When Brendan had written down the rule of the angel, and the rules of the saints of Erin, with their customs and devotional practices, he returned to Bishop Erc, and received ordination from him. It was then he heard in the Gospel: "Everyone who hath left father, or mother, or sister, or lands, shall receive an hundred-fold in this present time, and shall possess life everlasting." (St. Matt. c. xix., v. 29.) Thenceforth the love of the Lord grew exceedingly in his heart, and he (22) desired to leave his country and land, and parents and family, and he earnestly besought the Lord to grant him some place, secret, retired, secure, delightful, far apart from men. While he slept that night he heard the voice of the angel from heaven, saying to him: "Arise, O Brendan, for God will grant to thee what thou hast prayed for—even the Land of Promise." Then Brendan arose, and much was his heart gladdened by these words, and he retired alone to (23) *Sliabh-Daidche* (Brandon-hill), whence he gazed upon the vast and gloomy ocean on every side, and then he had a vision of the beautiful noble island, with the ministering of angels ar se, " o sunn imach maroen friut tria bhithu na betha, 7 múinfetsa duit an innsi n-álainn atconnarcais 7 is mian leat d'faghbail." Ciis Brenainn annsin codermhair ara fdæiltighi leis aitheasc in aingil fris, 7 doghni atlaigthi buidi do Dia.

Eirghes iarsin Brenainn asin tsleibh, 7 tic co a muinter, 7 atbert friu: " Dentar tri longa mora libh," ar se, " 7 tri sretha do rámhadhuibh for cech luing, 7 tri seola do croicnibh, 7 tricha fer an cach luing, acht nír bhat cleirig uile [*ut dixit poeta* :—

Tri longa seolais in saoi
Tar tonngar mara romaoi
Tricha fer in cech luing lais
Tar treathan mara mongmais.

Tri sretha do ramaib leo
Ar gach luing dib, caom an gleo,
Seol croicenn go loinne (o) lais
Isna tri longaib seolais.

Ṅochu cleirchiu luid uile
For loinges, caom in chaire,
Munter huathad (?), lom a lí
Isna tri longaib seolais.]

Seolais tra Brenainn Mac Finnlogha annsin for tonnghor in mara mongruaidh 7 for treathan na tonn toebhuaine 7 for beluibh ind aicein ingantaigh adhuathmhair agairbh, airm a bfacatar ilar na mbiast mbeilderg (co n-imad na mbleidmil mor) muiridhi; 7 fogeibhdis ailena aille ingantacha 7 ní tairistis inntibh (sin) beos.

thereon. After this he remained there for the space of three days, and again fell asleep. Then the angel of the Lord came to commune with him there, and spoke to him thus: "I will," said he, "be henceforth in close union with you for ever and ever, and I will teach you how to find the beautiful island of which you have had a vision, and which you desire to attain." Brendan thereupon wept exceedingly with joy at the words of the angel, and made fervent thanksgiving to God.

Then Brendan went away from the mountain, and comes to his community of monks, to whom he says: "Let there be constructed by you three large vessels, having three banks of oars in each, and three sails of hides, and (24) twenty men in each vessel." But they were not all clerics, as the poet said:—

Three vessels the sage sailed
Over the foaming surges of the ocean;
Twenty men in each vessel he had
On the waves of the boisterous sea.

Three sets of oars in each vessel,
Sweet the music of their rowing;
Three sails of hides to be unfurled
In each of the three vessels he sails.

(25) All were not clerics who went
On the voyage; sweet their mutual love;
The monks were humble—spare their looks—
Who sailed in the three vessels.

Then Brendan, son of Finlugh, sailed over the loud-voiced waves of the rough-crested sea, and over the billows of the greenish tide, and over the abysses of the wonderful, terrible, relentless ocean, where they saw in its depths the red-mouthed monsters of the sea and many great sea-whales. And they found therein beautiful, marvellous islands, wherein they tarried not.

Batur tra amlaid sin fria re .u. mbliadan for an aicen n-ingantach n-anaithnidh n-aineolach dhoibsium; et ni tharla duine dhoibh frisin re-sin, 7 ni roibhi esbaidh dhuini dia popul forru, 7 ni rofrithortadh corp na anum duini dib; et ba hingnadh inni sin, ar ni roleicc Brenainn doibh lon do breith leo, acht atbert ba tualuing Dia biadh doibh in cech dhu i mbeitis, amail roshasastar na .u. mile dona .u. aranaibh 7 don dhá n-iascaib.

In tan immorro ba comfhocraibh don chaisc, batar a muinter icca radh fria Brenainn dula for tír do cheileabhrad na casc. "As tualang Dia," ol Brenainn, "talam do thabairt duin in gach inadh bus ail dó." Iar toidhecht immorro na casc toccbhais in mil mor muiridi a fhormna a n-airdi uas treathan 7 uas tonnghor in mara, cur'bho talam comtrom cobhsaidh amail faichthe choimhreidh chomhaird. Et tiaghait-sium forsin talmain-sin 7 ceileabrait in caisc ann .i. oenla 7 da oidhchi. Iar ndul doibhsium ana longuibh sceinneas an blédmil fon muir fochedair. Et ba hamlaid sin docileabraitis in chaisc co cenn .uii. mbliadne for druim in mil moir, amail atbert (Cumin Coindire):

Carais Brenainn buanchrabudh
Doreir shenuid is shamhaidh:
Secht mbliadne ar drium in mil mhoir
Ba docair in coir chrabaidh.

Uair intan ba comhthocraibh don chaisc cacha bliadne no thocbhadh in mil mor a druim comba talam tirim techtaidhe.

They were thus for the space of (26) five years upon the ocean, so wonderful, so strange, and utterly unknown to them; and during all that time no man chanced to meet them, and not one of all the crews suffered any want, nor did any injury befall either body or soul of anyone. And this was a wonder, indeed, for Brendan had not allowed them to bring any provisions with them, but he told them that God would provide food for them, wherever they might be, just as He fed the five thousand with the five loaves and two fishes.

Now when the Easter-tide drew near, the brethren were urging Brendan to go on land to celebrate the paschal festival there. "God," said Brendan, "can provide land for us wheresoever He willeth." When Easter had come, the great sea-whale raised up its huge bulk over the breakers and noisy billows of the sea, so that it was level, firm land, like unto a green sward, evenly smooth and equally high. And they go forth upon that land, and they celebrate thereon the Easter festival, even for one day and two nights. And as soon as they returned to their vessels the whale at once plunged into the sea. In this manner they celebrated the festival of Easter to the end of seven years on the back of the whale, as (27) Cuimin of Connor tells :—

Brendan loved lasting devotion,
According to his synod and his equals.
Seven years on the back of the whale;
Severe was this mode of devotion.

Because each year, when Easter drew near, the whale would raise up its back, so that it was dry solid land.

Araili laithe dhoibh for an aicen n-ingantach co bhfacadar srotha doimne dubha in mara mongruaidh, 7 as inntibhsin dorimartus a longa dia mbadhuadh ar mhet na hainbthine. Gabhuidh cách iarsin ic fegad inagaid Brenainn, ár ba dermhair met in gabhuihd ir-rabutur. Tocbus Brenainn a ghuth cuhárd, 7 atbert: " As lor duit, a mhuir mhor-sa," ar se, " mhisi m-oenar do badhadh, 7 leicc uaid in lucht-so." Is ann sin tra rofhethnuig in mhuir, 7 toirnes fethedha na soebchoire focetoir. O sin amach iarum ni roerchoitset do neoch aile.

On certain days, while they traversed the wonderful ocean, they beheld the deep and black currents of the rough-crested sea, and in them their vessels were in danger of foundering, because of the vehemence of the storm. Then each would look intently on the face of Brendan, for exceeding great was the peril in which they were (28). Brendan raised his voice on high, and cried out: "Enough for thee, O mighty sea, that thou shouldst drown me alone, but suffer this people to escape." Then the sea grew calm, and the rushing of the whirlpools subsided at once. Thenceforth they harmed no one else. . . .

NOTES ON THE IRISH LIFE.

1.—Pedigree of St. Brendan.

Some copies of this Life give here the line of descent from Ciar (or Mogh Taoth), son of Fergus MacRoighe and Maebh, Queen of Connaught, in the first century. Duald MacFerbuis, in his *Book of Genealogies*, has it in three different forms. Comparing those with the most reliable pedigrees we have of St. Carthage Mochuda and St. Canice of Kilkenny, who came of the same stock as St. Brendan, we may set down his "stem" as follows:—Brendan, son of Finlug, son of Fioncadh, son of Olcu, son of Alt (*unde* Altraighe), son of Oghaman, son of Fiochur, son of Delmain, son of Eoghan (or End), son of Fualasgec, son of Moctha, son of Astomon, son of Mogh-Taoth, *alias* Ciar (*unde* Ciarriaghe), son of Fergus MacRoighe. Here we have thirteen generations from Fergus, whose "floruit" was early in the first century, to Brendan, born in 483, requiring more than the usual average allowed for a generation; but it is probable that some links have been lost. To the pedigree MacFerbuis subjoins a note, meaning: "He (Brendan) belonged to Kerry-luachra, in the district of Altraighe-cuile-beara or Kinbeara, and also to Corca-duibhne (Corcaguiney)." A similar note is added to the copies of the pedigree in the *Book of Leinster* and in the *Leabhar Breac*. The district of Altraighe ("Sept-land of the Ua Alta, or descendants of Alt") lay around the present Tralee, extending some miles, east and west; the portion of it called "Cuil-beara" by MacFerbuis was the *Cuil* ("corner" or "angle"), as it is called in Irish to the present day, extending from the Spa of Tralee to Fenit Island, and including the parish of Ballinahagluishe (hence called in Irish "Paroiste na Cuileac," or the Parish of the Corner). This district was also known, MacFerbuis says, as Kinbeara ("Heads of Beara"), often also called Rinbeara ("Points of Beara"), which was the name of the parish, in some mediæval records. The name "Beara" was probably given to the whole district from the curious rocky spurs or spits ("beara," or biora, in Irish) which crop up through the limestone "measures" there, in so many places, and which are specially remarkable in that portion of it anciently called *Ilaun Bearamhain* ("Island of the Beara"), now called Barrow, where alone the name survives. In the copies of the *Irish Life* that I have seen, "the precise place" of Brendan's birth is written "Altraighe-caille" ("of the wood"), not "Cuile," as given by MacFerbuis, which I believe to be the more correct, for the Altraighe "of the Wood" lay to the east of Tralee, towards the "great wood," that covered a wide expanse of the "plain of Kerry" in that direction in early times.

2.—Aengus Mac Nadhfraich

Was the first Christian King of Munster, having been

baptized by St. Patrick before he reached the throne. He was killed at the battle of Cill-osnadha (now Kelleston), in the present County of Carlow, in 490—about seven years after the birth of St. Brendan.

3. The mother of the saint is named "Cara" in the Latin *Lives*, preserved in the Burgundian Library, Brussels. The holy union of Finnlug and Cara, under the rule of Bishop Erc, was very fruitful of saints. In a marginal note to MacFerbuis's pedigree we find: "Brendan and Domaingin of Tuaim-musgire, and Faitleac of Cluaintuascairt and Faolan of Cill-tulac, were four sons of Finnlug." The festival of St. Domaingin is marked in the *Martyrology of Tallaght* on the 29th of April, but his church of Tuaim-musgire has not been identified. I believe I will not be far astray in suggesting that it was the church now called Kiltuomy, now a parish in the barony of Clanmaurice, where the ruins of an ancient church still remain, surrounded by a graveyard largely used for burials. We read in a very ancient *Life of St. Carthage-Mochuda*, that soon after his priestly ordination by his master, St. Carthage Senior, he built a small church at Kiltulach (now Kiltallagh, near Castlemain), where he wrought many miracles, and was highly honoured by those who attended his ministrations; but though he was ordained by St. Carthage, whose episcopal jurisdiction in Desmond, afterwards the diocese of Aghadoe, was limited by the river Maine, on the Kerry side of which lay Kiltulach, he was challenged as an intruder by two bishops who then ruled episcopal sees within the Kerry borders, and who insisted that he should

withdraw outside the sphere of their episcopal authority. Their names are given as Domaingen and Dubhlin, correctly, Dubhdin. This is a very early instance of fixed limits to diocesan jurisdiction in our primeval Irish Church. Carthage demurred to the challenge, and he appealed to his friend and patron, Moeltuile, King of Kerry, "whose castle lay beside the Shannon," to protect him from the molestation of those bishops. But his friend gave him a prudent advice: "My son, retire now; leave this small tract of land to those envious bishops, and hereafter it shall be thine, and much more, with all its inhabitants for ever." And so it came to pass; for after many years, while St. Carthage was still in his great monastery at Rathin, he and many of his favourite disciples founded churches within the district where those "envious bishops" ruled; namely, at Kilcarragh (Church of St. Carthage), now next parish to Kiltuomy. and at Kilfiachna (Church of Fiachna, a disciple of Carthage), now Kilfeighney, next parish to Kilmaniheen (Church of Maingen or Do-Maingen, the prefix "Do" being the usual expression of endearment, like "Mo"), now the parish of Brosna. I believe that this Bishop Domaingen, founder of Kilmaniheen, was founder also of Kiltuomy, the Church of "Tuaim-musgire," and that he was the saintly brother of St. Brendan. The Church of Faitleac of Cluaintuascairt was in the present County Roscommon. He probably had accompanied his brother, St. Brendan, in his missionary journeys in Connaught, and took part in the foundation of some of his monasteries within that province. The monastery of Cluantooskert (as the place is now called) may have been one of those founded by Brendan, in Roscommon, for the benefit of his countrymen from Kerry, who had migrated in large numbers thither, and occupied wide districts there, about the date of his later visits to Connaught; and he may have then placed Faitleac to govern it, as may be inferred from an entry in MacFerbuis, regarding this brother of Brendan's :—"Fergus MacRahilly made reverence to him (Faitleac) as successor to Brendan, for it was to him Brendan left his monks."

The Church of "Faolan of Kiltulach" may have been that of Kiltallagh, from which Carthage Mochuda was forced to withdraw, and which Bishop Domaingen may have then given in charge to his brother Faolan; a natural arrangement enough. There is a very ancient church within the present parish of Dingle bearing this saint's name, Kilfhaolain (pronounced Kilaoilane, or Killilane); it may have been founded by this brother of St. Brendan's before his migration to Kiltallagh. So far touching the holy brothers of the saint. The Irish *Life* tells us of the great holiness of his sister, Brig, who cared him so lovingly while in the tutelage of Bishop Erc. She very probably became a holy nun in St. Ita's Convent at Killeedy; and after many years, when her brother, St. Brendan, had founded the Convent of Nuns at Eanachduin (Annadown), on the east margin of Lough Corrib, he placed his holy sister to rule it; and there he died in the 93rd year of his age, while Brig was still living.

4. Bishop Erc is the earliest bishop of whom we have any trace in Kerry history, and the traces of his

connection with our early Kerry Church are vague and shadowy. There is no reasonable doubt, however, that this Bishop Erc, the patron of St. Brendan, was St. Erc of Slane, "the sweet-spoken Brehon," of St. Patrick, who is called in our *Annals*, "Bishop of Liolcach" (not identified), and who died, according to the *Annals of Ulster*, in 512. He must have assumed episcopal jurisdiction in Kerry-luachra some years before the birth of St. Brendan; and from what we read in this Irish *Life* of his relations with that saint, he must have resided there almost continuously for several years afterwards. It is very probable that he came to Kerry soon after the mission of St. Benignus, who was sent by St. Patrick, on his visit to Munster about 450, to evangelize the tribes of West Munster, and "to unite them to Holy Church by the saving waters of baptism," as his *Life* tells us. St. Benignus, who was then a priest, brought seven other priests, disciples of St. Patrick, with him, but did not remain long, being called away to North Clare and Connaught, where his apostolic labours may have been more urgently necessary, and where, as we know from his *Life*, they were continued for some years. To complete the work of the conversion of the *Ciarriaghe*, thus auspiciously commenced by St. Benignus and his companions, and to organize in a solid and permanent manner the infant Church of Christian converts there, St. Patrick sent one of his most zealous and devoted bishops, St. Erc—who must have got spiritual charge not only of Kerry-luachra, but also of a wide range of south-west Limerick, in the heart of which lay the

Convent of St. Ita, at Killeedy, over which he seems to have had jurisdiction. We have some vestiges yet remaining of his apostolic labours in Kerry. In the townland of Lerrig, parish of Kilmoyley, there are the ruins of a very ancient ecclesiastical establishment of some kind, which is known as Termon-Eirc (Church Sanctuary of Erc); but what it consisted of it is now impossible to ascertain, for all that remains are some grass-grown mounds of earth and stones, covering about half an acre, which are religiously preserved by the people from disturbance in any way. When I saw the place first, many years ago, I was told by the "oldest inhabitant" I met there, that he remembered from his boyhood the visit of some great scholars, as he called them, to the ruins; and that they told the people who were present on the occasion, that this "Tarmuin was one of the first churches called in Rome;" meaning, I suppose, that it was one of the earliest churches founded by St. Patrick and his disciples in Ireland; and I have no doubt that it was founded by Bishop Erc, the patron of St.Brendan—probably his first foundation in Kerry—and that for this reason it was specially honoured in after times, and became a "Tarmuin," having the high "privilege of sanctuary," as it was called.

There is another very ancient and interesting church on the southern slopes of Kerry-Head, within the parish of Ballyheigue, called *Kilvicadeaghadh* (Church of the Son of Deaghadh), which, I believe, bears the patronymic of St. Erc of Slane, for his father was "Deaghadh," as his pedigree shows; or "Dego," as it was latinized by our hagiographers. The church, at present in ruins, though very ancient, cannot date from St. Erc's time; but it was built on the site of some foundation of his there, and not far from a "holy well," which bears the same name as the church, being "the Well of Macadeaghadh." In connection with this well, there is most religiously preserved, by the head of a family in the neighbourhood, who alone still use the old church as their burial-place, a round stone amulet, called "the bauly," which is even yet used for the cure of "the ills that flesh is heir to," being immersed in the water from the holy well, which is then drunk "in honour of the saint of the well." I cannot say whether this amulet has come down from the days of Bishop Erc Macadeaghadh, or whether it may be a relic of his, such as "the white pebble which St. Columba blessed, by which God will effect the cure of many diseases;" but the preservation of it for many centuries, and the still enduring faith of the people in its healing virtues, indicate the hoar antiquity of the venerable church, and of its religious associations.

If Bishop Erc had his habitat here on the night of Brendan's birth, from which he could easily see the district of Altraighe-cuile "in one blaze of light," across the waters of what was afterwards called St. Brendan's Bay, how beautifully those lambent splendours, playing over the home of the infant Brendan, and "the ministering of angels in snow-white robes," must have arrested the attention and excited the wonder of the holy Bishop, and urged him to proceed "early on the morrow" in quest of the house where the child of so much heavenly predilection had been born! St. Erc, soon after ordaining St. Brendan to the priesthood, must have retired to his hermitage at Slane, "over the blue waters of the Boyne," where he died in 512.

5.—Airde MacFidaigh.

The mansion of this "brugaid" (great farmer) in which St. Becc was entertained when he prophesied the birth of Brendan, stood on the crest of a verdant knoll or hillock in the townland of Listrim, adjoining the parish of Ardfert, commonly called Cahirard (stone fortress on the height), but which an accurate map of the locality, more than three hundred years old, shows to be Cahirairde (fortress of Airde). From this Fenit lies due west, "between it and the open sea;' according to the prophecy of St. Becc, as given in the *Book of Leinster*: "this night thy king is born between thee on the west and the sea." On the top of this hillock can be easily traced at present the ring of the foundations of the Cathair, which crowned its swelling slopes, showing a diameter of more than one hundred feet inside the walls, which must have been at least seven feet in thickness at the base; but of those walls, and of whatever buildings lay within them, not a stone remains *in situ*, all having been drawn away for building purposes during many generations. But nothing can efface the tokens of early and long occupation of the surface all around its site, for its emerald verdure, which in early summer makes it conspicuous in the landscape for many miles in all directions, can only be accounted for by its uses for man's habitation for long centuries.

6.—St. Becc MacDe.

The *Annals of the Four Masters* record his death: "The age of Christ, 557; the nineteenth year of Diarmid; St. Becc, son of De, a celebrated prophet, died." His name is on the Calendars of Irish Saints for October the 12th, on which his festival was kept. He was son of De-Druad, sixth in descent from Mainne, son of Niall of the "Nine Hostages." There is no other reference, as far as I know, to his visit to Kerry, save what we find in the *Lives of Brendan;* but we may well believe that many of the early saints, such as he, came to Kerry, after St. Benignus, to visit the Christian converts there, and to promote the spread of faith and piety amongst them.

7.—Fenit ("spread over all Fenit").

This clearly shows that the "precise place" of the birth of Brendan lay within Fenit. This is a large townland, six miles west from Tralee, on the northern shore of its harbour, consisting of a promontory called Fenit Without, and an adjoining island, or rather peninsula, called Fenit Within. Though the area of the whole is less than seven hundred statute acres, it formed a separate parish, and an important one, in our early Celtic Church, and in later times it formed the *corpus* of the dignity of chancellorship in the Ardfert Cathedral, in union with the rectory of Kilmelchedor. There were two churches on the island, the ruins of which are marked on the Ordnance maps; of one of those, which seems to have been a small oratory, there is scarcely any vestige now remaining; of the other, which was the parish church, some of the walls are standing, three feet six inches thick, built of the limestone of the neighbourhood, but very rude and primitive in structure. It was about forty feet long by fifteen feet broad "in the clear," and was a plain rectangular building, of which neither door nor windows can now be traced. Within a few paces of those ruins there are vestiges of another ancient building, running at right angles to it, which may have been an earlier church, or some religious establishment attached to that whose ruins I have described; and around the site of those buildings, for many perches distance, there are unmistakable signs of an extensive burial-ground in ages long gone-by, but which has not been used for many generations. Among the people who at present occupy Fenit and its vicinity, I have found no tradition of the birth of St. Brendan there; nor is this surprising, for, during the many centuries that have elapsed since the date of the saint's birth, there has been more than once an entire change of the population, owing to the desolating wars, famines, and pestilence that have often scourged those districts, as well as to other causes; and the chain of local traditions has been thus completely broken.

Fenit must have been inhabited from the earliest times. In a long list of distinguished judges and scholars that lived in Ireland in the first century, which O'Curry quotes from the *Senchus Mor*, we find the name of Fergus *Fiannuite* ("of Fenit," O'Curry says); and in the next two centuries it was the resort and trysting-place of "Fianna Erinn" (the Fian Militia of Ireland), according to our oldest romantic tales, from whom, very probably, it got its name, "Fianan," as it reads in the Irish *Life* of Brendan. One of the most interesting and, as O'Curry pronounces it, one of the best authenticated of those ancient tales of the "Fianna Erinn," is a poem by their warrior poet, Oisin (Ossian), describing a visit of the whole host of Fians, led by the famous Fion MacCumhal their general, to Kerry and to the neighbourhood of Fenit, for the purpose of a grand horse-race on the magnificent strand extending from Fenit Island to within a short distance of Ballyheigue, for about seven miles, without a break. This poem of Oisin has not been published, but there is a spirited metrical version of it from the Gaelic, by Dr. Anster, in the volume of the *Dublin University Magazine* for 1852, from which I will give some extracts that may interest Kerry readers. The poem is supposed to have been composed by the warrior-bard, when he was old and blind; hence he was called "Guaire the blind." Thus it opens:—

> Guaire the blind! there was an hour,
> When Fion was in his pride and power,
> And led the hosts of Fian men;
> None called me blind and feeble then.
> *How my thoughts for ever stray,*
> *From the present evil day,*
> *To that bright time far away.*

The Fians mustered:—

> From valley deep and wooded glen,
> Fair Munster sent its mighty men,
> Six thousand gallant men of war,
> We sought the rath of Badamar;
> To the King's palace home we bent
> Our way; his bidden guests we went.

Here there was a horse-race, in which competed the most famous steeds in Munster:—

. . . .

They run; and foremost still is seen
Dill MacDacreca's coal-black steed;
At Crag Lochgur he takes the lead.

After the race, the King makes a present of this wonderful steed to Fion:—

And to Finn the King thus spake:
Take with thee the swift black steed,
Of thy valour fitting meed.

Fion, having received the gift:—

Stood before the Fian ranks,
To the King spake gracious thanks,

and then departed for Kerry:—

Finn rode over Luachair a joyous man,
'Till he reached the Strand of Barriman,
At the lake where the foam on the billows top
Leaps white, did Finn and the Fians stop.
'Twas then that our chieftain rode and ran
Along the Strand of Barriman,
Trying the speed of his swift black steed;
Who now but Finn was a happy man.
How my thoughts for ever stray
To that bright time far away.

Finn challenges Caoilte and Oisin to a race, and then

Myself and Caoilte at each side,
In wantonness of youthful pride,
Would ride with him where he might ride.

Finn's black steed easily wins the race at Barriman;

but, not content with this victory, he strikes across the country, followed by his companion racers :—

> Fast and furiously rode he;
> He urged his steed to far Tralee,
> On from Tralee to Lergduglas,
> And o'er Fraegmoy, o'er Finnas.

On still they go towards Killarney :—

> And where the fisher spreads his net
> To snare the salmon of Lemain,*
> And thence to where our coursers' feet
> Wake the glad echoes of Lochlein.
> Away to Flesk by Carnwood dun,
> And past MacScalve's Mangerton,
> Till Finn reached † Bearnac's hill at last.

Here they alighted, and spent a night of extraordinary adventures; after which they return to their starting-point :—

> With weariness, all weak and wan,
> We reach the Strand of Barriman;
> The well-known path again we meet,
> And friends with eager welcome greet.

All this may be pure romance and poetic fiction; but it is a fact worthy of note, that very near the Fenit end of the Strand of Barriman (*Traig Bearamhain*, in the Gaelic), and near "the lake where the foam on the billow's top leaps white," that is, where the "back strand" of Rathoneen now discharges its waters into the main sea, often causing the billows there to leap very high as well as white, there are within the adjoining sand-hills, on a cleared space, several mounds of what are known here about as *fulacth fiansa* (cooking

* River Laune.
† Cahir Barnac Mt., near the "Paps."

hearths of the Fians), consisting of immense quantities of burned stones, charcoal ashes and cinders, heaps of oyster-shells and various other shells, mixed with the bones of oxen and smaller animals, and the tines and other parts of deers' antlers, &c. There are many other such "kitchen-middens" through those sand-hills still visible; many others have, no doubt, been covered by the shifting sands; but this congeries of them is the most extensive I have discovered there. Whether "the hosts of the Fian men" actually prepared their grand feasts, and partook of them at this interesting place or not, we may safely assert that the residuum of the viands still found there would indicate "noble feasting," "fitting meed," for even "the ancient chivalry of Erin."

The coast along this strand, as well as the whole sea-board of the barony of Clanmaurice, is very inhospitable to sea-farers; and there is no safe harbour there except the small estuary opening between Fenit Island and Barrow; even this is dangerous and difficult of approach from the bay. In consequence of this, the sea-faring dwellers along that coast, who, O'Donovan tells us, were known as *feara feorna* ("men of the shore"), must have been hardy and daring mariners. Among these Brendan had his birth, and spent much of his youth and early manhood, and from them he may have imbibed his "love of ocean," and first felt his ardent longing

> To see the isles that gem
> Old ocean's purple diadem.

Often, perhaps, sauntering on the shore near the home

of his parents, when the sun was sinking in the west, he may

> Have watched the line of light that plays
> Along the smooth wave, tow'rd the burning west,
> And longed to tread that golden path of rays,
> And thought 'twould lead to some bright isle of rest.

Some years ago I was present at the launching of a lifeboat ("The Admiral Butcher") at Fenit. There was a *dejeuner,* and speeches, of course, on the occasion Dr. Haughton, Senior Fellow of Trinity College, was present as the friend of Surgeon Butcher, also of Trinity College; and in his genial, happy manner, proposed the toast of "The Church," to which he called upon me, as the senior clergyman there, to respond. Speaking at Fenit, the birthplace of the great sailor saint, and on such an occasion, I could not help referring to St. Brendan and his voyages, which I did in these words:—"As far as history and even legend carry us back, the people of this district have been brave and daring seamen. The earliest name we find for them in Irish history is 'Feara-feorna,' which may be Englished, 'long-shore men;' and from amongst them sprang the bravest and greatest sailor that perhaps the world has ever seen—I mean Brendan, the voyager, who was born and nurtured very near the spot where we are now assembled, at Fenit, close upon fourteen hundred years ago. We read in his *Life* that when he ventured 'to tempt the main' by his perilous voyages on the broad Atlantic, in his little *corrachs* or *corracles,* not half the size, probably, of our lifeboat of to-day, he was joined in his adventure by a crew of brave seamen, mostly from this district. The story tells us that when he was about to set sail, three other men from his monastery at Ardfert rushed into his boat, and were permitted, at their most earnest entreaties, to share in the dangers of the enterprise. Of such stuff are our sailors made, and I have no doubt that the men of to-day, the representatives of the 'feara-feorna' of old, are not degenerate sons of those 'sea-shore men, and will handle our lifeboat as bravely and deftly as befits worthy children of the great navigator, St. Brendan."

8.—" THE FOUNTAIN OF HIS BAPTISM (*Tubber-na-molt*, or Wether's Well).

This is a remarkable well, in the townland of Tubrid, parish of Ardfert, which still bears the name of "Wether's Well." It has been for many generations an object of great devotion and pious pilgrimage throughout large districts of Kerry and the adjacent counties; and there is not, I believe, any "holy well" in this county so frequently and generally visited for the purpose of "giving rounds," as the people say, or performing certain devotions about the well, as this Wether's Well. I do not think that the devout visitors there intend special honour to St. Brendan, or that many of the pilgrims know of that saint's personal relations with the sacred place; but there can be no reasonable doubt that his baptism there was the *fons et origo* of those pious pilgrimages which grew up, and have continued without ceasing for many centuries from generation to generation, though the original source and incentive to the devotion have been lost to popular remembrance in the lapse of ages.

The legend of the "three wethers bounding from the well," as the reason of its name, which probably arose at first from the handsome "turn or treat" ("*caomh cor*" in the Irish quatrain), contrived by Airde MacFidaigh for Bishop Erc, in presenting him, as "the fee for Brendan's baptism," with those wethers from his large flocks pasturing near the well, has held its ground in popular tradition to the present day, but in a curiously altered shape. The legend now runs that it was during "the dark and evil days" of the penal laws, when the faith of the people was banned, and a price set on the head of their priests, some religious celebration, at which there were three priests present, was being held in the hollow, or low ground, near this well. Suddenly the alarm was given by the watchers on the neighbouring heights, that the priest-hunters, with some bloodhounds, were at hand. When they reached the place the priests were nowhere to be seen, but three wethers sprung from the well before the bloodhounds, and led them a hot chase across the country for five miles or more until they suddenly disappeared near the sea, at a ford, hence called *Athcaorach* ("sheep-ford") to the present day, leaving their bloodhound pursuers, canine and human, completely at fault. In this manner the origin of the name is accounted for by people in this district who never heard of St. Brendan's baptism at the well, nor of the "baptismal fee" of the three wethers.

There is no record of such interference as this with any religious celebration there, nor of this wonderful deliverance of the priests engaged therein; but there is no doubt that Mass was often celebrated near this well in those dreadful times of persecution, and a rude stone altar stands there still, in the frontal of which is set up a carved panel of black marble, 3½ feet long by 2 feet high, showing three figures in excellent workmanship; the central one being that of a deceased bishop or abbot, in mortuary cerements, having on his right side the figure, probably, of St. Brendan; and on the other, that of a nun, probably St. Ita, who may have been the patron saints of the deceased. This beautifully carved panel had formed part of an altar-tomb, either at Ardfert Cathedral, or at the Abbey Church of Ardfert, or at that of Kyrie Eleison, Odorney, and was the work of the sculptor, in the thirteenth or fourteenth century; but in whose memory it was erected, there is no record or tradition. It was brought from one of those sacred shrines by some faithful Catholics, soon after the ruin and desolation wrought on their churches by triumphant heresy in the wars and confiscations of the sixteenth and seventeenth centuries; when it may have been said of each of those sacred temples and abbeys :—

Empty aisle, deserted chancel,
  Tower tottering to your fall;
Many a storm long since has beaten
  On the grey head of your wall!

Gone your abbot, rule, and order,
  Broken down your altar stones;
Nought see I beneath your shelter
  Save a heap of clayey bones.

Oh! the hardship, oh! the hatred,
  Tyranny and cruel war,
Persecution and oppression,
  That have left you as you are. *

* Collins's "Lament on Timoleague Abbey."

The faithful Catholic people, who were despoiled of those sacred shrines, loved them even in their desolation, and, in their love for the very stones of their sanctuaries, brought away this beautiful relic therefrom, and lovingly set it up "in the wilderness," into which they and their priests had been driven to worship their God, as a temporary altar near this "holy well," on which the holy Mass may be said, and from which the Bread of Life may still be broken to them, even in the desert, by their devoted priests; just as the Jews of old, in the darkest hour of their affliction, when they were driven into exile, torn away from home and country, and from the great temple of God they loved so much, sought, in many instances, to carry away with them into captivity stones from the sacred courts of the temple, as some solace in their sorrows, and as a reminder of the glories that had been, even as "they sat and wept by the rivers of Babylon."

This rude altar is still very much venerated by the people of the district, and to the present day all pilgrims to the well deposit upon it their simple votive offerings. It is told, that some time after this altar-panel was set up there, a Cromwellian settler near Tralee, in his bigoted hatred of the Catholics of the neighbourhood, resolved that they should not have even the poor comfort of possessing this one stone of their despoiled sanctuaries, and sent a cart and bullock with some men to remove it to his place at Killeen (Oakpark) near Tralee. These men succeeded in getting the stone into the cart, and were bringing it away, rejoicing on the high road by Dun-da-radharc, until they reached the place now called Bullock-hill, when all at once bullock and cart broke down, and could not be moved one inch further by all the powers of the Cromwellian bigot. There the stone remained, as the story tells, for some time, until the Catholic people mustered in force, and bore the stone back again in triumph, and set it up once more beside the well, where it still remains; while of the bigoted tyrant, who sought to remove and desecrate it, though a grantee of large estates in Kerry, not a vestige of his kith or kin is to be found in Old Killeen (new Oakpark) for many a day.

The well is distant about five miles from Fenit, where Brendan was born; and when Bishop Erc chose it as the place of his baptism, so far from the home of his parents, it must have attracted special veneration even then; very probably it was generally used as the baptismal font for the first Christian converts in the surrounding districts, before baptismal churches, or even the earliest Christian oratories, were erected there.

It must have been a remarkable fountain in those early times, for even now, when the volume of its waters is much reduced, there is an abundant spring of the purest water gurgling up from the native rock at all seasons. It supplies a large stream or river, now called "the Thyse," which flows on through Ardfert, beside the cathedral grounds, to the sea, and on the brink of which the Franciscans founded their house at Ardfert in 1253. This river was anciently called the "Gabhra" (Goura), and must have been much larger than it is at present; for it is told in local tradition, that it was one of those rivers (fifty in number, the Latin *Life* says) that, being fishless, were blessed by Brendan, and "caused to abound in fish;" but in the course of time, those who fished there churlishly refused a salmon to the monks of Ardfert, which they wanted for a special occasion; the blessing was withdrawn, and ever since the Thyse is a fishless stream, as it had been before Brendan's blessing.

9.—St. Ita, the Foster-Mother of Brendan.

This was the virgin-saint of Cluain-credhail, or Killeedy, County Limerick; patroness of the diocese of Limerick, often called the Brigid of Munster. She was born of noble parents, in the Decies, County Waterford, and died at her convent of Killeedy, full of years and sanctity, in A.D. 570, according to the *Annals of Ulster*. The date of the foundation of the convent at Cluain-credhail is uncertain. It may have been one of those established by St. Brigid herself, during her travels in Munster, with a community of her nuns, under the guidance and patronage of St. Erc of Slane, of which her *Lives* give a rather confused account. I think it may be fairly inferred from what we read in those *Lives* of her progress on the occasion, that she visited the *Ciarraighe*, "the relatives of her friend," St. Erc, "whom she desired to see;" and that having come into Kerry, she abode there "for some years" with the nuns, "in the house beside the sea," not far from where Bishop Erc dwelt. If the holy bishop did reside at Kilvicadagh, on the southern slope of Kerry Head, as I suggested in a previous note, I would take the "house beside the sea," where St. Brigid abode for some years, to be the very ancient church and convent at Glendathlion, over the Shannon, on the northern slopes of Kerry Head, near which there is a holy well in great repute, known as St. Brigid's Well to the present day. If these surmises are well founded, we may readily believe that St. Brigid, on her way towards Kerry, and under the direction of Bishop Erc, founded the nunnery at Cluain-creadhail, perhaps some years before St. Ita left her parents' home in the Decies, and sought refuge from the world in that remote and retired spot "at the foot of Slieve-luachra." She must have come there some time before St. Brendan's birth in 483, and must have already won the special friendship and entire confidence of the Bishop, St. Erc, when he placed the youthful Brendan, at the age of one year, under her fostering care for five years.

She seems to have had a special aptitude and grace in the fostering and education of youthful saints. Hence St. Cuimin of Connor, in his poem on the characteristics of our early Irish saints, devotes a stanza to the praise of St. Ita, beginning thus: "St. Ita loved much fosterage." One of her best-beloved foster-sons was her own nephew, St. Mochaomoge, or Pulcherius (as his name was latinized), whom she nurtured and educated in her convent from his childhood until he had reached early manhood, well trained in virtue and well stored with learning. One of the few popular traditions, from St. Brendan's time, I found surviving here in Ardfert, regards this saint and his foster-mother, St. Ita; it runs thus: Some time after St. Brendan had founded his first monastery at Ardfert, his foster-mother,

St. Ita, desired to visit the house and the monks there, of whose fervour she had heard much praise, and she also wished to ascertain whether her nephew, Mochaomoge, who had secretly left her some time before with the intention of entering a monastery, and of whose whereabouts she had no knowledge, had joined the holy community at Ardfert. Accompanied by one of her nuns and a holy priest who knew the way, she made the toilsome journey over Slieve-luachra and through the dense forests that then covered much of the plains of Kerry, and at length reached the high ground, now called Doon, in the parish of Tralee, where she was hospitably entertained by the lord of the Dûn. This elevated spot commanded an extensive view of the two great plains of Kerry, north and south; and the story tells that when Ardfert, on the west, and Rathoo, on the north, were pointed out to the saint as the sites of monasteries lately founded by St. Brendan, she burst forth into praises of God, who had blessed her eyes with that delightful vision, and declared that the Dûn, which afforded her so glorious a prospect, should henceforth be called *Dun-da-riarc* ("Fort of the beautiful prospect"), as it is called to the present day.

After some days' rest here, the saint proceeded on to Ardfert, visiting the well of St. Brendan's baptism, "Tubber-na-molt," on her way; and when she arrived at the monastery she found the monks on religious retreat for the day, and unable to admit her then. Some of the brethren had gone to the neighbouring strand, as was the custom, to gather shell-fish for their fasting fare, and met St. Ita on their return, but could not then speak to her. Next day, when the monks were off retreat, they received the saint with joyous welcome, and gave her the glad tidings that her dear foster-son, Mochaomoge, whom she sought so anxiously, was for some time a fervent member of their community. The story, as far as I heard, and "I tell the tale as 'twas told to me" many years ago by an old intelligent farmer, who was very much of a "shanachie" (Irish story-teller), does not say whether St. Brendan was then at his Ardfert house to welcome his dear friend and foster-mother, St. Ita, or not; but very probably he was away on one of his great Atlantic voyages at the time. The whole tale accords very well with what we read in the *Lives* of St. Ita and of Mochaomoge, of their habits of "travelling" on such visits to other monasteries, and especially of St. Mochaomoge's long wanderings in quest of "the place of his resurrection," which he found at Leamokevoge, near Thurles, Co. Tipperary, where he died, and where his memory is held in special honour.

There was very probably some religious establishment at Rathoo, even at that early period; but whether it was one of St. Brendan's foundations, cannot now be surely known. The earliest account I have met of the residence of a bishop there or near it, is the reference to St. Lughdach by the Scholiast on the "Festology of Ængus," at the 6th October: "*Lugdach espoc. . . . 7 ata hi raith muige tuaiscirt hi Ciarraige luachrai .i. oc daire mochua for bru feile* ("And Lughdach Bishop . . . also belonged to Rathoo, rath of the north plain, in Kerry-luachra; that is, to Derrymochua, or

Derricoe, on the brink of the Feale). Bishop Lughdach, according to Dr. Petrie, erected a church at Rathoo, and his festival day was October 6th. He was of the same Kerry stock as St. Brendan, but not in the same line or branch, for he was of the *Ui Ferba*, a very extensive sept in early Kerry, which afterwards gave its name to a large Cantred and rural deanery, stretching along the coast from Killury (Causeway) to Brandon-hill, which was known as "Offerba," and sometimes "Farbowe," in later records; while St. Brendan was of the royal branch of the *Altraighe*. St. Lughdach's "floruit" must have come very soon after St. Brendan's, judging from his pedigree, in the Martyrology of Donegal, and also from the fact that he was the uncle of St. Caoilin, of Termon-Caoilin, an illustrious Kerry saint, who was famous for her sanctity in Connaught, and who was able to protect there, before the King, her "Kerry cousins," the *Ciarraighe*, who migrated thither in such large numbers shortly before St. Brendan's death, as we may learn from John O'Donovan's account, taken from a MS. in Trinity College Library.

10. The Irish word here, *agh*, is given by O'Reilly as meaning "an animal of the cow kind." Dr. Stokes translates it, "hind;" but the adjective "wild" may better apply to "a wild cow" on the impassable wastes of Slieve-luachra at that time, than to any kind of deer, of which there were few tame ones then, to distinguish from those that were "wild;" and, surely, a cow's milk was more suitable for the youthful Brendan than that of "the hind with her fawn."

11. St. Brig, sister of St. Brendan; see note (3) *supra*.

12. The Irish text of those words of Brendan is somewhat obscure. Dr. W. Stokes and Dr. B. MacCarthy agree in giving them a sense that puts rather unseemly language into the mouth of this favourite pupil of Bishop Erc. Dr. MacCarthy translates them: "Go home, and take my curse; what brought you here?" while Dr. Stokes renders the passage: "Go away, and curse whoever brought thee here." Now I venture to say that both are needlessly vigorous in the rendering of "miscaidh" (*misguis*, in modern Irish), whether in an active or passive sense; for it may mean here "anger" or "resentment;" and the sense would be: "for this whipping you will get, don't blame me; but have blame and resentment to whoever left you here so carelessly, to disturb me at my reading."

The "flaxen-haired maiden" was the daughter of the princely chief of O'Flannan, an extensive sept-land on the slopes of *Crusuifhloin*, pronounced "crusiline" (O'Flannan's Cross), of which O'Heerin wrote the following quatrain:—

> Ui-Flannan, extensive land,
> A great land of delightful streams;
> O'Duibhduin is over the warm land;
> He is its king, and his care is upon it.*

O'Donovan could not identify "the situation of this territory of the O'Duibhduins;" but there is no difficulty about it now, since the publication of the "Taxation of the diocese of Ardfert" for A.D. 1300, in the *Calendar of Documents, Ireland*, brought out a few years ago. In this we find the rural deanery of

* O'Donovan's translation.

"O'Flannan and O'Dtorney," the first church therein being *Antrum Brendani* (cave of St. Brendan), now called O'Brennan, which locates "O'Flannan" beyond all doubt, and from which we may fairly infer that the O'Duibhduin of St. Brendan's day was the father of "the flaxen-haired maiden," and that one of the same family was the Bishop Duibhduin, mentioned above in note (3) as one of the "envious bishops" who disturbed St. Carthage Mochuda on his first mission in his native Kerry, and of whose church we still have some vestiges at Kilduff (Church of Duibh-din ?) on the sunny slopes, "the warm land" of O'Flannan, not far away from *Antrum Brendani*, or O'Brennan.

13. The *Uaimh Brenainn*, or cave where Brendan performed this penance, imposed by Bishop Erc, is well known for many centuries as the site of a parish church, and the name of a parish now called O'Brennan (the "O" representing the Irish "Uaimh" or cave), in the barony of Trughanacme, where there are the ruins of an ancient church, and a large and much-used grave-yard. The cave itself was preserved with religious care, perhaps from the days of Bishop Erc, through many centuries, and a little nunnery was built and maintained close beside it for many generations, for the education of the youth and the edification of the people of the district. Of this convent I heard an interesting story some years ago. At some remote period, when disorder and crime were rife in the country, a band of lawless men came to the little nunnery at night on evil intent, and loudly demanded instant admission from the affrighted nuns. These knew their dreadful peril, and

turning to God in fervent prayer, they called upon their holy patron, St. Brendan, to save his children from those wicked men. Their prayers were heard, and instantly delirium seized upon their assailants, who rushed wildly about until they tumbled into the "cave," from which they were utterly powerless to extricate themselves. There they had perforce to remain for some time, and though they shouted as loud even as Brendan "chanted the psalm" within the same cave, calling on the nuns to release them, they were left in durance, until the Bishop, who resided in the neighbourhood, was brought to impose wholesome penances upon them, and send them away wiser, if sadder men.

There is no trace now remaining of the little convent, and even the venerable cave itself cannot be identified with any certainty. It appears that some vandal in the vicinity, who wanted building stones, quarried into the "cave," some forty or fifty years ago, and destroyed almost every vestige of it.

14.—St. Finan Cam.

This saint was born in the early part of the sixth century, in Corcadhuine (now barony of Corcaguiney), of Christian parents, his father being Kennedigh, son of Maenach, son of Airde MacFidaigh (of whom see note (5) *supra*, and his mother Becnait. He was, probably, a near relative of St. Brendan's, and at a very tender age was placed under his tutelage and discipline, very likely in the monastery founded by Brendan on the western slopes of Brandon-hill some years before his Atlantic voyaging. Here Finan remained seven years, and so great was his progress in the practice of every virtue—so high the degree of sanctity he had attained, that his master, St. Brendan, said to him: "Brother Finan, it is not fitting that we should be any longer in the same house; but we should have communities in places apart; if you desire to remain here with brethren of your choice, do so, in God's name, and I will go elsewhere." "No, father," said Finan, "I am the younger, and I should not trespass longer on your labours; I will go away, therefore; and bless me, that my journey may be prosperous." Finan journeyed on, by Brendan's advice, to Slieve-Bloom, at the foot of which he founded soon after his famous monastery of Kinnitty (King's County). He returned frequently to his native Kerry, as his *Life* states, and dwelt for some years on the borders of Loch Lein (Lakes of Killarney), when, it is most probable, he founded the monastery at Innisfallen, though his namesake, St. Finan Lobhair, has been often credited with that foundation. He is also said to have spent some time in Iveragh, and founded some houses and churches there; but I believe the Finan of Loch-laoich, where the beautiful ancient oratory of St. Finan, remains, and of *Daire-Fhinain* (Derrynane) was quite a different person. In this opinion I am strengthened by the following quatrain in the *Dirge of Ireland*, by Mr. John O'Connell, the Iveragh poet, who wrote about 1660, and who knew the traditions, civil and religious, of that country remarkably well. Towards the close of his *Dirge* he makes what a competent judge has called "a supremely beautiful and pathetic appeal to

God and the Irish saints" to save his country and his faith from further calamity; among other saints he invokes:

> *Fionan Cluana-Iraird 'sa cleire,*
> *Finan Faithlin air an Lein-loch,*
> *Finan Locha-laoich, mo naomhsa,*
> *Do rug ón phlaig Uibhrathac saor leis.*

That is: "Finnian of Clonard and his disciples; Finan of Inisfallen on Loch-lein; and Finan of Loch-lee (or Loch Currane), my patron-saint, who brought Iveragh safe from the plague." Here the poet invokes the Finan of Iveragh, his own special patron saint, and the patron saint of the many branches of the O'Connell sept then in Iveragh, and distinguishes him unmistakably from the holy patron and founder of Inisfallen, St. Finan, whom I strongly believe to have been no other than Finan Cam.

In the Latin *Life* of the latter we have an interesting story. The saint used what is called a chariot (*carbad* in Gaelic) occasionally, and taking a drive one day on the shore of Loch-lein, his horse dropped dead under his humble *carbad.* Suddenly there came forth from the lake a beautiful pie-bald (the nearest English I can find for the Latin *hyachintinus*) horse, that at once submitted to be harnessed into the chariot, and drove the holy father on his journey. For three years this wonderful horse was his faithful servant, and when he had no further occasion for his services, he ordered him to return into the lake, which the obedient steed did without delay. Who has not heard of the legend of O'Donoghue's "White horse," careering on the Killarney

Lakes, of a May morning? Have we here in this story, in the *Vita Sti. Finani*, the earliest version of this Killarney legend; and is the "piebald steed" of the man of God, in the sixth century, "that returned into the Lakes," by his command, the original of the O'Donoghue's "white charger," so celebrated in after centuries, even to the present day?

I have some reason to surmise that this St. Finan was the founder also of ancient Achadeo, as well as Inisfallen, and perhaps Achadeo was the earlier foundation of the two. Dr. Lanigan (*Eccles. History*, vol. iii., page 19) suggests that *Kilachaid-conchinne* was founded by St. Finan Cam, in Corcadhuine (Corcaguiney), where the saint was born. Unfortunately, Dr. Lanigan, with all his marvellous knowledge of Irish ecclesiastical history, knew very little of Kerry topography. If he knew more of it, he might have found out that the church of *Achad-Gconchinne*, was not in Corcaguiney, but in *Magh-Gconchinne* (Magunihy, as given in *Four Masters*, A.D. 1581), and that the church of this *achad* (field), in Magunihy, was no other than the church of Achadeo (field of the two yews), the most conspicuous *achad* within the barony of Magunihy. It is not surprising, therefore, that St. Finan should be honoured as the patron saint of ancient Achadeo for so many centuries; but it is strange and regretable, that the patron-day should be given to another Finan, who had really no just claim to it; and that in the lapse of ages, March 16th, the feast day of St. Finan-Lobhair, should have supplanted April the 7th, the festival-day of St. Finan Cam, the special friend of St. Brendan;

and it is still more strange that this feast-day of Finan "the Leper," should be also the patron-day of St. Finan of Lochlaoich, the patron saint "who brought Iveragh safe from the plague," and who founded those beautiful churches and oratories, the ruins of which yet remain in that barony, where St. Finan-Lobhair never came.

15.—"The Pillar-stone that yet remains."

In the townland of Lerrig, within a short distance of Tarmuin-Eirc, of which I wrote in note (4) *supra*, there stands a very curious pillar-stone, called Gallane-Lerrigeh, which must have stood for centuries, perhaps, before St. Brendan's time, so notable are the tokens of hoar antiquity upon it. It bears an inscription, in Ogham characters, which, from the weathering of the stone and other causes, is now illegible. At a short distance it has the appearance of the mutilated trunk of a human figure, and it would not require a lively imagination to fancy that this curious stone was really that pillar-stone, in the shelter and shadow of which St. Brendan's *protégé* had his miraculous escape from his enemies.

16.—"Holy Orders" of Priesthood of St. Brendan.

St. Brendan was ordained priest after his journeys in Connaught and elsewhere in Ireland, by Bishop Erc, a short time before his death, in 512 or 514. The holy Bishop must have soon after withdrawn from Kerry to his hermitage over the "blue waters" of the Boyne, to prepare for a saintly death.

17.—St. Colman MacLenin.

St. Colman, bishop, founder, and patron of the Church of Cloyne, was of the royal family of Munster. In his earlier years he was distinguished for his poetic talents and was court poet at the royal court of Cashel, but after his conversion by St. Brendan he consecrated his poetic gifts to the service of religion. His conversion took place about the middle of the sixth century, for he assisted, it is said, about that date, as royal bard at the inauguration of Aodh Caomh, as King of Munster. The story of his conversion is given in the *Book of Munster* (Royal Irish Academy) as follows: A dispute arose between rival claimants of the kingship of Cashel. Aodh Caomh was declared king, but Brendan, who was present, and MacLenin, were given as guarantors to the other claimant, that the kingship should be given to him, after Aodh's death, or to his son, if he did not survive. Then it was that Brendan saw a watch of angels over Lothra (North Tipperary), and told of it to the king. Brendan sent one of his disciples with MacLenin (Colman) and witnesses from the king to ascertain what had occurred there. When they reached the place, they found the shrine of St. Ailbe (who had died some time before) in the form of a chest—which had been lately stolen, and the bodies of the young men, who had stolen it, dead in the neighbouring Lake—" whom God had drowned." " The shrine was brought by MacLenin to Brendan, and he knew that God's grace was upon MacLenin, who had brought it in his hands; then he said to him that it was not fitting that those hands that had touched and bore the holy shrine of the blessed Ailbe should ever after be employed save in the sacred ministry of God. Hence MacLenin left the court of the king and became a disciple of St. Brendan's."

The date of the foundation of his church at Cluain-uamha (Cloyne) is not certain. He died in the year 604, on the 24th of November, the day marked in all the calendars of Irish saints, and on which his festival is still observed in the diocese of Cloyne.

18.—The Poem of St. Colman, in honour of Brendan.

This poem consists of five quatrains, the first of which I give in the Irish text. Dr. Whitley Stokes says that the poem is not given in the Brussels MS., and as he had no other copy but that in the *Book of Lismore*, he could translate "only a few words of it." The language seems to be very archaic, and probably was carelessly transcribed. I sent my copy some years ago to an Irish scholar of some repute, and he returned it untouched. Another Gaelic scholar whom I employed sent me a translation which I do not consider reliable.

19.—St. Jarlath.

This great saint was born late in the fifth century, of a noble family. He was educated by St. Benignus, at his school of Kilbannon, which he established some years after his mission in Kerry. He founded a monastery at Cluainfois, not far from Kilbannon, and here it was that St. Brendan visited him and remained under his instruction for some time. St. Brendan foretold that "the place of his resurrection" should be, not at Cluainfois, but at *Tuaim-da-Guallan* (Tuam); and he accordingly removed thither afterwards, where he founded a church, which, in the course of time became the see of the Archbishop of Tuam. The year of his death is not known, and his festival, though marked in some calendars on the 26th of December, is observed in the Archdiocese on the 6th of June.

20.—The Poem composed by St. Brendan and St. Jarlath.

Dr. W. Stokes has not given a translation of this poem, as he could find no second copy to help in getting at the sense. I find a translation, or rather a paraphrase of it, in the *Notes on the Life of St. Brendan*, in vol. viii. of the *Irish Ecclesiastical Record*, page 85 (New Series, 1871-72). Where this was clearly too loose from the text, I have tried to bring it closer, and I think I have succeeded to some extent. The site of this *Ard Relig na n'angel*, was, it appears, the property of MacDuach, son of Duach Teangumbha, *alias* Galach (the Valorous), King of Connaught, who died in 504 (*Four Masters* in anno.), and Jarlath promises to give him for it "its full price," viz., abundance of temporal blessings and heaven without end.

21.—The Rule dictated by the Angel.

No fragments of this Rule are now extant, or have been discovered, though it was known to the writer of the Latin *Life of Brendan*, who must have compiled it many centuries after the saint's lifetime, for he says

" that Brendan shaped his life and that of his monks, according to that Rule, which is still preserved by the successors of the saint."

Other rules of this kind have come down to us from the immediate disciples of St. Patrick, who were the fathers and masters of monastic discipline in our early Church, even in St. Brendan's time. Perhaps the most valuable and most complete of those is the Rule of St. Ailbe of Emly, a good translation of which is given in those *Notes on the Life of St. Brendan* that I referred to before, and of which the writer says: " It is not too much to say that, in some respects, this is the most precious document that has been handed down to us by our fathers. It tells us the principles which guided the monks in their practices of religious perfection; it sets before us the daily routine of the community life; it mentions the various superiors, their special duties, the virtues to be practised, the faults to be shunned; it descends to the minutest details connected with the religious, and gives even the quantity and quality of the food to be used at their frugal repasts. This ancient Rule consists of sixty-nine strophes, and the Royal Library, Brussels, preserves a very old and complete copy." What a pity that the Rule of St. Brendan, which was so excellent that it was believed to have been dictated to him by an angel, has not been similarly preserved!

The Plain of Ai, where St. Brendan is said to have received his Rule of the religious life, and to have wrought the signal miracle stated in the text, was, according to John O'Donovan, in his Notes to *Leabhar na-g-Ceart,* "a beautiful plain in the county of Roscommon, extending from near the town of Roscommon to the verge of the barony of Boyle, and from the bridge of 'Cloonfree,' near Strokestown, westwards to Castlerea." These are, he says, the limits of this plain, according to a local tradition; but, he adds, the surmise that, from the position of the Ciarraidhe-Aei, a colony of Kerry people, who migrated to this part of Connaught, about St. Brendan's time, under the patronage of St. Caoilin, a Kerry saint who dwelt there, and through her influence with King Aedh MacEochaidh, were granted lands upon this plain, it must have extended farther to the west, beyond Castlerea, and may have included a portion of the county of Mayo, near the town of Turlough, in the barony of Carra.

In reference to the offer of land made to St. Brendan by the King, the *Latin Life of the Saint,* in the Burgundian Library, Brussels, tells us that "the man of God, not wishing to be puffed up with worldly favours, declined the proffered gift, but gave his blessing in return for the offer made to him, and took his departure for West Connaught, where he may conceal the great fame of his miracle. There, in some time, he converted many souls to Christ, and then returned, with many disciples, to Bishop Erc."

22.—The Motives of the Great Voyages on the Ocean.

These are variously represented in the Lives. In the *Irish Life,* the words of the Gospel, quoted in the text, urged the saint to leave home and family and country for "the love of God that grew in him exceedingly;" and to seek "the secret, retired, secure retreat in the ocean, far apart from mankind." In other accounts of his voyage, his motives are set down to his burning zeal for the salvation of souls that in those remote isles of the ocean, may still "gasp and faint for God's refreshing word;" as our national poet, D. F. MacCarthy, so well expresses it, in Brendan's person:—

I grew to manhood by the Western wave
  Among the mighty mountains on the shore;
My bed the rock, within some natural cave,
  My food whate'er the seas or seasons bore;
My occupation, morn and noon and night,
  The only dream my hasty slumbers gave,
Was Time's unheeding, unreturning flight,
  And the great world that lies beyond the grave.

And thus, where'er I went, all things to me
  Assumed the one deep colour of my mind;
Great nature's prayer rose from the murmuring sea,
  And sinful man sighed in the wintry wind;
The thick-veiled clouds by shedding many a tear,
  Like penitents, grew purified and bright,
And, bravely struggling through earth's atmosphere,
  Passed to the regions of eternal light.

And then I saw the mighty sea expand
  Like Time's unmeasured and unfathomed waves
One with its tide-marks on the ridgy sand,
  The other with its line of weedy graves.
And as beyond the outstretched wave of time,
  The eye of faith a brighter land may meet
So did I dream of some more sunny clime,
  Beyond the waste of waters at my feet.

Some clime where man, unknowing and unknown,
  For God's refreshing word still gasps and faints
Or, happier rather, some Elysian zone,
  Made for the habitation of the saints.

. . . .

The thought grew stronger with my growing days,
  Even like to manhood's strengthening mind and limb,
And often now amid the purple haze
  That evening breathed upon the horizon's rim—
Methought, as there I sought my wished-for home,
  I could descry amid the waters green,
Full many a diamond shrine and golden dome,
  And crystal palaces of dazzling sheen.

But angels came, and whispered, as I dreamt:
  "This is no phantom of a frenzied brain—
God shows this land from time to time, to tempt
  Some daring mariner across the main.
By thee the mighty venture must be made;
  By thee shall myriad souls to God be won;
Arise, depart, and trust to God for aid!"
  I woke, and kneeling, cried, "His will be done!"

In the valuable and interesting Preface to Jubenal's edition of the Latin *Life of St. Brendan*, we find another curious account of the reason of his great voyages, which, as it may help to explain the analogy "in the manner of life and character" of St. Thomas the Apostle, and St. Brendan, set forth in a "List of Saints who were similar in their manner of life," contained in the *Book of Leinster*, I will give it here.

Jubenal refers to an early version of the voyage of Brendan in ancient Low-German, or Low-Saxon, written, he thinks, in the fourteenth century. It is metrical, consisting of 1,752 verses, and agrees, in the main, with the Latin and French versions, but the opening is different:—

"Brendan, having read a book full of miraculous stories, so strange and incredible, waxed indignant at such extravagancies, and threw the book into the fire. Then God, to punish his incredulity, commanded him to forsake his country—to take ship and traverse the wide ocean for seven years, that he may see, with his own eyes, those wonders, and greater than those wonders, he deemed so unworthy of his belief." This is somewhat parallel with St. Thomas's incredulity, as narrated in the Gospel; and some story of the kind may have led to Brendan's being compared with St. Thomas by the old Irish writers.

23.—Sliebh-Daidche (Brandon-Hill.

From the context here, it seems that the place where Brendan first heard "the voice of the angel from heaven," was not far from this *Sliebh-Daidche*, to which "he retired alone," and from which "he gazed upon the vast and gloomy ocean on every side;" and there can be scarcely any doubt that this place was the house or monastery founded by him at the foot of this mountain on the west, where he had St. Finan Cam under his religious training for seven years, as stated in Note (14) *supra*, and where he dwelt occasionally for many years before his Atlantic voyages. The site of this foundation of the saint may be approximately determined by a story preserved in the *Itinerary of Geraldus Cambrensis*, quoted by Holinshed, in his quaint style and language, as follows:—

Legend of St. Brendan.*

"In the south part of Munster, between the maine sea coasting on Espaine (Spain) and St. Brandon's Hills, there is an island, of the one side encompassed

* From *Kerry Magazine*, vol. ii., p. 95.

with a river abundantlie stored with fish, and on the other part enclosed with a little brook, in which place St. Brendan was very much restante. This plot is taken to be such a sanctuary for beasts, as if anie hare, fox, stag, or other wild beaste be chased near that island by dogges, it making straight for the brooke, and as soon as it passeth the streame, it is *so cocksure*, as the hunter may perceive the beasts resting on the one bank, and the dogges questing on the other brim, being, as it were, by some invisible *railes* unbarred from dipping their feet in the shallow ford to pursue the beaste chased. On the other side of this island there runneth a river stored above measure with fresh fish, and especially with salmon, which abundance proceeded from God to provide the great hospitality that was kept there; and in order that the dwellers thereabout shall not, like pinching costrels, make any sale of the fish, let it be poudered (salted) as artificially as it may be, yet it will not keep above the first night or daie that it is taken, so that you may eat it within a short compasse, otherwise it putrifieth, and standeth to no steade."

This "plot that was so great a sanctuary for beasts," where "St. Brendan was very much restante," can be easily traced even at present. It was on the banks of the river Feoghanach, which flows from a lake on the western slope of Brandon-hill, and which forms a fine river for some miles before it reaches the sea near Smerwick harbour. For its size and the length of its course, it is one of the best and earliest salmon rivers in Ireland, its fish being of a singularly delicate and delicious quality. I had some experience of this on a certain occasion many years ago. A friend sent me a present of two salmon from the Feoghanach, for use on Christmas eve. When I received them it was, of course, the close season there, as on every other river in Kerry, and I thought my friend, while intending to be very kind, was not very judicious in his kindness, in sending me what I assumed to be "black," because unseasonable, salmon. However, I had the fish cooked, "within a short compasse;" and I certainly did not "pouder" (salt) any of them, when I found them both in splendid condition and of delicious quality. On the borders of this river, in the townland of Kilquane, there are the ruins of an ancient church, which gives a name to the parish as well as to the townland, Kilquane (Church of Cuan or Mochua), the founder of which lived very probably not long after the days of St. Brendan, and who seems to have been a very zealous and successful church-founder in Kerry, where we find no less than five very early churches bearing the name Kilquane; and, perhaps, as many more named from Mochua, an *alias* of the same holy man. But the church and monastery of Brendan's foundation lay on the other side of this river, somewhat nearer to the western slopes of Brandon-hill, where we find a townland named Shankeel (*Sean-Cill*, or Old Church), on which there had been a church of earlier date than Kilquane, which was called the "Old Church," when Kilquane was founded many years after it. Here, I surmise, lay the scene of Gerald Barry's marvellous story, though "the little brook" there has lost its wonderful virtues, and "the invisible railes" are no longer bars to the hunters' "dogges."

On this townland of Shankeel, and on the adjoining one, Ballynavinoorach, there are, or were some years ago, the remains of a large number of "Cloghanes," or ancient beehive cells or houses, which may have been the dwellings of the monks whom the great repute of St. Brendan had gathered around him in his monastery there; and higher up on the hill-side, where it slopes sharply towards the precipitous cliffs of that most picturesque coast, we find amid the moory wastes a green plot, called to the present day, "*fuithir-na-manac*" (the good land of the monks). There can be no doubt that St. Brendan had lived many years, in or near this district, in Corcaguiney. In the first of these notes, in which I gave his most reliable pedigree, it has been stated that, to all the copies of this pedigree, in MacFerbuis and the *Leabhar Breac*, there is added the *scholium*, "*Agus do Corcadubhne dho*" (he also belonged to Corcaguiney), plainly intimating his long residence there. And we are told in the Latin *Life*, that "soon after his priestly ordination," he founded cells and monastic houses in "his own country, but not many, before his voyage in quest of the land of promise." One of those I believe to have been the monastery of Shanakeel or Ballynavinoorach at the foot of Brandon-hill, which was founded about the same time as his proto-monastery at Ardfert-Brendan.

From this monastery the saint often retired into the mountain then called "Daidche," but with which his name has been associated for long centuries; and here he devoted much time to prayer and heavenly contemplation. And what a place for heavenly contemplation was this! How happily could the saintly soul here withdraw from cares of earth to commune alone with God while he knelt in lowly reverence on those heights of the eternal hills, surrounded on every side by the works of the Creator! Who can describe that glorious vision that fills the eye and bewilders the sense from Brandon Peak, at its elevation of 3,125 feet? It has been well said that no such prospect of sea and island, and mountain and plain, can be had in the three kingdoms; "from Aran of the Saints" on the north; along by the magnificent cliffs of Clare; across the Shannon estuary, which Arthur Young pronounced to be "the noblest mouth of a river in Europe;" by Kerry Head; round by those sublime cliffs and headlands that go out to meet the "league-long rollers" of the wide Atlantic, from Brandon Point to the Dursies, at the mouth of the Kenmare river, in the far south. Of the magnificent panorama which greeted the vision of the saint from this mountain height, may well be said:—

> And thus an airy point he won,
> Where, gleaming with the setting sun,
> One burnish'd sheet of living gold,
> Old ocean lay beneath him roll'd;
> In all her width far winding lay,
> With promontory, creek, and bay;
> And islands that empurpled bright,
> Floated amid the livelier light;
> And mountains that, like giants, stand
> To sentinel enchanted land.

Brendan gazed upon this gorgeous display of nature's

wealth of beauty in ecstacies of gratitude to the great Creator; and while he gazed upon that wondrous ocean, spread out before his eyes like a map, especially at evening, when " the line of light from the burning west" seemed a golden path to other climes where souls may be won to Christ, or where lay some shadowy land of the blessed, "reposing in the giant embrace of the deep," it is no wonder that thoughts and impulses "to tread that golden path" and resolves to go forth in quest of that "beautiful noble island" which he had seen in vision, should have seized upon him and filled his whole soul.

We read in a Life * of Columbus, that his friend, Fra Juan Peres, who welcomed and entertained him at his convent at La Rabida, near Palos, and afterwards secured for him the patronage of Queen Isabella, was well qualified by nature and study to sympathize with the thoughts and aspirations of the great discoverer. He, like Columbus, longed for the discovery of new lands, in order that Christ might be preached to more men; and the place of his abode was well suited to feed his restless imagination and Christian hopes. He had built an observatory on the roof of his convent, and he spent much of his spare time in contemplating the stars by night and the ocean by day. While he watched and peered far out upon the wide sea, the question ever recurred: "Did that *mare tenebrosum* really bound the world, or had it a farther shore, with races of men to be evangelized?" There was infinite room for speculation where all was conjecture.

* Father Knight's *Life of Columbus.*

In a like spirit had Brendan, centuries before Fra Peres, gazed upon that *mare tenebrosum* from his lofty observatory on Brendan Peak, discussed within himself like questionings, and was animated by like Christian hopes and yearnings for new lands where souls may be saved. This elevated scene of Brendan's retirement and contemplation must have become the object of devout pilgrimage in honour of the saint very soon after his lifetime. He may have built there one of those primitive oratories, of which so many examples are still preserved in that district, and blessed that marvellous well of purest water, that springs up yet at almost the highest level of the mountain. But whether he built an oratory there or not, in the course of time oratories and penitential stations were erected there, of which the remains are still to be seen; and these were thronged with pious pilgrims from very early times. To accommodate those devout visitors to the holy mountain, there was made, at some remote period, a passable causeway over hill and bog for seven miles, from Kilmelchedor Church to the summit of the hill, which can still be traced, and is known by the people as *Casan na Naomh* (path of the saints). The course of this is marked on the Ordnance Map (6 in.) as the "saint's road." Along this "way of the saints" many a long-drawn-out procession of clergy and laity moved from the church and house of Brendan at Kilmelchedor, up the mountain slopes, until they reached the highest peak, there to join in some devout celebration. Local tradition tells, that on some high festival, when there was a grand procession, it was found, when the head of the procession arrived at the holy place, the missal containing the Mass of the day had been left behind at the church, seven miles away, and then word was passed along the line of procession, which reached all the way back to the church, and the book, in a short time being sent on from hand to hand, was forthcoming on the hill-top.

The ascent of the mountain from that direction is comparatively easy, and along this "way of the saints," from the west and south, the toil of the pilgrim was not very severe; but the ascent from the east to the mountain top, that is, from the Cloghane side, was a very different matter: for here, indeed, there were stress and toil in the stiff and rather perilous climb up the dizzy heights that frowned over the way of the pilgrim. Rocks, chasms, and sharp declivities, appear on every side; but, as on the western side, the pathway of the devout visitor was improved and made comparatively easy, so also on this precipitous side, the ascent has been relieved of many of its difficulties and dangers by the thoughtful care of the monks. Steps are cut in the solid rocks; every difficult point of marsh, intersecting stream, or frowning declivity, is bridged over with solid stones, well worn by time and by the feet of the pilgrims, but still firmly and safely set in their position. This work is evidently one of remote antiquity, and it must have cost much time and labour, and required no ordinary degree of engineering skill to make a passable roadway over such difficult ground, for three miles, from Cloghane ancient church to the oratories on the summit of the hill. The construction of this *Via Sacra* would alone clearly indicate the wide-spread repute and esteem in which this mountain sanctuary of St. Brendan was held as a place of devout pilgrimage and penitential retreat; but the singular fact of its becoming a benefice church at a very early period, and receiving larger revenues as such than any church or benefice in the diocese of Ardfert, except two, as we learn from the *Taxation of Ardfert* before the year 1300, gives even a stronger proof of the multitude of the pilgrims, and the generosity of their votive offerings at this lofty shrine of the saint. There is no doubt that to receive and accommodate this concourse of pilgrims, larger churches and monastic buildings were erected on the sacred spot, than a visitor to the place at present would suspect. The remains visible now are not extensive nor remarkable in any way; but some years ago, when the public pilgrimage of July, 1868, was being organized, and a temporary altar set up within the ruins of one of the ancient oratories there; in providing stones for the purpose on the mountain-top, a number of sculptured stones were turned up, some of them arched, others carved, like the stones in the richly-carved doorway of Kilmecheder Church; many of them were of some foreign marble, and several of them were pierced through with dowel-holes for gudgeons and cramps to secure more durably the walls of a church built on this elevated site. All this would show that a church of goodly dimensions, and of some architectural merits had been erected there, as well as oratories and penitential stations, together with dwellings of some kind for the Fathers and monastic brethren, who ministered in the church and oratories, and attended to the spiritual and temporal needs of the pilgrims. It may well be questioned whether there has been anywhere in Europe, or perhaps in the world, a mountain sanctuary such as this *Sedes Brendani*, at so great an elevation, amid the clouds and mists and storms inseparable from the position, with groups of buildings so extensive, and the concourse of pilgrims so numerous, as graced and honoured for many centuries this sanctuary of St. Brendan on the loftiest peak of Brandon-hill.

This "Ecclesia Montis Brendani" was taxed in the rural deanery of O'Ferba, one of the five deaneries that composed the ancient diocese of Ardfert before its union with Aghadoe, and it was the terminal church of that deanery, which extended from Killury (Causeway) to Brandon-hill, and there touched the rural deanery of O'Souris, which wound along the coast from the western slopes of this hill, and from Dunquin in the extreme west to the "Villa Pontis," as it is designated in the *Taxatio*, now Castlemain, so called from the castle built on its very ancient bridge across the river Maine.

How long this sanctuary on Brandon-hill maintained its status of being third in point of revenue of all the churches of the diocese of Ardfert, which it held in the *Taxation* of 1300; or how long it continued to receive those rich votive offerings from the pilgrims who resorted to its shrines in such numbers as to give it that financially respectable position, it is now, I fear, impossible to ascertain. There is no reason to doubt that it long maintained a high repute as an approved penitential retreat, as well as a favourite place of devout pilgrimage, not only during the Middle Ages, but long after the religious fervours and the penitential rigours of those "ages of faith" had unhappily abated.

There is a remarkable case on record, of a penitential pilgrimage to Brandon-hill in the first half of the sixteenth century. In the Register of Primate Dowdall of Armagh we read of a great criminal, a parracide, guilty of the murder of his son, who, having publicly confessed his crime and submitted to a course of public penance, was directed by the diocesan penitentiary to make a pilgrimage to the principal "penitential stations" in Ireland before he would be canonically restored to the communion of the faithful. Among those principal "stations" *Knock-Brenain* (Brandon-hill) holds a foremost place in the list of them given in the "Register," ranking with "Ara of the Saints," "St. Patrick's Purgatory at Loughderg," "Skellig of St. Michael," "Holy Cross in Ormond," and the others enumerated. When the pilgrim returned to Armagh with proper certificates of his having visited all those penitential stations, and gave other satisfactory indications of sincere repentance, he was formally absolved and reconciled with the Church. This case may be taken as a fair illustration of the penitential practices of the faithful in Ireland long before, as well as long after, the date at which it occurred, while it furnishes a clear indication of how widely and generally through Ireland the "Station" on Brandon-hill was recognised as a suitable resort for such practices of penance. Though for many long years the sacred shrines on the

"Hill" lie ruined and desolate, many pilgrims still resort to it for purposes of devotion and penance, and some years ago a public pilgrimage thereto, joined in by many thousand persons, took place, an account of which will form the last *piece* in these "Brendaniana."

24.—"TWENTY MEN IN EACH VESSEL."

In the Irish *Life* there is no reference here to the voyage of Brendan to visit St. Enda of Aran for the purpose of taking counsel with him about his intended quest of the "Land of Promise of the Saints;" of which D. F. MacCarthy sings :—

Hearing how blessed Enda lived apart,
  Amid the sacred caves of Ara-mhor,
And how beneath his eye, spread like a chart,
  Lay all the isles of that remotest shore;
And how he had collected in his mind
  All that was known to man of the Old Sea,
I left the *Hill of Miracles behind,
  And sailed from out the shallow sandy Leigh.

. . . .

When I proclaimed the project that I nursed,
  How 'twas for this that I his blessing sought,
An irrepressible cry of joy outburst
  From his pure lips, that blessed me for the thought.
He said that he, too, had in visions strayed
  Over the untracked ocean's billowy foam;
Bade me have hope, that God would give me aid,
  And bring me safe back to my native home.

. . . .

Thus having sought for knowledge and for strength
  For the unheard-of voyage that I planned,
I left those myriad isles, and turned at length
  Southward my bark, and sought my native land.

In the *Navigatio*, of which I will give a literal and unabridged translation, this visit to St. Enda and Ara

* Ardfert (*Saltus Virtutum*—in the *Navigatio*).

of the Saints is mentioned in some detail before the account given of his sailing on his Atlantic voyage, and the number of those who accompanied him on this visit is stated to have been fourteen, while the number of his fellow-mariners on the great voyage is not distinctly stated. In the copy I have from the *Book of Lismore* of this Irish *Life,* the number is marked in Roman numerals (XX); that is, twenty in each vessel, making sixty in all; though in the text of the annexed poem of three quatrains, which is copied from the Egerton MS. (British Museum), the number in each vessel is given (*tricha*) "thirty." But I give in the translation "twenty"—which I have the warrant of the most reliable early Irish tradition for believing to be the correct number. It is now clearly proved that there was in the Calendar of our early Church a special festival in honour and commemoration of the "Egressio familiæ St. Brendani" (the Setting Sail of St. Brendan's Crew), and the number of this "family" or crew must have been well known to number "sixty," or twenty in each of the three vessels, when St. Ængus Cele-De invokes them in his *Book of Litanies,* thus:—"I invoke unto my aid the sixty, who accompanied St. Brendan in his quest of the Land of Promise." ("*Sexaginta qui comitati sunt Stum Brendanum in exquirenda terra promissionis invoco in auxilium meum.*") This festival of the "Egressio" is marked in the Martyrology of Tallaght on the 22nd of March, and must have been religiously observed in our Irish Church long before the date of the compilation of this Martyrology; that is, before A.D. 787, when it was compiled by St. Ængus and St. Mœlruin, at Tallaght, near Dublin ; and the *Book of Litanies* is believed to have been composed before the year 800. The tradition of the voyage of St. Brendan, and the number who sailed with him on his great enterprise, must have been well established at that period. Colgan,* after referring to this festival "in honour of the setting sail," mentions the Lives of saints who lived about St. Brendan's time, or soon after, which contain some references to his voyage, viz. : *The Life of St. Flannan*, chapter 5 ; of *St. Ita*, chapter 31 ; of *St. Munnu*, chapter 25 ; of *St. Brigid*, chapter 49 ; of *St. Machutus*, or *Maclovius*, by John A. Bosco, *passim;* and the *Life of St. Carthage*, senior. The passage in the *Life of St. Brigid*, to which Colgan refers, is very interesting. It is as follows :—" Now, Brendan came to Brigid to know why the monster of the sea had given honour to Brigid beyond the other saints. So, when Brendan reached Brigid, he asked her to confess in what degree she had the love of God. Said Brigid : " Make thou, O Cleric, thy confession first, and I will make mine thereafter." Said Brendan : " From the day I entered upon a devout life I never went over seven furrows without my mind being on God." " Good is the confession," said Brigid. "Do thou now, O Nun," said Brendan, " make thy confession." " The Son of the Virgin knoweth," said Brigid, " from the hour I set my mind on God, I never took it from Him for a moment." " It seems to us, O Nun," said Brendan, " that the monsters of the sea are right, when they give honour to

* *Acta SS. Hiberniæ*, page 731.

thee, beyond us." This story is given more at length in the Latin *Life*[*]—where the conflict of those monsters of the sea is described, and where it is told that one of them, being pursued by the other to imminent destruction, invoked St. Brendan and St. Patrick to defend it, but in vain, and at last commended itself to the protection of St. Brigid, when the monster, that was about to destroy it, at once ceased the pursuit, and its intended victim escaped unharmed. In this account in the Latin *Life*, St. Brigid closes her reply to St. Brendan, with the words: "The more one fixes the mind upon God and loves Him, so much the more do the beasts fear him." If this story be more than a pious allegory, and if an interview, such as this, really occurred between St. Brigid and St. Brendan, after his Atlantic voyage, this voyage must have been accomplished before the year 524, when St. Brigid died, and before St. Brendan had attained the fortieth year of his age, a period of life certainly most suitable for undertaking such an enterprise.

Though the Irish *Life* does not refer to St. Brendan's visit to St. Enda before his first Atlantic voyage, it mentions the visit he made to "Aran, the place wherein Enda dwelt," and where "he remained for the space of a month" before proceeding on his second voyage "in those wooden vessels," which he built by the advice of St. Ita, who told him "he would never find the land he was seeking from God in vessels made of dead stained skins, for it is a holy consecrated land, and men's blood hath never been shed therein;" but that he would find that land later on, in vessels built of wood. And when

* *Vita Sti. Brendani*, c. xvii.

a large wonderful vessel was fitted out, he embarked with sixty men, "who were all praising the Lord, and their minds were towards God."

It would appear from this narrative that the vessels in which he sailed on his first great voyage, which probably lasted five years, without accomplishing his purpose of reaching "the land of promise of the saints" were built in the style of *currachs*, covered with tanned hides, as was usual for such craft; and though they were, as the Irish text states, "*longa mora*" (large vessels), yet the crews in each could scarcely have been more than twenty in vessels of that quality.

25. The Irish text of this strophe is obscure, and Dr. W. Stokes does not translate some of the words. I give the translation partly from the *Notes on the Life of St. Brendan*, referred to above; and from my own study of the words, I think I have fairly made out the sense.

26. This reference to "five years upon the ocean," I believe implies that the first voyage lasted only that length of time, and that the voyage made in the great and well-appointed wooden vessels, which brought St. Brendan to the "land of promise of the saints," lasted two years, thus completing the traditional seven years devoted to the high and holy purpose. Hence, in the Irish version of the two voyages, we are told at the close of the narrative, that "then they reached the land which they had been seeking for the space of seven years, even the Land of Promise."

The *Navigatio*, which details the incidents of the seven years' voyage more fully than the Irish version, has no reference to the saint's return to Ireland, and his preparations for a second yoyage, within those seven years.

27.—The Back of the Whale.

This famous story of the great "Sea-whale" furnishing a secure and convenient place for the celebration of Easter, by St. Brendan and his brethren, during the seven years of their voyaging, is found in all the versions of the voyage that have appeared, whether in early Irish or in Latin, or in any mediæval or modern language, of which copies remain. It must have been well and widely known as a remarkable incident in the traditional history of the voyages of the saint, as early as the time of St. Cuimin of Connor, who employs it to illustrate the special characteristic virtue of St. Brendan, in the strophe, quoted from his *Characteristics of Irish Saints*, in our Irish text. St. Cuimin of Connor flourished, according to Colgan, about the year 656; that is, less than 100 years after the death of St. Brendan, when the traditions of his story must have been somewhat vivid.

It is a curious fact that in all the other tales and legends that have come down to us of early Irish "Imramha," or voyages, such as that of the "Sons of O'Corra," or that of "Maelduin," which have, in many respects, a great affinity with the "Voyage of Brendan," and embody some of its incidents almost *verbatim*, we find not the slightest trace of this wonderful story of the whale forming an island. The tale appears, it is true, in the mediæval *Life of St. Machutus*, or *St. Malo*, by

Bili, who attributes the celebrations on the whale's back to his patron, St. Malo, and gives only a secondary place therein to our St. Brendan; but this *Life* seems to be only a Breton version of our Irish voyage of St. Brendan, with the principal incidents therein slightly altered and thinly disguised; for instance, the wonderful sea-maiden whom Brendan restored to life and baptized, figures in Bili's *Life of St. Malo* as the more wonderful giant, Mildu, of dimensions even greater than those of the sea-maiden, whom St. Machutus restored to life likewise, and baptized in due form.

It may be interesting to give the passage in Bili's *Life of St. Malo*, touching the whale incident:—"When a rising wind had drifted their boat from its moorings, and they were sailing about until the morning of Easter Sunday, after sun-rise, near the hour of tierce, as the crew desired to go to prayer, the master requested St. Machut to sing the Mass on that day, but he excused himself, because there was no suitable place to celebrate; and behold, there came into view suddenly a small island, towards which they proceeded in all haste. Casting anchor, and disembarking thereon, they began to celebrate, St. Machutus singing the Mass. At the *Agnus Dei*, the ground on which they were was suddenly moved, and all who were hearing Mass there, cried out in great alarm: 'Oh! Brendan, we are being swallowed into the sea!' Then, the master said: 'Holy Machut, the demon (*dusmus*, in mediæval Latin) has put on this shape, in order to draw many to destruction.' Whereupon, St. Machut fearlessly spoke: 'Master, have you not preached to many, in my presence, that the whale, through the will of God, became once upon a time the living sepulchre of Jonas, the Prophet, when he refused to go to Nineveh? Here now, in like manner, is this whale provided as a helper for us by God.' Then ordering them all into the boat, he finished the Mass; and, as the whale submissively remained steady under him, he leisurely went into the boat after the others."

It has been said that this extraordinary story, as it is found in the *Voyage of St. Brendan*, or in that of his disciple, St. Machut, has been borrowed from the account of the adventures of Sinbad the Sailor, in the *Arabian Nights' Entertainment*, and was thence introduced into the Brendan legend; but it cannot be shown that those Arabian tales were known in Ireland, or could have been used in that manner so early as the middle of the seventh century, when St. Cuimin of Connor composed his poem on the *Characteristics of Irish Saints*, in which he commended St. Brendan's "severe mode of mortification for seven years on the whale's back." It is certainly much more probable that the whale was known to our Irish mariners, many of whom, from the earliest times, sailed the Northern Seas, the habitat of the "great beast," sooner and better than to the Arabians or other Oriental peoples, in whose seas the whale seldom or never appeared; and that the curious tale travelled from the West to the East, and found its way from Ireland into the *Arabian Nights*, where it figures in the adventures of Sinbad the Sailor.

From whatever source the story originally sprung, it is worthy of note that it had got very generally a firm hold on popular credence, not only in the East, but all over Europe, in mediæval times; for in all those curious books called "Bestiaries," or "Treatises on the natural history of animals, with spiritual meanings attached," that were in general use in the middle ages, this legend of the whale serving as an island on certain occasions, holds a prominent place. In one of those "Bestiaries," we read: "The whale is a great monster that dwells in the ocean. It covers its back with sea-sand, and raising itself out of the water, remains motionless, so that sailors mistake it for an island:—

> And they fasten the high-prowed ships,
> To that false land with anchor ropes;
> On that island they waken flame,
> And a high fire kindle.
> Then the whale, feeling the heat,
> Makes sudden plunge into the salt wave,
> And with the bark down goes the ocean's guest."

The "Bestiary" then gives the "moral," or "spiritual meaning" of this. "The whale signifies the devil; the sands are the riches of this world; the ship is the body that should be guided by the soul, acting as steersman; and the sea is the world. When we put our trust most in the pleasures of this life, and think we are quite safe, suddenly, without any warning, the devil drags us down to hell." *

A sound and excellent "moral," no doubt—one that must have been often happily applied by moralists in the middle ages. Later on we find the legend used by

* See *Mediæval Bestiaries.* A Lecture, by J. Romilly Allen, F.S.A.

Milton, in *Paradise Lost*, when he compares Satan in his huge and massive bulk :—

> . . . to that sea-beast
> Leviathan, whom God of all His works
> Created hugest that swim the ocean stream ;
> Him, haply, slumbering on the Norway foam,
> The pilot of some small night-founder'd skiff,
> Deeming some island, oft, as seamen tell,
> With fixèd anchor in his scaly rind,
> Moors by his side.

In those moral or poetical applications of the wonderful story, where the whale is supposed to typify or represent the demon, the spirit of the tale in the Brendan legend is entirely changed ; for in this, the great "sea-beast," far from showing any diabolical proclivities, co-operates, with great regularity, in the celebration of the Paschal festival, year after year, for seven years, and, in obedience to the servants of God, remains, with marvellous steadiness, "like a green sward evenly smooth," until each year's celebration had come to a satisfactory close, and then, "at once plunges into the sea," as the Irish *Life* narrates. Here, the "spiritual meaning" is evidently quite different from the "moral" deduced from the story in the mediæval "Bestiaries." But how did this "Mariner's tale" first take its rise, and why was it embodied in, and so fully identified with, the Brendan legend as almost to form its characteristic feature, while there is no trace of it in our other early Irish legends of the sea? Towards the solution of the question I venture a conjecture which will be taken at its worth.

It is generally held by those who are most familiar with the versions of the Brendan voyages in various languages, and who have written about them recently, that many of the incidents mentioned therein, and the descriptions of the islands visited in the course of the voyages, refer to, and were probably suggested by an acquaintance with, those islands on the Western Coasts of Ireland and Scotland, on which our early monks and hermits sought refuge from the world, and where they built cells and oratories, that in many instances remain to the present day. In a very interesting paper, which appeared some time ago in *The Irish Ecclesiastical Record*, on "Ardoilean," an island on the Galway Coast, the learned writer, Dr. Healy, suggests that this "island shrine" may have been the original of that "very high and rocky island" (*insula valde saxosa et alta*) which St. Brendan is stated, in the *Navigatio*, to have discovered first in his wanderings. So, with regard to the "Island of Sheep," the "Paradise of Birds," the "Island of St. Paul the hermit," and other islands described in the *Navigatio*, modern German writers who have written largely and learnedly about our Brendan legend, have identified them with well-known islands on the coasts of Ireland or Scotland. There are many islands on our western coasts that may well have suggested the incidents and imagery of the "Paradise of Birds," as given in the Latin version. On our Kerry coast there are at least two islands, which have been at all times true "paradises of birds" to the myriad fowl that congregate upon them, namely, the lesser Scellig and the Tearaght Rock in the Blasquet group. Here, the countless flocks of sea-fowl enjoyed an entire immunity from disturbance, and rested securely after their distant sea-flights, finding for themselves there a real paradise, "where the wicked cease from troubling, and the weary are at rest." The Tearaght, before the light-house was erected on it, "was the most remarkable resort of sea-fowl on our coast, for it was but rarely visited, except in the finest weather, being situated seven miles from the great Blasquet Island, surrounded by the heavy rolling seas of the Atlantic, and without any accessible approach or landing-place. Hence, on all points of the island are congregated myriads of fowl of many various kinds, and the ledges of the rock, up to the summit, present tiers of birds innumerable, in singular array, old and young, beside their nests." Such is the account given of the island by a gentleman who visited it about forty years ago.

Now, if this be true of the islands described in the *Navigatio*, or Latin version of the voyage, we may well believe that the incidents and descriptions in the Irish version had a like origin, and that even the extraordinary story of the whale may have sprung from a similar source, and may have been suggested by a reference to one of our "island shrines." Among the Magharees group of islands is one named *Ilaunamil*, to the present day, and it is so named on the Ordnance Maps. This means the "island of the whale" (*Miol-mor*, in Irish), or Whale Island. Whence came this name? Local tradition tells not. Whether from the fact of a whale being stranded on, or caught near its shore, in some pre-historic time; or, what is not improbable, from its curious shape, strangely like a whale, as may be seen on the maps, tapering towards its north-east point, which may be called the "head" of the whale," and again, sloping off towards the south-west, where we may suppose its tail to lie. At a point where the shoulder rounds off, there is a deep cavern on the face of the cliff, facing the Western Ocean, running into the island, nearly 300 ft. Into this the "league-long rollers" of Alantic rush with tremendous force, and are ejected to a great height from the mouth of the cavern. This is named on the map *Coosatrim*, which I take to mean the creek of the squirt, or spout (*Sram*, in Irish, having that sense) and this "spouting" may have quickened the fancy of some primeval visitor to liken the island to, and to name it from, a spouting whale.

There is no reason to doubt that the island had this name from the earliest times, and was known as such in St. Brendan's day. Now, it lies within a short distance of Brandon Point and Brandon-hill, being the nearest island sanctuary to which the saint could resort from his oratory on the mountain, and it is very probable that he did often resort thither, on occasions when he sought deeper solitude than was possible for him in any of his monasteries or oratories on the mainland. He may have retired to this "whale's island," on some of the great festivals—such as Easter-tide—in order to give himself more entirely to God in solitude, as some of our great saints have done on such solemnities; and thus may have sprung up the wonderful tale of his celebrating Easter on the whale's back, which grew and "improved," as we may expect, from generation to generation, until it became the characteristic trait in the saint's traditional history.

Whatever may be thought of this account of the *genesis* of the extraordinary tale, a description of the island, by a writer in the *Kerry Magazine*, who had often visited it many years ago, may be interesting:—"Ilaun-na-mill is an island of mountain limestone, surrounded by precipices, against which the sea is for ever breaking, or by ledges of rock, up which it rushes, and over which it seeths and foams. Chasms run into it, precipitous at the sides, but sloping at the ends; in one place the sea breaks through an arch, and sinks and rises with the swell outside." This is the place known as *Coosatrim*, or the "creek of the spout," where the sea often rises to a great height. From the description of the precipices and chasms that surround the island on all sides, it will be seen that making a landing upon it was no easy task; hence, the writer describes his effort to land as follows:—"Take down the sail—there, that little nook, we can land there; back a stroke with the bow-oar, so, and now you stand at the bow ready for a chance, when that coming swell has spent its force upon the rock before it falls away. Now, in she goes; steady, steady!—ah, too late, you could not do it; and she falls away, with the retiring waters, lest the advancing wave should dash her on the rocks. Here it comes, and breaks upon them, climbing up through crevices—now, again—well done!—Hasten up before the next wave comes on; and so, one by one, we get ashore, and clamber up the cliffs." It would seem from this graphic account that it required no ordinary deftness in handling a boat to effect a landing on this island, almost as much as would be needful to secure foothold on the back of a genuine whale; and perhaps it was this difficulty of access that led to its being never permanently, or even temporarily, inhabited, from the remotest times, though it has an area of about thirty statute acres; and though the soil is fairly good, there are little or no traces of cultivation: the description given of the "Whale Island" in the *Navigatio*, namely, that "there was no grass on the island, very little timber, and no sand on its shores," is literally true of *Ilaunamil*, the whale island of the Magharees at the present day.

28.—The Prayer of St. Brendan.

In this Irish version of the "Voyage," the prayer uttered by Brendan, when in extreme danger, from "the deep, fierce currents, and the vast black whirlpools of the rough-maned ocean," when lashed to fury by violent tempests, is given very briefly: "It is enough for you, O mighty sea, to drown me alone, but suffer my people to escape." What a noble spirit of self-sacrifice, of heroic devotion, and anxious solicitude for the safety of his brethren, the companions of his voyage, do these few words bespeak, on the part of the saint, who seemed not to heed his own peril, while he pleaded earnestly for the safety of his companions. Such a prayer, so generous and so disinterested, surely deserved the success it obtained; for the "sea grew still, and the whirlpools at once subsided, and thenceforth harmed no one."

This prayer of St. Brendan, during his voyages, has been considerably enlarged by later writers, and in mediæval times several forms of it were used in popular devotions in many countries of Europe, as well as in Ireland. A Latin version of one of those forms of the prayer was published for the first time, some years ago, by Cardinal Moran, in his *Acta Sti. Brendani*, of which MS. copies were found in the Sessorian Library, Rome, and in the monastery of St. Gall, in Switzerland. This *Oratio Sti. Brendani*, Cardinal Moran tells us, "is full of the deepest piety, and will be found to present a striking resemblance to the hymn of St. Colman, in the *Liber Hymnorum* and other prayers of our early Church."

To the copy in the Sessorian Library was affixed a rubric signifying that "St. Brendan the monk, when seeking the land of promise for seven successive years, made this prayer from the Word of God, through St. Michael the Archangel, while he sailed over the seven seas. Whosoever will sing or recite it one hundred times, on his bended knees or prostrate on the ground, either for himself, or for a friend or relative, living or dead, shall obtain pardon of all his sins, and shall be saved from the pains of hell."

This rubric most truly declares that the prayer was "made from the Word of God," for its petitions are mainly composed of extracts from and references to the text and history of the Old and New Testaments; and in this respect it was worthy of being inspired even "through St. Michael the Archangel," as the rubric states. It commences with the invocation of the Holy Trinity, Father, Son, and Holy Ghost; then there are fourteen petitions: "Spare me a sinner," addressed to the "Lord Jesus Christ, Son of the Living God," in honour of fourteen mysteries of His life, death, resurrection and ascension, and of the descent of the Holy Ghost. A long and beautiful prayer to the adorable Trinity, invoked as the Almighty Creator, "Who, out of shapeless matter, formed all things and creatures in their proper forms and species," introduces seven petitions: "Deliver me, O Lord," in honour of the special work of each of the seven days of creation, mentioned in some detail. Then come nine petitions: "Deliver me, O Lord," in honour of the nine choirs of angels, named at some length in their various orders. The same petition: "Deliver me, O Lord," is repeated forty-five times, in as many paragraphs, referring to facts and persons recorded in all the Books of the Old Testament, in some instances pretty fully, appealing for deliverance, in the first place, through the "blood of the righteous Abel, the first priest and martyr;" and lastly, "through the martyrdom of the seven Machabees, who, with their mother freely chose to be martyrs." Again, the same petition is addressed thirty times to the Lord, in as many paragraphs, referring to the miracles and wonderful deliverances recorded in the Books of the New Testament, from "the deliverance of the prophet Zachary from his dumbness, and of St. Elizabeth from barrenness," to many of the miraculous deliverances recounted in the history of St. Paul.

This portion of the prayer closes with a fervent and eloquent address to the Holy Trinity, to deliver him at all times from an evil death, and during his life, from every stain of soul and body; and to have mercy on the souls of his father and mother, his brothers and sisters, his relatives, his friends and his enemies, and all his benefactors, living and dead, especially those for whom he may have promised to pray.

The next portion is addressed directly to the saints and angels, beginning with: "Holy Mary, Mother of God," and then invoking the nine orders of angels—naming St. Michael, St. Gabriel, and St. Raphael; then St. John the Baptist, the twelve Apostles, and the Evangelists by name. A special prayer again to "Holy Mary, Mother of God, most chaste and most compassionate Virgin," asking her intercession "for him her unworthy servant;" then the mysteries of the life and death of Christ are briefly recited in a form not unlike that of the *Anima Christi* of St. Ignatius of Loyola to "defend me from the snares of the crafty enemy." Various classes and orders of saints are then invoked, that they may all prove a shield and safeguard before the Most Holy Trinity, for his soul; and for his body also, "from the soles of his feet to the crown of his head;" and the prayer concludes with a series of twenty petitions, full of unction and piety, addressed to the Persons of the adorable Trinity, for his deliverance from all manner of evil and misfortune, spiritual and temporal. Here is one of them: "I beseech the Father, through the Son; I beseech the Son, through the Father; I beseech the Holy Spirit, through the Father and the Son, and through every creature that praiseth the Lord, that all vice may be removed far from me, and that every saintly virtue may take root in my heart and soul.'

This "Oratio" occupies nearly eighteen large octavo pages in the *Acta Sti. Brendani,* so that the reciting of the whole, with due attention and devotion, would take some time, and the repetition of it, as the rubric prescribes, for "one hundred times, on bended knees or prostrate on the ground," would be a devotional exercise, involving no small labour, and well calculated to excite those salutary dispositions necessary to obtain the promised remission of sin, and freedom from the punishments due to it. It breathes throughout a spirit of the most fervent piety, and of an intimate and reverential knowledge of the Holy Scriptures, from Genesis to Revelations. In this respect it may compare favourably with many forms of prayer that are in popular use in latter times, which are not remarkable either for piety or knowledge, and not much to be recommended, as a competent authority has declared, "for either sentiment or expression." Certainly our ancestors in the faith, during past ages, who were familiar with such forms of popular devotion as this *Oratio Sti. Brendani,* and other beautiful prayers of our early Irish Church, so full of sound knowledge as well as sincere piety, were better able to comply with the advice of the Psalmist—to pray as well as "to sing wisely" in their devotions—than the faithful who use certain prayer-manuals in modern times.

The latest version of the prayer of St. Brendan that I am acquainted with, is the poetical one given by the late Denis F. M'Carthy, in his poem of the "Voyage of St. Brendan," from which I have already taken some extracts. It is well known that the poet had a tender devotion to the saint, and that his beautiful poem in his honour was the fruit of this devotion, and that it was to him truly "a labour of love." His rendering of the prayer is worthy of this tender piety, and not at all unworthy of his poetic genius. With the stanzas comprising it, I will conclude these notes on the *Betha Brenainn.*

THE PRAYER.

We were alone on the wide watery waste—
  Nought broke its bright monotony of blue,
Save where the breeze the flying billows chased,
  Or where the clouds their purple shadows threw.
We were alone—the pilgrims of the sea—
  One boundless azure desert round us spread;
No hope, no trust, no strength, except in Thee,
  Father, who once the pilgrim-people led.

And when the bright-faced sun resigned his throne
  Unto the Ethiop Queen who rules the night,
Who, with her pearly crown and starry zone,
  Fills the dark dome of heaven with silvery light—
As on we sailed, beneath her milder sway,
  And felt within our hearts her holier power,
We ceased from toil, and humbly knelt to pray
  And hailed with vesper hymns the tranquil hour!

We breathed aloud the Christian's filial prayer,
  Which makes us brothers even with the Lord;
Our Father, cried we, in the midnight air,
  In heaven and earth, be Thy great name adored;
May Thy bright kingdom, where the angels are,
  Replace this fleeting world, so dark and dim.
And then, with eyes fixed on some glorious star,
  We sang the Virgin-Mother's vesper hymn!

Hail, brightest star! that o'er life's troubled sea
  Shines pitying down from heaven's elysian blue!
Mother and maid, we fondly look to thee,
  Fair gate of bliss, where heaven beams brightly through.
Star of the morning! guide our youthful days,
  Shine on our infant steps in life's long race;
Star of the evening! with thy tranquil rays,
  Gladden the aged eyes that seek thy face.

Hail, sacred maid! thou brighter, better Eve,
  Take from our eyes the blinding scales of sin;
Within our hearts no selfish poison leave,
  For thou the heavenly antidote can'st win.
O sacred Mother! 'tis to thee we run—
  Poor children, from this world's oppressive strife;
Ask all we need from thy immortal Son,
  Who drank of death, that we might taste of life.

Hail, spotless Virgin! mildest, meekest maid!
  Hail, purest Pearl that time's great sea hath borne!
May our white souls, in purity arrayed,
  Shine, as if they thy vestal robes had worn;
Make our hearts pure, as thou thyself art pure;
  Make safe the rugged pathway of our lives;
And make us pass to joys that will endure
  When the dark term of mortal life arrives.

'Twas thus in hymns and prayers and holy psalms,
  Day tracking day, and night succeeding night,
Now driven by tempests, now delayed by calms,
  Along the sea we winged our varied flight.

THE VOYAGE OF ST. BRENDAN.

INTRODUCTION.

THE earliest version of the "Voyage" that has come down to us is undoubtedly that contained in the *Betha Brenainn*, as we find it in the *Book of Lismore*, and other MSS. I have already given the commencement of this, as far as the beautiful prayer, whereby Brendan hushed the storm-lashed ocean and saved his companions from all hurt. Then it goes on to tell that on a certain day the demon appeared in "awful, hideous form" on the sail of Brendan's vessel, visible only to the saint, who asked him why he had come there before his proper time. Satan answered that he sought his hell in the gloomy abysses of the dark sea. He was then permitted to reveal to Brendan "the gate of hell;" and a lengthened description is given of the horrors and terrors of that place of torments, in terms that show the wonderful copiousness of the Irish language. The brethren asked Brendan with whom he conversed; he told them, and related some of the awful torments he had witnessed. Thereupon one of the brethren desired through curiosity to behold some of those torments. On being permitted, he was seized with terror, crying out: "Woe, woe, woe, to him who may come into that prison," and died immediately, but was at once restored to life by the prayers of Brendan.

Another day they found a beautiful flaxen-haired maiden, "whiter than the snow, or the foam of the sea," but of a preternatural size. She was dead, being pierced through the body with a spear. Brendan restored her to life, and ascertaining from her that "she was of the dwellers in the sea, who pray and expect their resurrection," he gave her baptism. Then he asked her whether she preferred to go at once to heaven or return to her people. "To heaven," she said in language that Brendan alone understood, "for I hear the voices of the angels praising the mighty Lord." After receiving the holy Viaticum she breathed forth her spirit and received Christian burial there.

Soon after they came to an island beautiful and lofty, but could find no landing-place, though they searched for twelve days. They saw a splendid church upon it, and they heard the chanting of men who were praising the Lord therein, but the voices only lulled them all to sleep. At length a waxed tablet was cast down to them, inscribed with the words: "Waste no more time or toil in seeking to enter this island, for you cannot come in, but the island you are in quest of, you will find elsewhere." They turn away from the island, taking with them reverently the waxed tablet, in remembrance of the visit.

On another occasion the crew were tormented with a great thirst, and they discovered a stream of limpid water gushing from a rock, from which they desired to drink. "First bless it," said Brendan, "that you may test its quality." Then Brendan pronounced a blessing, and instantly the stream dried up, and the devil appeared, mocking their thirst, which, however, at once left them. ...

The version then relates the return of Brendan and his brethren again to their own country, after their five years' voyaging, and the cordial welcome they received everywhere from their people, especially St. Brendan, who is said to have then "performed many miracles, healing the sick and expelling demons and vices." After some stay at home, he visits his foster-mother St. Ita, who, after an affectionate greeting, reminds him that he had not taken counsel with her about his voyage, and assures him that he could not find the "Land of Promise" in vessels made of the skins of dead beasts—but in wooden vessels, properly constructed for his voyage. Thereupon Brendan proceeded to Connaught, where a large and commodious ship was built and provided with the needful equipment for a voyage. Then he embarked, having a crew of sixty men, among whom were the shipwright and the smith, who had worked at the construction of the ship. A man called "Crosan," which Dr. W. Stokes translates "Buffoon," besought Brendan, on his knees, that he might go with him, and he was admitted into the ship at the last moment. Then they sailed forth into the ocean, calling first to Aran, where St. Enda dwelt; and here they stay for the space of a month. Proceeding on their voyage westwards, they soon reached a large, lofty, beautiful island, on the shore of which they saw a great number of sea-cats, which threatened to devour them. To save the rest of the crew from destruction, the *Crosan* consented to sacrifice himself, and having received the last sacraments, leaps ashore with joy, and is instantly devoured by those monsters; thus, as the text has it, "the notoriously sinful man, who came last into the ship, should be chosen the first to go to heaven . . . in illustration of the words of Christ. 'The first shall be last, and the last first.'" Soon after the smith falls grievously ill and likely to die. Brendan asked him whether he preferred a longer life to an immediate admission into heaven. The smith declares that "he has heard the voice of the Lord calling him," and therefore choses to go to heaven at once. After receiving the Viaticum he dies, and is buried in the sea, as no land was near; where his body, wonderful to relate, lay peaceably, without sinking or moving in any direction.

Soon after they come to a small island, but they are met at the landing-place by a crowd of demons, like coal-black pigmies, who opposed their landing. These they will not combat, according to Brendan's advice, and after some delay they wished to weigh anchor and depart; but their anchor got so firmly fixed in the rocks, they could not hoist it up, and were obliged to sail on without it. This was a serious embarrassment, for the smith who could forge a new anchor was dead; but Brendan desired a priest in the company "to do smith's work for a month:" and he blessed his hands for the purpose, so that in a short time he supplied an anchor of excellent workmanship.

They sailed on still westwards, and they reach a small but beautiful island, with its many bays well supplied with fish. Here they see a church built of stone, and an ancient penitent praying therein, without flesh or blood, and only the skin, like shrivelled leather, on his bones." He warns them of their danger from the attack of a monstrous sea-cat that was on the island, and they sail quickly away, pursued by the monster. The rest of this story can be found in the *Legend of the Three Students who went on a Pilgrimage.*

This venerable hermit had revealed to Brendan the land he was seeking, even the Land of Promise; and soon afterwards, when the term of seven years had expired, the saint at last attained the object of his desires, and happily reached the earthly paradise. Here, while he and his companions search for a landing-place, they hear the voice of a venerable old man, who invited them to land, and to rest now from their toilsome quest, and enter upon and enjoy those "happy plains of paradise, and the delightful fields of this "radiant land." Then follows an eloquent description of the beauties and delights of this Island of the Blessed, which closes with a declaration from the ancient dweller therein that: "Happy is he who through his well-deservings and good works merits, in union with Brendan, son of Finlug, to inhabit for ever this island whereon we stand."

Here the narrative breaks off abruptly, and the Irish text concludes with a long passage from the *Fis Adhamhnan* (Vision of Adamnan), which has no relevance with the Voyage of Brendan.

This is a brief but accurate outline of the Irish version of the Voyage, from which it will be seen that the incidents of the story, as told therein, are few and baldly related, while the structure of the tale is rather disjointed and fragmentary, seemingly made up of scraps and fragments from two or more earlier versions in Irish that have been lost. It differs considerably in those respects from the Latin version (the *Navigatio*), of which I will now give a literal and complete translation into our modern English, the first of its kind that has been published. In this version the incidents related are numerous and consecutive, are told more circumstantially, and the current of the story runs on smoothly to the end. This was the most popular version during the Middle Ages, as the story itself was certainly the most popular of all the mediæval legends of which we have any account. Hence there is scarcely a public library in Europe that does not contain some MS. copies of it, and in one library, the Bibliothèque Royale, Paris, there are no less than eleven MS. copies, some of them written in the eleventh century; one MS. copy in the Vatican library, which Cardinal Moran consulted in preparing his edition of the *Navigatio* in his *Acta Sti. Brendani*, is referred by a competent judge to the ninth century. From this Latin version sprung many of the versions into early German, early French, and other languages. One of those composed in the Romanz language by an Anglo-Norman trouvere, "who wonned in the English court of King Henry Beauclerc, and basked in the smiles of his queen," the beautiful Adelais of Louvain, was translated from the Latin, and addressed to the "Lady Adelais," or "Auliz," about the year 1121. There is a learned and interesting paper upon this in the number of *Blackwood's*

Magazine for June, 1836, in which the writer* gives a spirited translation from the "Romanz" into racy, if somewhat quaint, English, of many passages of this "Voyage of St. Brendan," commencing thus:—

> Lady Adelais, who queen
> By the grace of heaven hath been
> Ycrowned, who this land hath blest
> With peace and wholesome laws, and rest,
> Both by King Henry's stalwart might
> And by thy counsels mild and right—
> For these, thy holy benison
> May the Apostles shed each one
> A thousand. thousand-fold upon thee;
> And, since thy mild command hath won me
> To turn this goodly historie
> Into romanz, and carefully
> To write it out, and soothly tell
> What to St. Brandan erst befel—
> At thy comand I undertake
> The task right gladly, but will make
> No light or silly pleasantrie
> Unfit in such grave work to be.

I will, in my translation, follow the division into chapters, and the headings thereof, as marked off in Cardinal Moran's edition, and at the end of certain chapters I will append the corresponding translated passages from Blackwood's *Anglo-Norman Trouveres*—as well as certain poems of modern English poets, who have treated in verse some incidents of our "goodly historie."

* I have tried to ascertain from Messrs. Blackwood, who kindly gave me permission to use this paper, the name of the writer, but they could not tell me.

THE VOYAGE OF ST. BRENDAN.

CHAPTER I.

ST. BRENDAN IS STIMULATED BY THE EXAMPLE OF ST. BARINTHUS TO SEEK THE LAND OF PROMISE.

ST. BRENDAN, son of Finnlug Ua Alta, of the race of Eoghan, was born in the marshy district of Munster* He was famed for his great abstinence and his many virtues, and was the patriarch of nearly three thousand monks. While he was in his spiritual warfare, at a place called Ardfert-Brendan† there came to him one evening, a certain father, named Barinthus, of the race of King Nial, who, when questioned by St. Brendan, in frequent converse, could only weep, and cast himself prostrate, and continue the longer in prayer; but Brendan raising him up, embraced him, saying: "Father, why should we be thus grieved on the occasion of your visit? Have you not come to give us comfort? You ought, indeed, make better cheer for the brethren. In God's name, make known to us the divine secrets, and refresh our souls by recounting to us the various wonders you have seen upon the great ocean." Then Barinthus, in reply, proceeds to tell of a certain island: "My dear child,

* Ciarriagho Luachra.

† "Saltus Virtutis Brendani," in some of the texts.

Mernoc, the guardian of the poor of Christ, had fled away from me to become a solitary, and found, nigh unto the Stone mountain, an island full of delights. After some time I learned that he had many monks there in his charge, and that God had worked through him many marvels. I, therefore, went to visit him, and when I had approached within three days' journey, he, with some of the brethren, came out to meet me, for God had revealed to him my advent. As we sailed unto the island the brethren came forth from their cells towards us, like a swarm of bees, for they dwelt apart from each other, though their intercourse was of one accord, well grounded in faith, hope, and charity; one refectory; one church for all, wherein to discharge the divine offices. No food was served but fruits and nuts, roots and vegetables of other kinds. The brethren, after complin, passed the night in their respective cells until the cock crew, or the bell tolled for prayer. When my dear son and I had traversed the island, he led me to the western shore, where there was a small boat, and he then said: "Father, enter this boat, and we will sail on to the west, towards the island called the Land of Promise of the Saints, which God will grant to those who succeed us in the latter days." When we entered the boat and set sail, clouds overshadowed us on every side, so dense that we could scarcely see the prow or the stern of the boat. After the lapse of an hour or so, a great light shone around us, and land appeared, spacious and grassy, and bearing all manner of fruits. And when the boat touched the shore, we landed, and walked round about the island for fifteen days, yet could not reach the limits thereof. No plant saw we there without its flower; no tree without its fruit; and all the stones thereon were precious gems. But on the fifteenth day we discovered a river flowing from the west towards the east, when, being at a loss what to do, though we wished to cross over the river, we awaited the direction of the Lord. While we thus considered the matter, there appeared suddenly before us a certain man, shining with a great light, who, calling us by our names, addressed us thus: "Welcome, worthy brothers, for the Lord has revealed to you the land He will grant unto His saints. There is one-half of the island up to this river, which you are not permitted to pass over; return, therefore, whence you came."

When he had ceased to speak, we asked him his name, and whence he had come. But he said: "Why do you ask these questions? Should you not rather inquire about this island. Such as you see it now, so has it continued from the beginning of the world. Do you now need food or drink? Have you been weighed down by sleep, or shrouded in the darkness of the night? Know then for certain that here it is for ever day, without a shadow of darkness, for the Lord Jesus Christ is the light thereof, and if men had not transgressed the commandment of God, in this land of delights would they have always dwelt."

Hearing this we were moved to tears, and having rested awhile, we set out on our return journey, the man aforesaid accompanying us to the shore, where our boat was moored. When we had entered the boat, this man was taken from our sight, and we went on into the thick darkness we had passed through before, and thus unto the Island of delights. But when the brethren there saw us, they rejoiced with great joy at our return, as they had long bewailed our absence, and they said: "Why, O fathers, did you leave us, your little flock, to stray without a shepherd in the wilderness? We knew, indeed, that our abbot frequently departed somewhere from us, and remained away sometimes a month, sometimes a fortnight, or a week more or less." When I heard this I tried to console them, and said: "Brethren, harbour no thought of evil, for your lives here are certainly passed at the very portals of paradise. Not far away from you lies the island, called the 'Land of Promise of the Saints,' where night never falls nor day closes; thither your abbot, Mernoc, resorts, as the angels of God watch over it. Do you not know, by the fragrance of our garments, that we have been in the paradise of God?" They replied: "Yes, father, we knew well that you had been in the paradise of God, for we often found this fragrance from the garments of our abbot, which lingered about us for nearly forty days." I then told them that I had abided therein with my dear son, for a fortnight, without food or drink; yet, so complete was our bodily refreshment, that we would seem to others to have been filled to repletion. When forty days had passed, having received the blessings of the abbot and the brethren, I came away with my companions, that I may return to my little cell to which I will go on to-morrow.

Having heard all this, St. Brendan and his brethren

cast themselves on the ground, giving glory to God in these words: "Righteous Thou art, O Lord, in all Thy ways, and holy in all Thy works, who hast revealed to Thy children so many and so great wonders; and blessed be Thou for Thy gifts, who hast this day refreshed us all with this spiritual repast." When these discourses were ended, St. Brendan said: "Let us now proceed to the refection of the body, and the "new commandment."* The night having passed, St. Barinthus, receiving the blessing of the brethren, returned to his own cell.

NOTE.—In the beginning of this chapter is given the earliest Latin translation that I have met of the name of *Ardfert-Brendan*, or *Clonfert-Brendan*, in the form "Saltus virtutis Brendani," as some of the earliest MSS. have it, or "Saltus virtutum B.," as others give it. I translate this *Ardfert-Brendan*, for I believe the context points to that location of the scene of the story, while I am aware that "saltus" is curiously ambiguous, and may mean a "clearance in a wood," or a "wood-pasture" (in Irish, *cluain*), as well a "height or bluff" (in Irish *Ard*) in land or river; and that therefore, the Latin may mean either *Ardfert-Brendan* or *Clonfert-Brendan*. The Latin word *virtus*, given by those early writers who must have been familiar with the ancient Gaelic, as an equivalent for the second part of the name, *feart*, clearly indicates the true etymology of those names, for it shows that the word *feart*, or its earlier form *firt*, was simply borrowed from the Latin *virtus*, and had exactly the same meaning. *Ardfert-Brendan* does not, therefore, mean the "height of the grave" (*fert* in Irish), as some authorities have suggested, but the *Ard* or bluff of the "virtue," or the powers of St. Brendan; that is, of the house or place where the virtues or spiritual powers of the saint and his children were exercised, and which was the scene of many of his marvellous works. The name, when fully

* *i.e.* the washing of the feet, as at the Last Supper.

and correctly given, is *Ardfert-Brendan*, and this could not refer in any way to "the grave" of St. Brendan, which was certainly not at Ardfert, but, as all his Lives tell us, at Clonfert, where his remains were interred, and from which, as far as we know, they were never translated.

The interesting story of the visit of Baruin, or as the name is Latinized, Barinthus, to St. Brendan, told so circumstantially and dramatically in this chapter of the *Navigatio*, has no counterpart in any Irish version of the Voyage of St. Brendan that has been as yet discovered; nor is there, as far as I have heard, any trace of this very curious tale of the Voyage of St. Barinthus and his "dear son Mernoc" to the "Land of Promise of the Saints," such as we find it detailed here, in any other account of such early voyages that has come down to us in ancient MSS. Whether the tale is purely legendary, fancifully devised to explain why St. Brendan "had set his heart" upon his ocean quest of this same "Land of Promise of the Saints," or whether there had been an old-world tradition of some voyage on the Atlantic by a real Father Baruin, which was dressed up in this form, as a preface to Brendan's Voyage, by some writer or reciter of that wonderful tale in later times, it is now, I suppose, impossible to determine. We know, indeed, that there existed a real Father Baruin, who was abbot of a monastery at Druimcuillen, on the borders of Munster and Leinster (now Drumcullen parish, King's County), and whose feast is noted in the *Martyrology of Tallaght* on the 3rd of May, and also on the 21st of that month; but his period does not fit in with the date of such a tale as this visit to St. Brendan, which should be early in the sixth century; whereas the abbot of Drumcullen is stated "to have flourished" at the end of that century, many years after St. Brendan's death.

There is a very ancient church at Baruin, now Barrow, a few miles west from Ardfert, which is still called in Irish *Teampul Baruin* (Church of Barun). This old church, now a desolate ruin, with a few remains still existing, dates probably from the eleventh century, when the district around it may have been formed into a distinct parish, which was valued and taxed as a separate benefice, in the Taxation of Ardfert Diocese, in 1300, as "ecclesia de Barun" (Church of Barun or Barrow). From the appearance of the site and the surroundings of this old church, we can infer that there had been a much earlier religious foundation at the place, which may have been, in fact, contemporaneous with St. Brendan's foundation of his monastery at Ardfert; and here, at ancient Barun, may have stood the "little cell" (*cellula*, in the Latin text) or oratory, to which, we are told, St. Barinthus returned on the close of his visit to his saintly brother at Ardfert. However this may be, the name still survives in the little church and district of Baruin, and it is not improbable that the founder of the oratory there, where he had the harbour beside Fenit, opening into the Atlantic, near at hand, was a sea-faring saint, like so many of the earliest founders of such oratories and monastic houses along the coast of Ireland, who may have made some voyages on the great ocean, and recounted his adventures thereon to his neighbours at the Ardfert Monastery, which he, no doubt, visited occasionally. Hence may have come the germ of this interesting legend of Baruin and Mernoc, as narrated in this chapter.

CHAPTER II.

ST. BRENDAN AND HIS COMPANIONS SET SAIL.

ST. BRENDAN soon after selected from his whole community fourteen monks [amongst whom was the youthful Machutus, so famous and worthy of God's favour, who had been chosen of God from his infancy, and who persevered to the end of his life in the divine praises, as anyone may know who reads his venerable *Acts*, wherein his early and latest renowned works are recorded].* Taking these apart, the venerable

* The words within brackets are found only in two late MSS., and are clearly an interpolation.

father Brendan retired with them into an oratory where he thus addressed them:—"Dearly beloved fellow-soldiers of mine, I request your advice and assistance, for my heart and mind are firmly set upon one desire; if it be only God's holy will, I have in my heart resolved to go forth in quest of the Land of Promise of the Saints, about which Father Barinthus discoursed to us. What do you think? What is your advice?" But they, well knowing the purpose of their holy father, replied, as with one voice:—"Father-abbot, your will is our will also. Have we not forsaken our parents? Have we not slighted our family prospects? Have we not committed into your hands even our very bodies? We are, therefore, ready to go with you, whether unto life or unto death, provided only we find such to be the will of God."

St. Brendan and the chosen brethren then decided to make a fast of forty days, at three days' intervals,* and afterwards to take their departure. Those forty days having elapsed, St. Brendan, affectionately taking leave of his monks, and commending them to the special care of the Prior of his monastery, who was afterwards his successor there, sailed forth towards the west, with fourteen brethren, to the island wherein dwelt St. Enda, and remained there three days and three nights. Having received the blessing of this holy father and all his monks, he proceeded to the remotest part of his own country, where his parents abode. However, he willed not to visit them, but went up to the summit of the mountain†

* *i.e.*, taking food only every third day.

† *Hodie*, Brandon-Hill.

there, which extends far into the ocean, on which is "St. Brendan's Seat;" and there he fitted up a tent, near a narrow creek, where a boat could enter. Then St. Brendan and his companions, using iron implements, prepared a light vessel, with wicker sides and ribs, such as is usually made in that country, and covered it with cow-hide, tanned in oak-bark, tarring the joints thereof, and put on board provisions for forty days, with butter enough to dress hides for covering the boat and all utensils needed for the use of the crew. He then ordered the monks to embark, in the name of the Father, and of the Son, and of the Holy Ghost; but while he stood on the shore and blessed the little creek, behold three more monks from his monastery came up, and cast themselves at his feet, saying: "O dearest father, suffer us, for the love of Christ, to accompany you on your voyage, otherwise we will die here of hunger and thirst, for we are resolved to travel with thee all the days of our lives." When the man of God saw their great urgency, he ordered them to embark, saying: "Have your will, my children;" but adding: "I know well why you have come hither. One of you has acted well, for God had provided for him an excellent place; but for two others, He has appointed harm and judgment."

St. Brendan then embarked, and they set sail towards the summer solstice. They had a fair wind, and therefore no labour, only to keep the sails properly set; but after twelve days the wind fell to a dead calm, and they had to labour at the oars until their strength was nearly exhausted. Then St. Brendan would encourage and exhort them: "Fear not, brothers, for our God will be unto us a helper, a mariner, and a pilot; take in the oars and helm, keep the sails set, and may God do unto us, His servants and His little vessel, as He willeth." They took refreshment always in the evening, and sometimes a wind sprung up; but they knew not from what point it blew, nor in what direction they were sailing.

CHAPTER III.

Their First Discovery of Land.

At the end of forty days, when all their provisions were spent, there appeared towards the north, an island very rocky and steep. When they drew near it, they saw its cliffs upright like a wall, and many streams of water rushing down into the sea from the summit of the island; but they could not discover a landing-place for the boat. Being sorely distressed with hunger and thirst, the brethren got some vessels in which to catch the water as it fell; but St. Brendan cautioned them: "Brothers! do not a foolish thing; while God wills not to show us a landing-place, you would take this without His permission; but after three days the Lord Jesus Christ will show His servants a secure harbour and resting-place, where you may refresh your wearied bodies."

When they had sailed round the island for three days, they descried, on the third day, about the hour of none, a small cove, where the boat could enter; and St. Brendan forthwith arose and blessed this landing-place, where the rocks stood on every side, of wonderful steepness like a wall. When all had disembarked and stood upon the beach, St. Brendan directed them to remove nothing from the boat, and then there appeared a dog, approaching from a bye-path, who came to fawn upon the saint, as dogs are wont to fawn upon their masters. "Has not the Lord," said St. Brendan, "sent us a goodly messenger; let us follow him;" and the brethren followed the dog, until they came to a large mansion, in which they found a spacious hall, laid out with couches and seats, and water for washing their feet. When they had taken some rest, St. Brendan warned them thus: "Beware lest Satan lead you into temptation, for I can see him urging one of the three monks, who followed after us from the monastery, to a wicked theft. Pray you for his soul, for his flesh is in Satan's power."

The mansion where they abode had its walls hung around with vessels made of various metals, with bridle-bits and horns inlaid with silver.

St. Brendan ordered the serving brother to produce the meal which God had sent them; and without delay the table was laid with napkins, and with white loaves and fish for each brother. When all had been laid out, St. Brendan blessed the repast and the brethren: "Let us give praise to the God of heaven, who provideth food for all His creatures." Then the brethren partook of the repast, giving thanks to the Lord, and took likewise drink, as much as they pleased. The meal being finished, and the divine office discharged, St. Brendan said: "Go to your rest now; here you see couches well dressed for each of you; and you need to rest those limbs overwearied by your labours during our voyage."

When the brethren had gone to sleep, St. Brendan saw the demon, in the guise of a little black boy,at his work, having in his hands a bridle-bit, and beckoning to the monk before mentioned: then he rose from his couch, and remained all night in prayer.

When morning came the brethren hastened to perform the divine offices, and wishing to take to their boat again, they found the table laid for their meal, as on the previous day; and so for three days and nights did God provide their repasts for His servants. Afterwards St. Brendan set out on his journey with the brethren, first cautioning them not to take away any property from the island. "God forbid," said they, "that any of us should dishonour our journey by theft;" whereupon St. Brendan said: "Behold the brother of whom I spoke to you on yesterday has concealed in his bosom a silver bridle-bit which the devil gave him last night." When the brother in question heard this he cast away the bridle-bit out of his bosom, and fell at the feet of the saint, crying aloud: "O father, I am guilty; forgive me, and pray that my soul may not be lost;" and all the brethren cast themselves on the ground earnestly beseeching the Lord for his soul's sake. When they rose from the ground, and St. Brendan had raised up the guilty brother, they all saw a little black boy leap out of his bosom, howling loudly: "Why, O man of God, do you expel me from my abode, where I have dwelt for seven years, and drive me away, as a stranger, from my secure possession?" Then St. Brendan said: "I command thee, in the name of the Lord Jesus Christ, that thou injure no man until the day of judgment;" and turning to the penitent brother, he told him to prepare without delay to receive the body and blood of the Lord, for that his soul would soon depart from his body, and that there would be his burial-place; but that the other brother who accompanied him from the monastery would be buried in hell. Soon after the soul of the brother who received the Holy Viaticum departed this life, and was taken up to heaven by angels of light in the sight of his brethren, who gave him Christian burial in that place.

St. Brendan and the brethren came to the shore where the boat lay, and embarked at once; whereupon a young man presented himself to them, bearing a basket full of loaves of bread and a large bottle of water, and said: "Accept this blessing from your servant, for a long way lies before you ere you obtain the comfort you seek; but this bread and water will not fail you from this day until Pentecost." Under this blessing they sailed forth upon the ocean, partaking of food only every second day, while the boat was borne along in divers directions, until one day they came within view of an island, not far off, towards which they sailed with a favourable wind.

THE PALACE ON THE ISLAND.

Right before them there,
A noble castle, large and fair,
Like kingly hall, most rich to see,
Or emperor's palace—royally
Within, without was it arrayed—
The walls of hardest opal made,
The palace marble, pure and bright
(*No wood was there*), and dazzling light
Of gems and gold shone gorgeously
From the inlaid walls, and joyfully
They entered,—but their marvelling
Was that they found no living thing;
Then to the topmost tower they hied,
But human being ne'er espied.
Now in the palace Brendan stood;
Then sate him down in wondering mood,
Looking around, and then he said:
"Brethren, for our support and aid,
Seek ye if aught of food is here."
They sought, and found with gladsome cheer
Both food and drink most plentiful,
And silver vessels beautiful
As ere could be, and golden too,
Fairer than aught that man could view;
With daintiest cheer the stores abound,
Whate'er they wished for, that they found;
So gladly sate they down to dine,
But praising first that hand divine
That led them hither o'er the sea,
And prayed His mercy large and free.

Anglo-Norman Trouvere.

CHAPTER IV.

They visit Sheep-Island, and celebrate the Easter Festival.

When the boat touched a landing-place, the man of God ordered all to disembark, he being the last to leave the boat. In making a circuit of the island, they saw great streams of water flowing from many fountains, full of all kinds of fish. St. Brendan said to the brethren: "Let us here perform the divine office, and sacrifice unto God the Lamb without spot, for this day is the festival of the Lord's Supper;" and they remained there until Easter Saturday.

In the island they found many flocks of sheep, all pure white, so numerous as to hide the face of the land. Then the saint directed the brethren to take from the flocks what was needful for the festival; and they caught one sheep, which, being tied by the horns, followed at their heels, as if it were tame; and he also told them to take one spotless lamb. When they had obeyed those orders, they prepared to celebrate the office of the next day; and there came to them a man with a basket of hearth-cakes and other provisions, which he laid at the feet of the man of God, prostrating himself three times, and saying, with tears: "Oh, precious pearl of God, how have I deserved this, that thou shouldst take food at this holy season from the labour of my hands." St. Brendan, then raising him up from the ground, said: "My son, our Lord Jesus Christ has provided for us a suitable place wherein to celebrate His holy resurrection."

Afterwards he proceeded to perform the "ministering to the servants of God,"* and to prepare what was needful for to-morrow's festival. When the supply of provisions was taken into the vessel, the man who brought them said to St. Brendan: "Your boat can carry no more now, but after eight days I will send you food and drink sufficient until Pentecost." Whereupon the man of God said to him: "How can you know for certain where we will be after eight days?" and he replied: "This night you will spend on that island you see near you, and to-morrow also until noon; then you will sail on to the island not far from it towards the west, called the "Paradise of Birds," and there will you abide until the octave of Pentecost."

St. Brendan asked him also why the sheep were so very large on that island, larger even than oxen; and he told him that they were so much larger there than in the lands known to St. Brendan, because they were never milked, and felt not the stress of winter, having at all seasons abundant pasture.

They then went on board their vessel, and having given and received parting blessings, they proceeded on their voyage. When they drew nigh to the nearest island, the boat stopped ere they reached a landing-place; and the saint ordered the brethren to get out into the sea, and make the vessel fast, stem and stern, until they came to some harbour; there was no grass on the

* The "New Commandment" of the washing of their feet.

island, very little wood, and no sand on the shore. While the brethren spent the night in prayer outside the vessel, the saint remained in it, for he knew well what manner of island was this; but he wished not to tell the brethren, lest they might be too much afraid. When morning dawned, he bade the priests to celebrate Mass, and after they had done so, and he himself had said Mass in the boat, the brethren took out some uncooked meat and fish they had brought from the other island, and put a caldron on a fire to cook them. After they had placed more fuel on the fire, and the caldron began to boil, the island moved about like a wave; whereupon they all rushed towards the boat, and implored the protection of their father, who, taking each one by the hand, drew them all into the vessel; then relinquishing what they had removed to the island, they cast their boat loose, to sail away, when the island at once sunk into the ocean.

Afterwards they could see the fire they had kindled still burning more than two miles off, and then St. Brendan explained the occurrence: "Brethren, you wonder at what has happened to this island." "Yes, father," said they; "we wondered, and were seized with a great fear." "Fear not, my children," said the saint, "for God has last night revealed to me the mystery of all this; it was not an island you were upon, but a fish, the largest of all that swim in the ocean, which is ever trying to make its head and tail meet, but cannot succeed, because of its great length. Its name is Jasconius."

When they had sailed beside the island, where they

had already been, for three days, and reached the end thereof, they saw towards the west another island, not far off, across a narrow sound, which was very grassy, well-wooded, and full of flowers; and they bore away towards its landing-place.

> Then Brandan said: "Brothers know well
> Wherefore this strange mischance befel,
> No land was that but monstrous *beast*
> Whereon you sought to hold your feast.
> Nor marvel thus why this should be,
> Hugest of all are fish in sea,
> For they were formed by heaven's great King
> Before all other earthly thing."
>
> *Anglo-Norman Trouvere.*

CHAPTER V.

THE PARADISE OF BIRDS.

WHEN they had sailed to the southern side of this island they found a rivulet flowing into the sea, and there they brought the boat to land. The saint ordered them to leave the boat, and tow it up against the stream, which was only wide enough for its passage; and thus they towed it for a mile up to the source of the rivulet, the saint sitting on board the while.

After some consideration, St. Brendan said to them: "Behold, my brothers, God has provided for us a suitable place wherein to abide during the Paschal time; and if we had no other provisions, this fountain would, I believe, serve for food as well as drink;" for the fountain was, in truth, a very wonderful one. Over it hung a large tree of marvellous width, but no great height, covered over with snow-white birds, so that they hid its boughs and leaves entirely. When the man of God saw this, he was considering with himself why this immense number of birds were thus brought together in one assemblage; and the question grew so irksome to him that he with tears besought the Lord, on his bended knees, thus: "O God, who knowest what is unknown, and revealest what is hidden, Thou seest the anxious distress of my heart; therefore I beseech Thee that Thou wouldst vouchsafe, in Thy great mercy, to reveal Thy secret in what I see here before me; not for any desert of my own worthiness, but solely in regard to Thy clemency, do I presume to ask this favour."

Thereupon one of the birds flew off the tree, and in his flight his wings had a tinkling sound like little bells, over to the boat where the man of God was seated; and, perching on the prow, it spread out its wings in token of gladness, and looked complacently towards St. Brendan. Then the man of God, understanding from this that his prayer was granted, addressed the bird: "If you are a messenger from God, tell me whence have those birds come, and why this concourse of them here?" The bird at once made answer: "We are partakers in the great ruin of the ancient enemy, having fallen, not by sin of our will or consent, but soon after our creation our ruin resulted from the fall of Lucifer and his followers. The Almighty God, however, who is righteous and true, has doomed us to this place, where we suffer no pain, and where we can partially see the Divine presence, but must remain apart from the spirits who stood faithful. We wander about the world, in the air, and earth, and sky, like the other spirits on their missions; but on festival days we take the shapes you see, abide here, and sing the praises of our Creator. You and your brethren have been now one year on your voyage, and six more years' journeying awaits you; where you celebrated your Easter this year, there will you celebrate it every year, until you find what you have set your hearts upon, the "Land of Promise of the Saints." When it had spoken thus, the bird arose from the prow of the vessel, and flew back to the other birds.

On the approach of the hour of vespers, all the birds, in unison, clapping their wings, began to sing: "*A hymn, O Lord, becometh Thee in Sion, and a vow shall be paid to Thee in Jerusalem*" (Ps. lxiv.); and they alternately chanted the same psalm for an hour; and the melody of their warbling and the accompanying clapping of their wings, sounded like unto a delightful harmony of great sweetness.

Then St. Brendan said to the brethren: "Take bodily refreshment now, for the Lord has sated your souls with the joys of His divine resurrection." When supper was ended, and the divine office discharged, the man of God and his companions retired to rest until the third watch of the night, when he aroused them all from sleep, chanting the verse: "Thou, O Lord, wilt open my lips;" whereupon all the birds, with voice and wing, warbled in response: "Praise the Lord, all His angels, praise Him all His virtues." Thus they sang for an hour every night;

and when morning dawned, they chanted: "May the splendour of the Lord God be upon us," in the same melody and measure as their matin praises of God. Again, at tierce, they sang the verse: "Sing to our God, sing; sing to our King, sing wisely;" at sext: "The Lord hath caused the light of His countenance to shine upon us, and may He have mercy on us;" and at none they sang: "Behold how good and how pleasant it is for brethren to dwell in unity." Thus day and night those birds gave praise to God. St. Brendan, seeing all this, made thanksgiving to the Lord for all His wonderful works; and the brethren were thus regaled with such spiritual viands until the octave of the Easter festival.

At the close of the festival days, St. Brendan said: "Let us now partake of the water of this fountain; hitherto we had need of it only to wash our hands or feet." Soon after this the man with whom they had been three days before Easter, who had supplied them with provisions for the Paschal season, came to them with his boat full of food and drink; and having laid it all before the holy father, he said: "My brothers, you have here abundance to last until Pentecost; but do not drink of that fountain, for its waters have a peculiar virtue, so that anyone drinking thereof, though it seems to have the taste and quality of ordinary water, is seized with sleep, and cannot awaken for twenty-four hours." After this, having received the blessing of St. Brendan, he returned to his own place.

St. Brendan remained where he was with his brethren until Pentecost, the singing of the birds being a delight ever new to them. On the feast of Pentecost, when St. Brendan and the priests had celebrated Mass, their venerable procurator, or provider, brought sufficient food for the festival; and when they had sat down together at their repast, he said to them: "My brothers, you have yet a long journey before you; take, therefore, from this fountain vessels full of its water, and dry bread that may keep for another year, and I will supply as much as your boat can carry." He then departed with a blessing from all; and St. Brendan, eight days afterwards, got the boat laden with the provisions brought by this man, and all the vessels filled with water from the fountain.

When they had brought everything down to the shore, the bird before mentioned flew towards them, and alighted on the prow of the boat; and the saint, understanding that it would make something known to him, stood still where he was. Then the bird, in human voice, addressed him: "With us you have celebrated the Paschal time this year; you will celebrate it with us also next year, and where you have been in the past year on the festival of the Lord's Supper, there will you also be on the same festival next year. In like manner, you will celebrate the festival of the Lord's Pasch, as you did before on the back of the great fish Jasconius; and after eight months you will find the island of St. Ailbe, where you will celebrate the Nativity of Jesus Christ." Having spoken thus, the bird returned to its place on the tree.

THE WARBLING OF THE BIRDS.

At this the abbot stood amazed,
And wondering, on their beauty gazed,
And prayed to Heaven, that it might show,
Both whence they came, and where they go,
And who they were—when instantly
One of those birds from off the tree
Flew toward him, lightly hovering;
While at each stroke of that bright wing
Burst forth such harp-like melody,
That tranced in joy and bliss was he.
Then mildly to the bird he said:
"If thou by hand of God wast made
To serve Him, swiftly to me tell
What isle is this? and what befel
Thee and thy feathered company,
That far from all society
Of men ye won—for ye are fair
As disembodied spirits are."
Then sang the bird: "Erst we were high
In power and glory in the sky,
For angels were we, but we fell
When pride drove Sathanas to hell:
For we his vassals were, and driven
Thus for his surquedie* from Heaven—
Now exiled for a space to stay
Upon this island, till the day
That shall restore us to the skies,
For we are birds of Paradise.
But ye have much," said he, "to do
And bear ere Paradise ye view,
And six years' toils must suffer still,
Rocked by the winds and waves at will;
And aye each year your Pasch shall keep
Upon some monster of the deep."
When thus he said, away he flew
Back to his tree; and when the dew,
And slanting shade, and sun's soft shining,
Showed that the day was fast declining,

* *i.e.* Rebellion.

These snowy birds, with dulcet throats
Poured in sweet unison their notes ;--
And sang so softly, clearly, sweetly ;
With voice and heart, aye so completely
Joined in God's praise that ye might ne'er
The solace of that compare
With aught that human song could do
Tho' man might learn a lesson too.
Then said the abbot : "Brethren, see,
These birds a lesson teach to ye ;
Tho' fallen from their high state, and driven
Unto this isle, yet praise they Heaven,
And thank the Lord, who unto us
Hath been by far more bounteous ;
And hence should we prepare more praise."
With joyful hearts their chant they raise,
They quit the ship, and range along
The shore ; and now the complin song
They chant with pleasant melody.
Then free from all anxiety,
Commend themselves to Jesus' care,
And soon they slumber sweetly there.

Anglo-Norman Trouvere.

CHAPTER VI.

THE ISLAND OF ST. AILBE.

THE brethren got the boat ready, and set sail forth into the ocean, while all the birds sung in concert: "*Hear us, O God our Saviour, the hope of all the ends of the earth, and in the sea afar off.*" After this St. Brendan and his brethren were tossed about to and fro on the billows of the ocean for the space of three months, during which they could see nothing but sea and sky, and they took refreshment only every second day. One day, however, an island came into view, not far off; but when they drew near the shore the wind drove them aside, and thus for forty days they sailed round about the island without finding a landing-place. The brethren meanwhile besought the Lord with tears that He would vouchsafe to help them, for their strength was almost exhausted because of their great fatigue; and when they had thus persevered in frequent prayer for three days, and in fasting also, at length they found a narrow creek fit to receive one boat, and beside it two fountains, one foul and the other limpid. When the brethren hastened to take some of the water, the man of God said to them: "My children, do nothing that may be unlawful. Take nothing here without the leave of the venerable fathers who are on this island, and they will freely give what you would take by stealth."

When all had landed and were considering in what direction they should go, there came to them an old man, wasted from extreme old age, whose hair was white as snow and his face pellucid like glass. He prostrated himself thrice, before he went to embrace the man of God, who, raising him up from the ground, embraced him, as did all the brethren, in like manner. Then this aged man, taking the holy father by the hand, led him to the monastery, about a furlong distant, when St. Brendan stood at the entrance, and asked his guide whose monastery this was, and who was its superior. He put to him various questions in this way, but could get no reply, only manual signs, indicating silence with much gentleness. As soon as the holy father recognised that silence was the rule of the place, he cautioned his brethren: "Restrain your tongues from much talking, lest the monks here may be scandalized by your foolish speeches."

After this, there came forth to meet them eleven monks, in their habits and crosses, chanting the versicle: "Arise, you holy ones from your dwellings, and come forth to meet us; sanctify this place; bless this people, and vouchsafe to guard us, thy servants, in peace." The versicle being ended, the abbot embraced St. Brendan and his companions in due order, and in like manner his monks embraced the brethren of the holy man. When the kiss of peace was thus mutually given and received, they conducted them into the monastery, according to the custom in western countries; and the abbot and his monks proceeded to wash the feet of their guests, and to chant the "New Commandment."

Then he led them all into the refectory, in strict silence; and when they had washed their hands he gave them a signal to take their seats, when one of the monks, on a given signal, rose up and supplied the table with loaves of bread of marvellous whiteness and roots of delicious flavour. The monks had taken places at table alternately with their guests, in due order, and between each pair a whole loaf was served, when the ministering brother set before them also some drink. Father abbot, in much cheerfulness, pressed his guests: "Brothers, from the fountain, out of which to-day you wished to drink stealthily, make now a loving cup in gladness and in the fear of the Lord. From the other fountain of foul water, which you saw, are the feet of the brethren washed, for it is always tepid. Those loaves of bread which you now see before you, we know not where they are prepared, or who brings them to our cellar; but we know well that, by the free gift of God, they are supplied to us, as an alms, by some obedient creature of His; and thus is fulfilled in our regard the words of divine truth: 'Those who fear God want for nothing.' Here we are twenty-four brothers, having each day twelve loaves for our support, one loaf for two brothers; but on Sundays and great festivals the Lord allows us a full loaf for each brother, so that of what remains we may have a supper; and now, on your advent, we have a double supply; thus it is that from the days of St. Patrick and St. Ailbe, our patriarchs, for eighty years until now, Christ provides us with sustenance. Moreover, neither old age nor bodily infirmities increase upon us here, neither do we need cooked food, nor are we oppressed with heat or distressed with cold; but we live here, as it were, in the paradise of God. When the hours for the divine office and for Mass arrive, the lamps in our church, which, under God's guidance, we brought with us from our own country, are set alight, and burn always without growing less."

When the repast was over, and they had thrice taken some drink, the abbot gave the usual signal, and all the brethren, in great silence, rose from table, giving thanks to God, and preceded the fathers to the church, at the door of which they met twelve other monks, who readily bent the knee, as they passed. Then St. Brendan said: "Father abbot, why have not those monks dined with us?" "For your sakes," said the abbot, "as our table could not seat us all together. They will now take their meal, for through God's holy will they shall want for nothing. We will now enter the church and sing vespers, so that the brethren who are now dining, may sing the office afterwards in proper time." When vespers had concluded, St. Brendan took heed of the structure of the church: it was a perfect square of equal length and breadth, and in it were seven lamps, so arranged that three of them hung before the central altar, and two before each of the side altars. All the altars were of crystal, and the chalices, patenas, cruets, and the other vessels required for the Divine Sacrifice were also of crystal. Around the church were ranged twenty-four benches, with the abbot's seat between the two choirs of monks in rows on either side. No monk from either choir was allowed to intone the chant of the office, but the abbot; and throughout the monastery no voice was heard, nor any sound whatever; but if a brother needed anything, he went to the abbot, and on his knees made signs that he wanted aught; and then the father wrote on a tablet what God had intimated to him to be needful for the brother.

While St. Brendan was pondering all these things, the abbot said to him: "Father, it is now time to return to the refectory, that all may be done with day-light, as it is written: 'He who walketh in the light, stumbleth not.' So it was done, and when all things were completed in due order of the daily routine, all hastened with alacrity to complin. Then the abbot intoned the versicle: "Incline unto my aid, O Lord," invoking at the same time the Most Holy Trinity; and they subjoin the antiphon: "We have sinned; we have acted unrighteously; we have worked iniquity; Thou, O Lord Christ, who art all mercy, have pity on us. In peace unto the selfsame, I will sleep and take my rest;" and they proceed to chant the office of complin.

When the office had concluded, the brethren went to their cells, taking their guests with them; but the abbot remained with St. Brendan, in the church, to await the lighting of the lamps. The saint asked the father abbot about the rule of silence they observed; how such a mode of intercourse in a community was possible to flesh and blood. The abbot, with much reverence and humility, replied: "Holy father, I declare before the Lord, that during the eighty years that have passed since we came to this island, none of us has heard from the other the sound of the human voice, save only when we sing the praises of God. Amongst us twenty-four brothers, no voice is raised; but signs are made by the fingers or the eyes; and this is permitted only to the elder monks. None of us, since we came here, have suffered any infirmity of body or mind, such as may be fatal to mankind." Upon this St. Brendan said with many tears: "Vouchsafe, I beseech thee, father abbot, to let us know whether we are permitted or not to abide here." The abbot rejoined: "You are not permitted, for such is not the will of God; but why do you ask me, when God had revealed to you, before you came to us, what you must do? You must return to your own country, where God has prepared for you, as well as for your fourteen companions, the place of sepulture. Of the other two monks, one will have his pilgrimage in the island of the anchorites; but the other will suffer in hell the worst of all deaths;" and these events afterwards came to pass.

While they were thus conversing, behold, as they looked on, a fiery arrow, passing in through a window, set alight all the lamps that hung before the altars, and passing out through the same window, left the lamps burning. Then St. Brendan inquired who would extinguish those lamps in the morning, and the abbot replied: "Come, and see the secret of all this: you observe those tapers burning in the vases; yet none of them is consumed, nor do they grow less, nor do any ashes remain in the morning, for the light is entirely spiritual." "How," said St. Brendan, "can a spiritual flame thus burn in a material substance?" "Have you not read," said the abbot, "of the burning bush, near Mount Sinai, which remained unconsumed by the burning?" "Yes," said the saint, "I have read of this; but what analogy has it to this case?"

When they had thus remained on watch until morning, St. Brendan asked permission to depart from the island, but the abbot replied: "No, O man of God, you must celebrate with us the festival of our Lord's Nativity, and afford us the joy of your company until the Octave of Epiphany." The holy father, therefore, with his brethren, remained until that time, on this Island of St. Ailbe.

THE ABBEY OF ST. AILBE.

So forth they hie with glee
The abbot and his company,
When, lo! they found a wond'rous spring,
From whence two streams their waters fling,
The one was foul, the other bright—
Much gazed the faithful at the sight;

But faint were they, so blithe they go
To slake their thirst : " No, brothers, no,"
Brandon out cried ; " first seek and know
If this strange spring be wholesome drink."
Affright they hastened from the brink,
Tho' sorely pained with thirst ;—then nigh
An old man came, and when his eye
Glanced on St. Brendan, and he saw
The holy freres, with mickle awe
He prostrate fell, and kissed the hands
Of the abbot, who now bade him stand,
And soothly tell by word or sign
Where were they. Well could he divine,
Although he spoke not what was said,
And joyfully and swiftly led
The abbot and his companie,
With care and all humilitie
Unto an abbey, fair and good
(Beneath the moon none holier stood)
The abbot of that saintly place,
With honour due his guests to grace,
Caused bring forth from his treasurye
Relics of rich orfeverie—
Crosses and shrines, and caskets fair,
With amethysts beset, and rare
Open-wrought gold, most rich y-chased,
And precious gems all featly placed
Around, and censers fair y-dight
Of solid gold, and jewels bright,
And vestments rich, not wrought alone
With silk, but many a priceless stone,—
Garnet and ruby, sardonis,
Topaz and jasper precious,
Gleamed on the clasps most gorgeously.

Anglo-Norman Trouvere.

CHAPTER VII.

THEY VISIT OTHER ISLANDS.

WHEN those festival days had passed, St. Brendan, with the blessing of the abbot and all his monks, and with a supply of the necessary provisions, set sail into the ocean; and there the vessel, without the use of oar or sail, drifted about in various directions, until the beginning of Lent. One day they saw an island not far off, and quickly made sail towards it; for they were harassed with hunger and thirst, their store of food and water having been exhausted three days before. When St. Brendan had blessed the landing-place, and all had landed, they found a spring of limpid water, and herbs and vegetables of divers kinds around it, and many sorts of fish in the stream that flowed from it to the sea. Then St. Brendan said: "Brothers, God has surely given us comfort, after our wearisome labours. Take of those fishes sufficient for your repast, and dress them on the fire, and gather also those herbs and roots which God has provided for His servants." When this was done, they poured out some of the water to drink; but the man of God cautioned them: "Take heed, my brethren that you use this water in moderation. But the brethren paid not equal heed to this caution, for while some drank only one cup of the water, others drank two cups, and others again drank three of them; so that upon some of them there fell a sudden stupor, which lasted for the space of three days and nights; when upon others it befell only for one day and night; but St. Brendan prayed without ceasing to God for them, as they incurred this great danger through ignorance. When three days had passed, the father said to his companions: "Let us, my children, hasten away from this fatal place, lest greater evil befall you; the Lord had given you refreshment, but you have turned it to your detriment. Go forth, therefore, from this island, taking with you as much fish as you may want for a meal on every third day, until the festival of the Lord's Supper; and also one cup of this water for each man, with a like supply of the vegetables." Having laden the boat with those provisions, as the man of God directed, they set sail into the ocean in a northerly course.

After three days and nights the wind ceased, and the sea became like a thick curdled mass, so great was the calm. Then the holy father said: "Take in your oars, and cast loose the sails, for the Lord will guide our boat whithersoever He willeth." In this manner was the boat kept in motion for the space of about twenty days, until at length God sent a favourable wind; when they put on sail, and worked their oars also in an easterly direction, taking refreshment every third day.

On a certain day there came into view an island, like a cloud, at a distance, when St. Brendan asked the brethren whether they recognised it. On their replying that they did not, the holy father said to them: "I know it well, my children, for we were on it last year, on the festival of the Lord's Supper, and therein our good procurator abides." Hearing this the brethren, in great joy, plied their oars vigorously, putting forth all their strength; but the man of God said to them: "Senseless you are thus to tire out your limbs. Is not the Almighty God the pilot of our vessel? Leave her, therefore, in His hands, for He will guide her course as He willeth.

When they drew near to the island, their procurator came out to meet them; and, giving glory to God, led them to the same landing-place where they had landed the year before, where he embraced the feet of St. Brendan and all the brethren, saying: "Wonderful is God in His saints." Having finished the versicle, and everything being removed from the boat, he set up a tent, and prepared a bath for them, for it was the festival of the Lord's Supper; and he provided new garments for all the brethren, as well as for St. Brendan, performing all other services to them as was his wont.

The brethren then celebrated with great diligence the festival of the Passion of our Lord, until Holy Saturday, when all the offices and ceremonies of the day being ended, and the festival of the Lord's Supper being fully completed, the procurator said to them: "Go now to your boat, in order that you may celebrate the vigil of Easter, where you celebrated it last year, and also the day itself, until the hour of sext; then sail on to the Paradise of Birds, where you were last year, from Easter until the Octave of Pentecost. Take with you all you require of food and drink, and I will visit you on next Sunday week." And the brethren acted accordingly.

St. Brendan, giving his blessing to this good brother,

embarked with all his brethren, and made sail to another island. When they drew near to the landing-place they found the caldron, which in their flight the year before they had left on the back of Jasconius. Then St. Brendan, going on land, sung the "Hymn of the Three Children" to the close, and cautioned the brethren: "Watch and pray, my children, that you enter not into temptation; consider well, how the Almighty God has placed under us, without difficulty, this greatest monster of the deep." The brethren made their vigils here and there over the island, until the morning watch, when all the priests said their masses until the hour of tierce; but St. Brendan, getting into the boat, with the brethren, there offered to God the holy sacrifice of the Immaculate Lamb, saying: "Last year we celebrated here our Lord's resurrection; and I desire, if it be God's holy will, to celebrate it here also this year."

Proceeding thence they came to the island called the Paradise of Birds; and when they reached the landing-place, all the birds sang in concert: "Salvation to our God, who sitteth on the throne, and to the Lamb;" and, again: "The Lord is God, and He hath shone upon us; appoint a solemn day, with shady boughs, even to the horn of the altar." (Ps. cxvii.) Thus with voice and wing they warbled, until St. Brendan and his companions were settled in their tent, where they passed the Paschal time, until the Octave of Pentecost.

The procurator already mentioned came to them, as he had promised, on Low Sunday, bringing what was needed for their sustenance; and in mutual joy all gave thanks to God. When they were seated at their repast, behold! the bird before spoken of perched on the prow of the boat, spreading out and clapping its wings with a loud sound, like a great organ, and St. Brendan knew that it wished to convey to him this message, which it spoke as follows: "The Almighty and merciful God has appointed for you four certain places, at four different seasons of the year, until the seven years of your pilgrimage will be ended; on the festival of our Lord's Supper you will be each year with your procurator, who is here present: the vigil and festival of Easter you will celebrate on the back of the great whale; with us here you will spend the Paschal time, until the Octave of Pentecost, and on the island of St. Ailbe you will remain from Christmas until the festival of the Purification of the Blessed Virgin Mary. After those seven years, through many and divers perils, you will find the Land of Promise of the Saints which you are seeking, and there you will bide for forty days; then will God guide your return to the land of your birth."

When St. Brendan had heard this, he, with many tears, cast himself prostrate, as did also the brethren, giving thanks and praises to the great Creator of all things. The bird then flew back to its place on the tree, and when the meal was ended, the procurator said: "I will, with God's help, come to you again on Pentecost Sunday with provisions." And with a blessing from all, he took his departure.

CHAPTER VIII.

They are Miraculously Saved from Destruction.

The venerable father remained here for the appointed time, and then ordered the brethren to make ready the boat, and to fill all the water vessels from the fountain When the boat was launched, the procurator met them in his boat laden with provisions, which he quickly transferred into the boat of the man of God ; and, with a parting embrace, returned whence he had come ; but the saint sailed forth into the ocean, and the boat was borne along for the space of forty days.

One day a fish of enormous size appeared swimming after the boat, spouting foam from its nostrils, and ploughing through the waves in rapid pursuit to devour them. Then the brethren cried out to the Lord : "O Lord, who hast made us, deliver us, Thy servants;" and to St. Brendan they cried aloud: "Help, O father, help us ;" and the saint besought the Lord to deliver His servants, that this monster may not devour them, while he also sought to give courage to the brethren in these words: "Fear not, you of little faith ; for God, who is always our protector, will deliver us from the jaws of this monster, and from every other danger." When the monster was drawing near, waves of immense size rushed on before it, even up to the gunwale of the boat, which caused the brethren to fear more and more ; but St. Brendan, with hands upraised to heaven, earnestly prayed : "Deliver,

O Lord, Thy servants, as Thou didst deliver David from the hands of the giant Goliah, and Jonas from the power of the great whale."

When these prayers were uttered, a great monster came into view from the west, and rushing against the other, spouting flame from its mouth, at once attacked it. Then St. Brendan spoke: "Behold, my children, the wonderful work of our Saviour; see here the obedience of the creature to its Creator: await now the end in safety, for this conflict will bring no evil to us, but only greater glory to God." Thereupon the rueful monster that pursued the servants of God is slain, and cut up in their presence into three parts, and its victor returned whence it came.

Next day they saw at a distance an island full of herbage and of wide extent. When they drew near it, and were about to land, they found the hinder portion of the monster that was slain. "Behold," said St. Brendan, "what sought to devour you. Do you now make your food of it, and fill yourselves abundantly with its flesh, for you will have a long delay upon this island. Draw the boat higher up on the land, and seek out a suitable place whereon to fix our tent."

When the father had selected a site for their tent, and the brethren had, in compliance with his directions, placed therein the requisite fittings, he said to them: "Take now, of this monster's flesh, sufficient provision for three months, as this night will its carcass be devoured by the great fishes of the sea." The brethren acted accordingly, and took as much of its flesh as was needed; but they said to St. Brendan: "Holy father, how can we live here without water to drink?" "Is it more difficult," said the saint, "for the Almighty to give us water than to give us food? Go to the southern side of the island, and there you will find a spring of clear water and abundance of herbs and roots, of which you will take a supply sufficient for your wants." And they found everything as the man of God had told them.

St. Brendan remained on this island for three months, for violent storms prevailed at sea, and severe stress of weather, from hail and rain. The brethren went to see what had become of the remains of the great monster, of which the saint had spoken; and they found, where its carcass had lain, only its bones, as the father had told them; and when they mentioned this to him: "If you needed to test the truth of my words," said he, "I will give you another sign; this night will a large part of a fish, breaking loose from a fisher's net, be cast ashore here, and to-morrow you will have your repast on it." Next day they went to the place indicated, and finding there what the man of God had foretold, brought away as much fish as they could carry. The venerable father then said to them: "Keep this carefully, and salt it, for it will be much needed, as the Lord will grant calm weather to-day and to-morrow; and on the third day, when the turbulence of the sea and the waves will have subsided, we will take our departure from this island."

THE CONFLICT OF SEA-MONSTERS.

Toward them a serpent of the sea
Rushed swift as wind most savagely—
The fire that from his nostrils came
Was like the roaring furnace flame,

Unmeasured was his length, I trew—
His very breadth was huge enew,
Full fifteen feet, and all around him
The waves were seething. Nought could found him,
He near the frighted pilgrims drew;
Then Brendan spoke, right bold and true
His words—" O sirs, now wherefore stand,
Fearing that God's all powerful hand
Is short to save! O guard, I pray,
'Gainst senseless fear, that would gainsay
God's word, and take this truth away,—
Who puts his trust in Heaven's high King,
Hath need to fear no living thing."
Then, lo! another monster rose
That huge sea-serpent to oppose—
Right toward the ship his swift course steering,
And when the other saw him nearing,
Full well, I trew, his foe he knew,
And backward from the vessel drew.
And now they close in deadly fight,
With huge heads reared, a fearful sight!
While from their nostrils flames spout high
As are the clouds in the upper sky;
Blows with their fins each gives his brother,
Like clashing shields on one another :—
With murd'rous teeth each other biting,
Like trenchant swords each other smiting.
Spouted the blood, and gaping wide
Were teeth-prints in each monster's side;
And huge and deadly deep each wound—
And blood-tinged all the waves around,
And all a-seething was the sea,
And still the fight raged furiously.
The first now fought with failing might,
The second triumphed in the fight,
With stronger teeth he overbore him,
And into three huge pieces tore him;
And then the victory gained, he goes
Back to the place from whence he rose.

Anglo-Norman Trouvere.

CHAPTER IX.

THE THREE CHOIRS OF SAINTS.

WHEN those days had elapsed, St. Brendan ordered them to load their boat with the skins and water-vessels filled from the fountain, and with a supply of herbs and roots also, as much as may be needful; for the saint, since he was ordained a priest, eat of nothing in which had been the breath of life. Having thus laden the boat, they set sail in a northerly direction. One day they saw an island afar off, when St. Brendan said to the brethren: "On that island, now in view, there are three classes of people: boys, young men, and elders; and one of our brothers will have his pilgrimage there." The brethren asked him which of them it was; but he was loath to tell; when, however, they pressed the question, and seemed grieved at not being told, he said: "This is the brother who is to remain on this island." He was one of the monks who had come after the saint from his own monastery, about whom he had made a prediction when they embarked in their own country. They then drew near to the island, until the boat touched the shore.

The island was remarkably flat, almost level with the sea, without a tree or anything that waved in the wind; but it was of wide extent, and covered over with white and purple flowers.* Here, as the man of God had told, were three troops of monks, standing apart, about

* *Calthus*, the Marigold.

a stone's cast from each other, and keeping at this distance asunder when they moved in any direction. One choir, in its place, chanted: "The saints shall advance from virtue to virtue; God shall be manifest in Sion;" and then another choir took up the same chant; and thus they chanted unceasingly. The first choir was of boys, robed in snow-white garments; the second was of young men, dressed in violet; and the third of the elder men, in purple dalmatics.

When the boat reached the landing-place it was the fourth hour; and at the hour of sext, all the choirs of monks sung together the Psalm: "May God have mercy on us, and bless us" (Ps. lxvi.), to the end; and "Incline unto my aid, O Lord;" and also the psalm, "I have believed, therefore have I spoken" (Ps. cxv.), with the proper prayer. In like manner, at the hour of none, they chanted three other psalms: "Out of the depths I have cried to thee, O Lord" (Ps. cxxix.); "Behold how good and how pleasant it is for brethren to dwell together in unity" (Ps. cxxxii.); and "Praise the Lord, O Jerusalem; praise thy God, O Sion" (Ps. cxlvii.). Again, at Vespers, they sung the psalms: "A hymn, O Lord, becometh Thee in Sion" (Ps. lxiv.); "Bless the Lord, O my soul" (Ps. cii.); and "Praise the Lord, ye children; praise ye the name of the Lord" (Ps. cxii.); then they chanted, when seated, the fifteen gradual psalms.

After they had finished this chanting, a cloud of marvellous brightness overshadowed the island, so that they could not see what was visible before; but they heard the voices, without ceasing, in the same chant until the morning-watch, when they sung the psalms: "Praise the Lord from the heavens" (Ps. cxlviii.); "Sing unto the Lord" (Ps. cxlix.); and "Praise the Lord in his saints" (Ps. cl.); and then twelve psalms, in the order of the psaltery, as far as the psalm: "The fool saith in his heart" (Ps. xiii.). At the dawn of day, this cloud passed away from the island, and then the choirs chanted the three psalms: "Have mercy on me, O Lord" (Ps. l.); "The Lord is my refuge" (Ps. lxxxix.); and, "O God, my God" (Ps. lxii.). Again, at the hour of tierce, they sang three other psalms: "Oh, clap your hands, all ye nations" (Ps. xlvi.); "Save me, O God, by Thy name" (Ps. liii.); and, "I have loved, because the Lord will hear the voice of my prayer" (Ps. cxiv.), with the Alleluia. Then they offered the Holy Sacrifice of the Immaculate Lamb, and all received the Holy Communion with the words: "*This Sacred Body of the Lord and the Blood of our Saviour receive unto life everlasting.*"

When the Holy Sacrifice was ended, two members of the choir of the young men brought a basket full of purple grapes, and placed it in the boat of the man of God, saying: "Partake of the fruit of the isle of the Strong Men, and deliver to us our chosen brother; then depart in peace." St. Brendan then called this brother to him, and said: "Give the kiss of peace to your brethren, and go with those who are inviting you. I say to you, that in a happy hour did your mother conceive you, because you have deserved to abide with so holy a community." St. Brendan then, with many tears, gave him the kiss of peace, as did also the brethren, and said to him: "Remember, my dear son, the special favours to which God has preferred thee in this life; go thy way, and pray for us." Bidding them all farewell, the brother quickly followed the two young men to the companies of the saints, who, on seeing him, sang the verse: "Behold how good and pleasant it is for brethren to dwell together in unity;" and in a higher key intoned the *Te Deum laudamus* ("We praise Thee, O God"); and then, when all had embraced him, he was admitted into their society.

St. Brendan set sail from the island, and when meal-time had come, he told the brethren to refresh themselves with the grapes they got on the island. Taking up one of them, and seeing its great size, and how full of juice it was, he said, in wonder: "Never have I seen or read of grapes so large." They were all of equal size, like a large ball, and when the juice of one was pressed into a vessel, it yielded a pound weight. This juice the father divided into twelve parts, giving a part every day to each of the brethren; and thus for twelve days, one grape sufficed for the refreshment of each brother, in whose mouth it always tasted like honey.

When those days had passed, St. Brendan ordered a fast for three days, after which a resplendent bird flew towards the boat, bearing in its beak a branch of an unknown tree, on which there was a cluster of very red grapes; and dropping it near the man of God, flew away. Then he said to the brethren: "Enjoy this feast the Lord hath sent us;" and the grapes being as large as apples, he gave some to each of them; and thus they had food enough for four days, after which they resumed their previous fasting.

Three days after, they saw near at hand an island covered all over with trees, closely set, and laden with such grapes as those, in surprising abundance, so that all the branches were weighed down to the ground, with fruit of the same quality and colour, and there was no tree fruitless or of a different kind in the whole island. The brethren then drew up to the landing-place; and St. Brendan, leaving the boat, walked about the island, where the fragrance was like that of a house stored with pomegranates; the brethren the while remaining in the boat awaited his return, and the wind laden with those odours blew towards them, and so regaled them with its fragrance, that they heeded not their long fast. The venerable father found on the island six fountains, watering the greenest herbage and vegetables of divers kinds. He then returned to the brethren, bringing with him some samples, as first-fruits of the island: and he said to them: "Leave the boat now, and fix up your tent here; be of good cheer, and enjoy the excellent fruits of this land which God has shown to us." And thus for forty days they feasted on the grapes, and herbs, and vegetables watered by those fountains.

After that period, they embarked again, taking with them some of the fruits of the island, and sailed along as the winds shaped their course, when suddenly there appeared flying towards them the bird called *Gryphon*. When the brethren saw it, they cried out to the holy father: "Help us, O father, for this monster comes to devour us." But the man of God told them to fear it not, for God was their helper. And then another great bird came into view, and in rapid flight flew against the Gryphon, engaging it in a combat, that seemed for some time of doubtful event; but at length, tearing out its eyes, it vanquished and slew it; and the carcass fell into the sea, in the sight of all the brethren, who thereupon gave thanks and praises to God; while the bird which gained the victory flew away, whence it had come.

They went to the island of St. Ailbe, to celebrate the Christmas festival, and afterwards taking leave of the abbot, with mutual blessings, they sailed about the ocean for a long time, taking rest only at Easter and Christmas on the islands before mentioned.

THE GRYPHON AND THE DRAGON.

A flaming griffin in the sky,
With fearful hearts they now espy
With crooked claws to seize, I ween,
And flaming wings and talons keen;
And o'er the ship he hovereth low,
And vainly may the strong wind blow;
More swift is he, than barque more strong,
And fierce he chaseth them along,
But, lo! a dragon takes his flight,
With outstretched neck, and wings of might:
A flaming dragon he, and grim,
And toward the griffin beareth him.
And now the battle furiously
In mid air rageth fell to see,
Sparks from their teeth fly thick around,
And blows, and flames, and many a wound
Is given. The pilgrims anxiously
Gaze up; oh! which shall victor be?
The griffin's huge—the dragon slight,
But far more lightsome for the fight;
And lo! the griffin in the sea
Falls dead. The dragon victory
Hath won—O then they joyed outright,
And thanked the God of power and might.

Anglo-Norman Trouvere.

CHAPTER X.

Some Wonders of the Ocean.

On a certain occasion, when St. Brendan was celebrating the festival of St. Peter, in the boat, they found the sea so clear that they could plainly see what was at the bottom. They, therefore, saw beneath them various monsters of the deep, and so clear was the water, that it seemed as if they could touch with their hands its greatest depths; and the fishes were visible in great shoals, like flocks of sheep in the pastures, swimming around, heads to tails. The brethren entreated the man of God to say Mass in a low voice, lest those monsters of the deep, hearing the strange voice, may be stirred up to attack them; but the saint said: "I wonder much at your folly. Why do you dread those monsters? Is not the largest of them all already devoured? While seated, and often chanting upon its back, have you not chopped wood, an d kindled a fire, and even cooked some of its flesh? Why, therefore, should you fear those? For our God is the Lord Jesus Christ, who can bring to nought all living things." Having thus spoken, he proceeded to sing the Mass in a louder voice, as the brethren were still gazing at the large fishes; and these, when they heard the voice of the man of God, rose up from the depths, and swam around the boat in such numbers, that the brethren could see nothing but the swimming fishes, which, however, came not close to the boat, but swam around at some distance, until the Mass was ended, when they swam away in divers directions, out of the view of the brethren. For eight days, even with a favourable wind, and all sails set, they were scarcely able to pass out of this pellucid sea.

One day, on which three Masses had been said, they saw a column in the sea, which seemed not far off, yet they could not reach it for three days. When they drew near it, St. Brendan looked towards its summit, but could not see it, because of its great height, which seemed to pierce the skies. It was covered over with a rare canopy, the material of which they knew not; but it had the colour of silver, and was hard as marble, while the column itself was of the clearest crystal. St. Brendan ordered the brethren to take in their oars, and to lower the sails and mast, and directed some of them to hold on by the fringes of the canopy, which extended about a mile from the column, and about the same depth into the sea. When this had been done, St. Brendan said: "Run in the boat now through an opening, that we may get a closer view of the wonderful works of God." And when they had passed through the opening, and looked around them, the sea seemed to them transparent like glass, so that they could plainly see everything beneath them, even the base of the column, and the skirts or fringes of the canopy, lying on the ground, for the sun shone as brightly within as without.

St. Brendan then measured an opening between four pavilions, which he found to be four cubits on every side. While they sailed along for a day by one side of the column, they could always feel the shade as well as the heat of the sun, beyond the ninth hour; and after thus sailing about the column for four days, they found the measurement of each side to be four hundred (?) cubits. On the fourth day, they discovered on the south side, a chalice of the same material as the canopy, and a patena like that of the column, which St. Brendan at once took up, saying: "The Lord Jesus Christ has displayed to us this great marvel, and has given to us two gifts therefrom, in testimony of the fact to others." The holy father then directed the brethren to perform the divine office, and afterwards to take refreshment; for they had taken none since they came in sight of this column. Next day they rowed towards the north, and having passed out through an opening, they set up the mast, and unfurled the sails again, while some of them held on by the fringes, or skirts of the canopy, until all was right in the boat. When they had set sail, a favourable wind came on in the rear, so that they had no occasion to use the oars, but only to hold the ropes and the tiller. And thus for eight days were they borne along towards the north.

THE ICEBERG.

Right in their course they clearly see
A pillar rising in mid-sea;
A wondrous building round appeared,
Not as a common structure reared,
But founded all of sapphire stone—
(Nought with more brightness shone),
And to the clouds upreared high,
While in the deep ye might descry
Its base, and round about outspread
A fair pavilion, to the sea
Descending, while clear overhead,
Like dazzling gold the canopy

Shone; ne'er on earth was such a sight!
Then Brendan with swift course sailed right
Onward, and until within that tent,
He and his monks, and vessel went.
And then he saw an altar,
Where the pillar stood, 'twas emerald rare,
Sardonyx formed the sacristy,
The pavement was chalcedony,
And right above that pillar spread
A golden drapery overhead.
And there were beryl lamps—they saw
Well pleased these marvels, for no awe
Of peril had they, and three days
They lingered in that pleasant place,
Ceaseless the holy service singing.

Anglo-Norman Trouvere.

CHAPTER XI.

A VOLCANIC ISLAND.

WHEN those days had passed, they came within view of an island, which was very rugged and rocky, covered over with slag, without trees or herbage, but full of smiths' forges. St. Brendan said to the brethren: "I am much distressed about this island; I have no wish to enter it or even to approach it—yet the wind is driving us directly towards it, as if it were the aim of our course." When they had passed on further, about a stone's cast, they heard the noise of bellows' blowing like thunder, and the beating of sledges on the anvils and iron. Then St. Brendan armed himself all over his body with the sign of the Cross, saying: "O Lord Jesus Christ, deliver us from this malign island." Soon after one of the inhabitants came forth to do some work; he was all hairy and hideous, begrimed with fire and smoke. When he saw the servants of Christ near the island, he withdrew into his forge, crying aloud: " Woe! Woe! Woe! "

St. Brendan again armed himself with the sign of the Cross, and said to the brethren: " Put on more sail, and ply your oars more briskly, that we may get away from this island." Hearing this, the savage man, above mentioned, rushed down to the shore, bearing in his hand a tongs with a burning mass of the slag, of great size and intense heat, which he flung at once after the servants of Christ; but it did them no hurt, for they were protected by the sign of the Cross. It passed them at a furlong's distance, and where it fell into the sea, it fumed up like a heap of burning coals, and a great smoke arose as if from a fiery furnace. When they had passed on about a mile beyond the spot where this burning mass had fallen, all the dwellers on the island crowded down to the shore, bearing, each of them, a large mass of burning slag, which they flung, every one in turn, after the servants of God; and then they returned to their forges, which they blew up into mighty flames, so that the whole island seemed one globe of fire, and the sea on every side boiled up and foamed, like a caldron set on a fire well supplied with fuel. All the day the brethren, even when they were no longer within view of the island, heard a loud wailing from the inhabitants thereof, and a noisome stench was perceptible at a great distance. Then St. Brendan sought to animate the courage of the brethren, saying: " Soldiers of Christ, be strong in faith unfeigned and in the armour of the Spirit, for we are now on the confines of hell; watch, therefore, and act manfully."

CHAPTER XII.

JUDAS ISCARIOT.

ON another day there came into view a large and high mountain in the ocean, not far off, towards the north, with misty clouds about it, and a great smoke issuing from its summit, when suddenly the wind drove the boat rapidly towards the island until it almost touched the shore. The cliffs were so high they could scarce see the top, were black as coal, and upright like a wall. Here the monk, who remained of the three who followed St. Brendan from his monastery, leaped from the boat, and made his way to the foot of the cliff, wailing and crying aloud: "Woe is me! father, for I am forcibly torn away from you, and cannot return." But the brethren, seized with a great fear, quickly drew off from the shore; and, lamenting loudly, cried unto the Lord: "Have mercy on us, O Lord, have mercy on us!" St. Brendan plainly saw how the wretched man was carried off by a multitude of demons, and was already burning amongst them, and he exclaimed: "Woe is yours, unhappy man, who has made you so evil an end of your life."

Afterwards a favourable breeze caught the boat, and drove them southwards; and as they looked back, they saw the peak of the mountain unclouded, and shooting up flames into the sky, which it drew back again to itself, so that the mountain seemed a burning pyre. After this dreadful sight, they sailed for seven days towards the south, and then St. Brendan observed a very dense cloud, on approaching which there came into view what had the shape of a man, sitting on a rock, with a veil before him as large as a sack, hanging between two iron prongs; and he was tossed about like a small boat in a storm. When the brethren saw this, some thought it was a bird; others, that it was a boat; but the man of God told them to cease the discussion, and to steer directly for the place; where, on his arrival, he finds the waves all around motionless, as if frozen over. They found a man sitting on a rugged and shapeless rock, with the waves on every side, which in their flowing beat upon him, even to the top of his head, and in their ebbing exposed the bare rock on which the wretched man was sitting; and the cloth which hung before him, as the winds tossed it about, struck him on the eyes and on the forehead.

When the saint asked him who he was, for what crime he was sent there, and how he had deserved to suffer so great a punishment, he answered: "I am that most unhappy Judas, the most wicked of all traffickers; not for any deserving of mine, but through the unspeakable mercy of Jesus Christ, am I placed here. I expect no place for repentance; but through the forbearance and mercy of the Redeemer of the world, and in honour of His Resurrection, I have this cooling relief, as it is now the Lord's Day; while I sit here, I seem to myself to be in a paradise of delights, considering the agony of the torments that are in store for me afterwards; for when I am in my torments, I burn like a mass of molten lead, day and night, in the heart of that mountain you have seen. There Leviathan and his satellites dwell, and there was I when it swallowed down your lost brother, for which all hell exulted, and belched forth great flames, as it always does, when it devours the souls of the reprobate. But that you may know the boundless mercy of God, I will tell you of the refreshing coolness I have here every Sunday from the first vespers to the second; from Christmas Day to the Epiphany; from Easter to Pentecost; on the Purification of the Blessed Virgin Mary, and on the festival of her Assumption. On all other days I am in torments with Herod and Pilate, with Annas and Caiphas; and, therefore, I adjure you, through the Redeemer of the world, to intercede for me with the Lord Jesus, that I may remain here until sunrise to-morrow, and that the demons, because of your coming here, may not torment me, nor sooner drag me off to my heritage of pain, which I purchased at an evil price."

The saint then said: "The will of the Lord be done; you will not be taken away by the demons until to-morrow." And he asked him what meant that cloth in front of him. Judas replied: "This cloth I once gave to a leper, when I was the purse-bearer of the Lord; but as it was not my own, I find no relief from it, but rather hurt; those iron prongs on which it hangs, I once gave to the priests for supporting their caldrons; and the stone on which I am sitting, I placed in a trench on a public road before I became a disciple of the Lord's."

When evening came, a multitude of demons gathered round in a circle, shouting: "Depart from us, O man of God, for we cannot come near our comrade unless you retire from him, and we dare not see the face of our prince until we bring back to him his pet victim; give us therefore, our prey, and keep it not from us this night." The saint then said: "I protect him not, but the Lord Jesus Christ has permitted him to remain here this night." The demons cried out: "How could you invoke the name of the Lord on behalf of him who had betrayed Him?" The man of God then commanded them in the name of Jesus Christ to do him no hurt until morning.

When the night had passed, at early dawn, when St. Brendan was proceeding on his way, a countless multitude of demons covered the face of the deep, uttering dreadful cries: "O man of God, accursed be thy coming and thy going, for our chief has this night scourged us with cruel stripes, because we had not brought back his wretched captive." "Not on us," said the saint, "but on yourselves shall those curses be; for blessed is he whom you curse, and accursed is he whom you bless." The demons shouted: "He will suffer double punishment for the next six days, because you saved him from his punishment last night." But the man of God warned them: "You have no power, neither has your chief, only whatever power God may give you; and I command you in the name of the Lord, that you increase not his torments beyond those you were wont to inflict before." "Are you," said they, "the Lord of all, that we should thus obey your command?" "No," rejoined the saint, "but I am the servant of the Lord of all; and whatsoever I command in His name, it is done, and I am His minister only in what He grants to me." In this manner they pursued him with their blasphemies until he was far away from Judas ; and they bore off this wretched soul with great rushing and howling.

SAINT BRENDAN AND JUDAS ISCARIOT.

Saint Brendan sails the northern main ;
  The brotherhoods of saints are glad.
He greets them once, he sails again ;
  So late !—such storms !—The saint is mad.

He heard, across the howling seas,
  Chime convent-bells on wintry nights ;
He saw, on spray-swept Hebrides,
  Twinkle the monastery lights ;

But north, still north, Saint Brendan steered,
  And now no bells, no convents more !
The hurtling Polar lights are neared
  The sea without a human shore.

At last—(it was the Christmas night ;
  Stars shone after a day of storm)—
He sees float past an iceberg white,
  And on it—Christ !—a living form.

That furtive mien, that scowling eye,
  Of hair that red and tufted fell—
It is—oh, where shall Brendan fly ?—
  The traitor Judas, out of hell !

Palsied with terror, Brendan sate ;
  The moon was bright, the iceberg near.
He hears a voice sigh humbly : "Wait !
  By high permission I am here.

"One moment wait, thou holy man !
  On earth my crime, my death, they knew ;
My name is under all men's ban—
  Ah ! tell them of my respite, too !

"Tell them one blessed Christmas night
  (It was the first after I came,
Breathing self-murder, frenzy, spite,
  To rue my guilt in endless flame)—

"I felt, as I in torment lay
  'Mid the souls plagued by heavenly power,
An angel touch mine arm, and say:
  'Go hence and cool thyself an hour!'

"'Ah! whence this mercy, Lord?' I said.
  'The Leper recollect,' said he,
'Who asked the passers-by for aid,
  In Joppa, and thy charity.'

"Then I remembered how I went,
  In Joppa, through the public street,
One morn when the sirocco spent
  Its storms of dust with burning heat;

"And in the street a leper sate
  Shivering with fever, naked, old;
Sand raked his sores from heel to pate,
  The hot-wind fevered him five-fold.

"He gazed upon me, as I passed,
  And murmur'd: 'Help me, or I die!'—
To the poor wretch my cloak I cast,
  Saw him looked eased, and hurried by.

"O Brendan, think what grace divine,
  What blessing must full goodness shower,
When fragment of it, small like mine,
  Hath such inestimable power!

"Well-fed, well-clothed, well friended, I
  Did that chance act of good, that one.
Then went my way to kill and lie—
  Forgot my good as soon as done.

"That germ of kindness, in the womb
  Of mercy caught, did not expire;
Outlives my guilt, outlives my doom,
  And friends me in the pit of fire.

"Once every year, when carols wake,
  On earth, the Christmas-night's repose
Arising from the sinner's lake,
  I journey to these healing snows.

"I stanch with ice my burning breast,
With silence balm my whirling brain.
O Brendan! to this hour of rest
That Joppan leper's ease was pain."

Tears started to Saint Brendan's eyes;
He bowed his head, he breathed a prayer.
Then looked, and lo! the frosty skies,
The iceberg, and no Judas there!

MATHEW ARNOLD'S *Poems.*
(With kind permission of Macmillan & Co.)

CHAPTER XIII.

THE ROCKY ISLAND OF THE HOLY HERMIT ST. PAUL.

ST. BRENDAN afterwards made sail for some time towards the south, in all things giving the glory to God. On the third day a small island appeared at a distance, towards which as the brethren plied their oars briskly, the saint said to them: "Do not, brothers, thus exhaust your strength. Seven years will have passed at next Easter, since we left our country, and now on this island you will see a holy hermit, called Paul the Spiritual, who has dwelt there for sixty years without corporal food, and who for twenty years previously received his food from a certain animal."

When they drew near the shore, they could find no place to land, so steep was the coast; the island was small and circular, about a furlong in circumference, and on its summit there was no soil, the rock being quite bare. When they sailed around it, they found a small creek, which scarcely admitted the prow of their boat, and from which the ascent was very difficult. St. Brendan told the brethren to wait there until he returned to them, for they should not enter the island without the leave of the man of God who dwells there. When the saint had ascended to the highest part of the island, he saw, on its eastern side, two caves opening opposite each other, and a small cup-like spring of water gurgling up from the rock, at the mouth of the cave in which the soldier of Christ dwelt. As St. Brendan approached the opening of one of the caves, the venerable hermit came forth from the other to meet him, greeting him with the words: "Behold how good and how pleasant for brethren to dwell together in unity.'" And then he directed St. Brendan to summon all the brethren from the boat. When they came he gave each of them the kiss of peace, calling him by his proper name, at which they all marvelled much, because of the prophetic spirit thus shown. They also wondered at his dress, for he was covered all over from head to foot with the hair of his body, which was white as snow from old age, and no other garment had he save this.

St. Brendan, observing this, was moved to grief, and heaving many sighs, said within himself: "Woe is me, a poor sinner, who wear a monk's habit, and who rule over many monks, when I here see a man of angelic condition, dwelling still in the flesh, yet unmolested by the vices of the flesh." On this, the man of God said: "Venerable father, what great and wonderful things has God shown to thee, which He has not revealed to our saintly predecessors! and yet, you say in your heart that you are not worthy to wear the habit of a monk; I say to you, that you are greater than any monk, for the monk is fed and clothed by the labour of his own hands, while God has fed and clothed you and all your brethren for seven years in His own mysterious ways; and I, wretch that I am, sit here upon this rock, without any covering, save the hair of my body." Then St. Brendan asked him about his coming to this island, whence he came, and how long he had led this manner of life. The man of God replied: "For forty years I lived in the monastery of St. Patrick, and had the care of the cemetery. One day when the prior had pointed out to me the place for the burial of a deceased brother, there appeared before me an old man, whom I knew not, who said: 'Do not, brother, make the grave there, for that is the burial-place of another.' I said 'Who are you, father?' 'Do you not know me?' said he. 'Am I not your abbot?' 'St. Patrick is my abbot,' I said. 'I am he,' he said; 'and yesterday I departed this life. and this is my burial-place.' He then pointed out to me another place, saying: 'Here you will inter our deceased brother; but tell no one what I have said to you. Go down on to-morrow to the shore, and there you will find a boat that will bear you to that place where you shall await the day of your death.' Next morning, in obedience to the directions of the abbot, I went to the place appointed, and found what he had promised. I entered the boat, and rowed along for three days and nights, and then I allowed the boat to drift whither the wind drove it. On the seventh day, this rock appeared, upon which I at once landed, and

I pushed off the boat with my foot, that it may return whence it had come, when it cut through the waves in a rapid course to the land it had left.

"On the day of my arrival here, about the hour of none, a certain animal, walking on its hind legs, brought to me in its fore-paws a fish for my dinner, and a bundle of dry brushwood to make a fire, and having set these before me, went away as it came. I struck fire with a flint and steel, and cooked the fish for my meal; and thus, for thirty years, the same provider brought every third day the same quantity of food, one fish at a time, so that I felt no want of food or of drink either; for, thanks to God, every Sunday there flowed from the rock water enough to slake my thirst and to wash myself.

"After those thirty years I discovered these two caves and this spring-well, on the waters of which I have lived for sixty years, without any other nourishment whatsoever. For ninety years, therefore, I have dwelt on this island, subsisting for thirty years of these on fish, and for sixty years on the water of this spring. I had already lived fifty years in my own country, so that all the years of my life are now one hundred and forty; and for what may remain, I have to await here in the flesh the day of my judgment. Proceed now on your voyage, and carry with you water-skins full from this fountain, for you will want it during the forty days' journey remaining before Easter Saturday. That festival of Easter, and all the Paschal holidays, you will celebrate where you have celebrated them for the past six years, and afterwards, with a blessing from your procurator, you shall proceed to that land you seek, the most holy of all lands; and there you will abide for forty days, after which the Lord your God will guide you safely back to the land of your birth."

CHAPTER XIV.

The Paradise of Delights.

St. Brendan and his brethren, having received the blessing of the man of God, and having given mutually the kiss of peace in Christ, sailed away towards the south during Lent, and the boat drifted about to and fro, their sustenance all the time being the water brought from the island, with which they refreshed themselves every third day, and were glad, as they felt neither hunger nor thirst. On Holy Saturday they reached the island of their former procurator, who came to meet them at the landing-place, and lifted every one of them out of the boat in his arms. As soon as the divine offices of the day were duly performed, he set before them a repast.

In the evening they again entered their boat with this man, and they soon discovered, in the usual place, the great whale, upon whose back they proceeded to sing the praises of the Lord all the night, and to say their Masses in the morning. When the Masses had concluded, Jasconius moved away, all of them being still on its back; and the brethren cried aloud to the Lord: "Hear us, O Lord, the God of our salvation." But St. Brendan encouraged them: "Why are you alarmed?

Fear not, for no evil shall befall us, as we have here only a helper on our journey."

The great whale swam in a direct course towards the shore of the Paradise of Birds, where it landed them all unharmed, and on this island they sojourned until the Octave of Pentecost. When that solemn season had passed, their procurator, who was still with them, said to St. Brendan: "Embark now in your boat, and fill all the water-skins from the fountain. I will be the companion and the conductor of your journey henceforth, for without my guidance you could not find the land you seek, the Land of Promise of the Saints." Then, while they were embarking, all the birds of the island, as soon as they saw St. Brendan, sung together in concert: "May a happy voyage under his guidance bring you safely to the island of your procurator." They took with them provisions for forty days, as their course lay to the west for that space of time; during which the procurator went on before them, guiding their way.

At the end of forty days, towards evening, a dense cloud overshadowed them, so dark that they could scarce see one another. Then the procurator said to St. Brendan: "Do you know, father, what darkness is this?" And the saint replied that he knew not. "This darkness," said he, "surrounds the island you have sought for seven years; you will soon see that it is the entrance to it;" and after an hour had elapsed a great light shone around them, and the boat stood by the shore.

When they had disembarked, they saw a land, extensive

and thickly set with trees, laden with fruits, as in the autumn season. All the time they were traversing that land, during their stay in it, no night was there; but a light always shone, like the light of the sun in the meridian, and for the forty days they viewed the land in various directions, they could not find the limits thereof. One day, however, they came to a large river flowing towards the middle of the land, which they could not by any means cross over. St. Brendan then said to the brethren: "We cannot cross over this river, and we must therefore remain ignorant of the size of this country." While they were considering this matter, a young man of resplendent features, and very handsome aspect, came to them, and joyfully embracing and addressing each of them by his own name, said: "Peace be with you, brothers, and with all who practise the peace of Christ. Blessed are they who dwell in Thy house, O Lord; they shall praise Thee for ever and ever."

He then said to St. Brendan: "This is the land you have sought after for so long a time; but you could not hitherto find it, because Christ our Lord wished first to display to you His divers mysteries in this immense ocean. Return now to the land of your birth, bearing with you as much of those fruits and of those precious stones, as your boat can carry; for the days of your earthly pilgrimage must draw to a close, when you may rest in peace among your saintly brethren. After many years this land will be made manifest to those who come after you, when days of tribulation may come upon the people of Christ. The great river you see here divides this land into two parts; and just as it appears now, teeming with ripe fruits, so does it ever remain, without any blight or shadow whatever, for light unfailing shines thereon." When St. Brendan inquired whether this land would be revealed unto men, the young man replied: "When the Most High Creator will have brought all nations under subjection, then will this land be made known to all His elect." Soon after, St. Brendan, having received the blessing of this man, prepared for his return to his own country. He gathered some of the fruits of the land, and various kinds of precious stones; and having taken a last farewell of the good procurator who had each year provided food for him and his brethren, he embarked once more, and sailed back through the darkness again.

When they had passed through this, they reached the "Island of Delights," where they remained for three days, as guests in the monastery; and then St. Brendan, with the abbot's parting blessing, set sail in a direct course, under God's guidance, and arrived at his own monastery, where all his monks gave glory to God for the safe return of their holy patron, and learned from him the wonderful works of God, which he had seen or heard during his voyage.

Afterwards he ended in peace the days of his life, on the nones of July, our Lord Jesus Christ reigning, whose kingdom and empire endure for ever and ever. Amen!

THE EARTHLY PARADISE.

And now that fair youth leads them on,
Where Paradise in beauty shone,
And there they saw the land all full
Of woods and rivers beautiful;

And meadows large, besprent with flowers,
And scented shrubs in fadeless bowers,
And trees with blossoms fair to see,
And fruit also deliciously
Hung from the boughs; nor briar, nor thorn,
Thistle, nor *blighted tree forlorn*
With blackened leaf, was there, for spring
Held aye a year-long blossoming;
And never shed their leaf the trees,
Nor failed their fruit, and still the breeze
Blew soft, scent-laden from the fields.
Full were the woods of venison;
The rivers of good fish each one,
And others flowed with milky tide
(No marvel, all things fructified).
The earth gave honey, oozing through
Its pores, in sweet drops like the dew;
And in the mount was golden ore,
And gems and treasures wondrous store;
There the clear sun knew no declining,
Nor fog nor mist obscured his shining;
No cloud across that sky did stray,
Taking the sun's sweet light away;
Nor cutting blast, nor blighting air,
For bitter winds blew never there;
Nor heat, nor frost, nor pain, nor grief,
Nor hunger, thirst; for swift relief
For every ill was there; plentíe
Of every good right easily
Each had according to his will,
And aye they wandered blightly still,
In large and pleasant pastures green,
Oh! such as earth hath never seen!
And glad was Brendan, for their pleasure
So wondrous was, that scant in measure
Their past toils seemed, nor could they rest,
But wandered aye in joyful quest
Of somewhat fairer, and did go
Hither and thither, to and fro,
For very joyfulness; and now
They climb a mountain's lofty brow,
And see afar a vision rare
Of angels—I may not declare

What there they saw, for words could ne'er
The meaning tell; and melodie
Of that same heavenly company
For joy that they beheld them there
They heard, but could not bear its sweetness,
Unless their natures greater meetness
To that celestial place hath borne :—
But they were whelm'd with joy. "Return,"
Said they, "we may not this sustain."
Then spoke the youth in gentle strain.
"O Brendan, God unto thine eyes
Hath granted sight of Paradise;
But know, it glories hath more bright
Than ere hath dazed thy mortal sight;
One hundred thousand times more fair
Are those abodes, but thou could'st ne'er
The view sustain, nor the ecstacy
Its meanest joys would yield to thee;
For thou hast in the body come,
But, when the Lord shall call thee home,
Thou, fitted then, a spirit, free
From weakness and mortality,
Shalt aye remain, no fleeting guest;
But taking here thy endless rest.
And while thou still remainest below
That heaven's high favour all may know,
Take hence these stones, to teach all eyes
That thou hast been in Paradise."

Anglo-Norman Trouvere.

ST BRENDAN'S RETURN.

We were about to cross its placid tide,
When, lo! an angel on our vision broke,
Clothed in white, upon the further side
He stood majestic, and thus sweetly spoke:
"Father, return, thy mission now is o'er;
God, who did call thee here, now bids thee go,
Return in peace unto thy native shore
And tell the mighty secrets thou dost know.

"In after years, in God's own fitting time,
This pleasant land again shall re-appear;
And other men shall preach the truths sublime
To the benighted peoples dwelling here.

But ere that hour, this land shall all be made,
  For mortal man, a fitting, natural home,
Then shall the giant mountain fling its shade,
  And the strong rock stem the white torrent's foam.

" Seek thy own isle—Christ's newly-bought domain,
  Which Nature with an emerald pencil paints:
Such as it is, long, long shall it remain,
  The School of Truth, the College of the Saints,
The student's bower, the hermit's calm retreat,
  The stranger's home, the hospitable hearth,
The shrine to which shall wander pilgrim feet
  From all the neighbouring nations of the earth.

" But in the end upon that land shall fall
  A bitter scourge, a lasting flood of tears,
When ruthless tyranny shall level all
  The pious trophies of its early years:
Then shall this land prove thy poor country's friend,
  And shine a second Eden in the west;
Then shall this shore its friendly arms extend,
  And clasp the outcast exile to its breast."

He ceased, and vanished from our dazzled sight,
  While harps and sacred hymns rang sweetly o'er;
For us again we winged our homeward flight
  O'er the great ocean to our native shore.
And, as a proof of God's protecting hand,
  And of the wondrous tidings that we bear,
The fragrant perfume of that heavenly land
  Clings to the garments that we wear.

D. Fl. M'Carthy's " *Voyage of St. Brendan.*"

THE LATIN LIFE OF ST. BRENDAN.

INTRODUCTION.

I PROPOSE to give here an English translation of that portion of the *Vita Sti. Brendani*, published in Cardinal Moran's *Acta Sti. Brendani*, which relates incidents in the life of the saint after his famous voyages on the ocean. The earlier portion of this Latin Life is substantially a translation of the *Betha Brenainn* (Irish Life), narrating the same incidents, in the same order, and in almost equivalent terms, that have been already related in my translation of the biographical portion of this Irish Life; and I will therefore, to avoid tiresome repetition, omit the translation of that part of the *Vita*.

The text of this Latin version was printed from the fine copy in what is called the *Codex Kilkenniensis*, "a most valuable repertory," Cardinal Moran tells us, "of the Lives of our early saints, which is now preserved in Marsh's Library, Dublin," and which is supposed to have been written in the thirteenth century. The late Dr. Reeves, in a paper read by him before the Royal Irish Academy, in January, 1875, proves that this important collection of Lives of Irish saints was really the *Codex Armachanus* referred to and quoted by Fathers Fleming and Colgan, under that title; that it had for a time belonged to Archbishop Usher; and that it received its present name within the past generation from a gentleman who mistook it for another MS. often quoted as the *Liber Kilkenniensis,* by our Irish hagiographers. There is a MS. volume in the Library of Trinity College, Dublin, classed E. 3, 11, which Dr. Reeves shows to have been almost identical with the *Codex Armachanus,* or *Kilkenniensis,* as far as its subject-matter goes ; but this seems to be only a fragment, for many lives are omitted that are contained in the *Codex.* It had belonged to the house of Canons Regular on "All Saints Island," in Loughree, near the Longford shore of the Shannon, when the famous scholar and scribe, Augustin MacGradin, who died in A.D. 1405, was Canon Prior there. It is very probable, as Dr. Reeves suggests, that both these MSS. had been copied from a larger compilation of the Lives of Irish saints of a much earlier date, which is not now known to exist. At what period such a compilation may have been first made, and at what time the various Lives embodied therein may have been written, it is, I fear, now impossible to ascertain. No doubt those Lives were composed at various dates, and by different authors, some of them coming down from an early period, while others were some centuries later. I believe that the *Vita Sti. Brendani,* of which we have the most complete copy known to exist, in the *Codex,* from which Cardinal Moran published it, may be contemporaneous with, if not anterior to, the *Navigatio,* the earliest known copy of which dates from the ninth century.

In this Latin Life of Brendan we find incidents of the later history of the saint, more in detail than in any other ancient account that has come down to us. The Irish version of the Life, as far as it is known to exist, does not touch on that period of his life at all; and other Latin versions, such as those in the *Codex Salmanticensis*, lately edited by the Bollandist Fathers, from the MS. in the Burgundian Library, Brussels, are apparently mere abridgments of this *Vita* or of the *Navigatio*, of which I have given a translation in the preceding pages.

But though this Life of the saint be the most detailed account of his later history that is now accessible, it is, alas! only a very meagre and fragmentary one, furnishing but a shadowy and imperfect outline of the holy life and apostolic labours of St. Brendan. It seems to consist of "scraps and gatherings" from dim and confused popular traditions, strung together very much at haphazard, sometimes without chronological order or sequence of incidents, and probably committed to writing after some centuries had elapsed. This was, no doubt, inevitable with regard to the histories of many of our early saints, even when their lives were written soon after their demise, like that of St. Columba, by one of his successors, Adamnan; for in the waste and wreck of ages, many such memorials have been completely lost, leaving nothing to us but vague and confused traditions, such as those strung together in this *Vita Sti. Brendani*. In my translation, I will follow the division into chapters or sections, with the titles thereof, as given in Cardinal Moran's edition; and I will append, beeween brackets, to each section any reference to its subject-matter that I have been able to glean from other sources within my reach, such as may help to elucidate or supplement it. I will commence with Chapters XI.-XII., wherein the "Voyage" is mentioned.

THE LATIN LIFE OF ST. BRENDAN.

XI.-XII. St. Brendan, after his Return from his Voyage, founds many Monasteries, in which Three Thousand Religious serve God under his Rule.

When St. Brendan had been ordained a priest by St. Erc, he then received the holy habit of a monk; and many persons, forsaking the world, came to him from various directions, to be admitted by him to the monastic life. After some time he founded oratories and monastic houses in his native district, though not many at that period; but when he returned from his voyage in quest of the "Land of Promise of the Saints," his religious foundations were widely extended through many parts of Ireland. It was then that many persons brought large offerings to St. Brendan, in the name of Christ; and many others, relinquishing their worldly possessions, were received into the religious life, by the man of God, who founded divers oratories and monasteries in many parts of Ireland, in which, as our elders relate, three thousand monks were under his rule. And he made his own father a monk, and his mother a consecrated widow.

Meanwhile the saint had visited his foster-mother,

St. Ita, who welcomed him most tenderly, with an affectionate embrace, and who received great mental recreation from the recital of the marvellous things he had seen on the ocean. Soon after the saint took his departure from her, with mutual benedictions.

He proceeded to a place called *Inis-da-dromand*, which lies in a northern estuary of the lower Shannon, the river flowing between the countries of *Corcabaiscin* (West Clare) and Kerry; and there he founded a famous monastery, where, within a brief period, seven members of the community died in the odour of sanctity, about whose sacred relics the mortuary chapel of that place was erected.

About the same time the saint gave his blessing to fifty streams in various districts, which had been fishless, and thenceforth, through the blessing of the man of God, they abounded in fish. In the course of time he passed into the province of Connaught, where land was granted to him, whereon he founded the famous city of Clonfert, in which he was interred.

[Among the religious houses founded by St. Brendan "in his native district," before his famous voyages, we may mention the monastery of Ardfert-Brendan, probably the earliest of all his foundations. He was ordained priest by St. Erc, about 510, and admitted by him soon after to his religious profession as monk, when, as the text states, "many persons, forsaking the world came to him from various directions, to be admitted to the monastic life." To receive and accommodate those postulants of the religious state, who thus crowded to him, he founded his first monastery, probably under St. Erc's guidance, on a site not far from that saint's own sanctuary at Lerrig (*Tarmuin-Eirc*, for which see page 38, *supra*). This site, as a local tradition tells, was on the table-land forming the back of the limestone ridge that runs for some miles through the plains of the present Clanmaurice, on which there are traces of an old pagan cemetery and of some very early Christian foundations also. The name of one of the townlands on this ridge, Kileacle, as it is commonly called; or, in the older and correct form, Kilkeacle, belonged to one of those primitive Christian oratories (the *cell* or church of *Caochal*, of whom tradition is otherwise silent) that may have existed there before St. Brendan's time. Here our saint and his monks were laying down the lines of the new monastery—marking off the cells, enclosure, &c., according to a written plan or sketch which one of the brethren had placed beside him on the ground, when suddenly a large bird flew past, bearing in its beak the paper on which the plan was traced, towards Ardfert about a mile distant on the south, where it dropped the scroll on the *ard* or high ground, where Ardfert Cathedral now stands. This, according to the tradition, was accepted by St. Brendan as an intimation of the heavenly will that his new monastery should be founded there, and not on the ground first chosen, and he accordingly founded his proto-monastery at Ardfert-Brendan. This was, no doubt, a more eligible site for a religious house, in every respect, than the elevated situation on the Kilkeacle ridge, for it was more accessible, and had an abundant supply of water for all purposes in the river Thyse, that flowed at the base of the *ard*, as well as in the great fountain of purest spring water, ever since known as Brandon-Well, that sends forth its copious streams at a short distance to the west of Ardfert.

Another foundation of the saint, "in his native district," was at Kilfinoora, a townland adjoining Fenit, where he was born, in which there are at present the remains of a large mediæval church, which in an ancient map of the locality is marked *Kilmore* (great church). Here there are vestiges of an earlier foundation, which bore the name Kilfinora, or the Church of Finabhair, which I surmise was the name of Brendan in an *alias* form, for the best interpretation we have of the old Gaelic word *Finabhair*, is that given by an excellent Irish scholar, the late Mr. O'Beirne Crowe—viz., "Bright Gleam," which may have been aptly applied to St. Brendan, because of those "bright gleams" that shone over the home of his parents on the night of his birth, as all his Lives tell us. However this may be, it is a singular fact that the site and surrounding district of this ancient church, though in the centre of another parish, belonged from the earliest times, as they do at present in ecclesiastical mearings, to the cathedral parish of Ardfert, and were apportioned, with the revenues of that parish, among the dignitaries of the cathedral down to a recent period. I would infer from this that ancient Kilfinora had early and close relations with Ardfert-Brendan, and had very probably been founded by St. Brendan, in connection with that monastery, and about the same time.

We find this name *Finabhair* borne by another early foundation of the saint in or near "his native district"—namely, the monastery at Shanakeel (old church), or Ballynavenoorah (Homestead of *Finabhair*), on the western slopes of Brandon-Hill, of which I have written in a Note on the *Irish Life* (*supra*, page 75), and which was certainly founded before his famous voyages. To this period we may attribute also the erection of a very primitive oratory on Inistuascairt, one of the Blasquet islands; the remains of which are still known as those of St. Brendan's oratory. There is a dim tradition that he founded also the ancient "Laura," or group of early monastic cells, known as *Kilabounia*, in the Glen, parish of Kilemlagh, barony of Iveragh, and that he occasionally visited his religious establishment there, sailing in his *currach*, across Dingle Bay, from his island oratory in the Blasquets. On one of those visits, when his little corracle neared the coast of Valentia Island, he was suddenly hailed by a man on the cliffs, imploring him to attend two persons who were dying without the sacraments. This story will be found, as local tradition has it, in the "Legend of the Well of Brendan's anointing," further on in this volume. I am inclined to think that this most interesting ancient "Laura," of *Kilabounia*, was founded at a later time, not by St. Brendan himself, but by one of his early disciples, St. Beoanus, whose name occurs in the Visions of St. Fursey, in conjunction with that of St. Meldan, another early disciple of St. Brendan.

Of the many religious foundations made by St. Brendan after his great voyage, within "his wide-spread jurisdiction" ("parochia ejus dilatata," in Latin text) "through many parts of Ireland," we have very scant record, even of their names. The only foundation of his mentioned here is that at *Inisdadromand* (the island of the two ridges), an island in that great estuary of the Shannon, which receives the waters of the River Fergus. It is now called *Inisdadroum*, and is shown on the Ordnance maps under that name, as containing nearly five statute acres. There is within this estuary a much larger island, named Coney Island on the maps, containing over two hundred and forty-four statute acres, on which there are still some remains of religious foundations, described in one of the Ordnance Survey letters in the Royal Irish Academy collection as " the ruins of a church on the south side which is not very ancient, as it has a pointed doorway in the south wall, and another more ancient church on the east side." This island is said by the writer of this letter to be the *Inisdadromand* of St. Brendan's foundation; and I notice that Dr. Healy, in his learned *Ancient Schools and Scholars*, adopts this view. It is possible that the small island that still bears the name may have been the earliest site of the monastery which, in the course of time, was transferred to the larger and more commodious one, now called Coney Island. This monastery must have been from the first a remarkable centre of religious life and missionary enterprise, as we may infer from the edifying notice of these seven great saints among its monks, who died there soon after its foundation, and were specially honoured by the mortuary-chapel or cemetery (*leviciana*, in Latin text) erected to receive their sacred relics.

Of the histories of those great saints, even of their names, I can find no trace whatever. Another indication of the eminent repute of this religious house, we find in the account of its foundation, given in the life of Brendan, in the *Codex Salmanticensis*, referred to above: " When Brendan came to the island Da Dromand, he founded a house there, and thence thoroughout wide districts of Munster the saving seed of holy faith was sown by him; on every side the heavenly trumpet of the Gospel loudly resounded; the religion of Christ was firmly planted; monasteries are founded, and the miracles of saintly men and holy virgins shine resplendent (*coruscant*, in text)." There is no reason to doubt that about this period St. Brendan laboured as a zealous and devoted missionary in several parts of Munster, and founded many churches and monasteries in various districts thereof, within which it is no exaggeration to state, as our text does, that three thousand monks lived in religious obedience under his rule. Of some of those foundations of the saint we find traces still remaining; for instance, in Cork, near the city,* "on the north side of the river, beside the road leading to Youghal, where there is still a burial-ground," there was an ancient church, dedicated to St. Brendan, which may have been the scene of his early missionary labours. Also in the diocese of Cork there are two parish churches, viz., *Kilmoe* and *Canaway*, according to Dr. Smith, dedicated to the same saint, and probably for a similar reason.

In Clare, not far from the banks of the Fergus, near Ennis, we find notice of another foundation of the saint's, namely, at *Dubhdoire*, now Doora, according to O'Curry, an extensive parish in that county: "Brendan MacFinloga was at his church in *Dubhdoire* in Thomond. His nearest neighbour on the north was Dobharcha, chief of the *Ui Dobharcon* (now O'Liddies). This man had a grass field or meadow near Loch Lir, into which Brendan's cows strayed to graze, and Dobharcha killed them for the trespass. When this was told to Brendan, he waxed indignant, and prayed, if it were God's will, that this wicked tyrant should suffer condign punishment."† This befell him soon after, when he was drowned in that lake, on the borders of which he had killed Brendan's cows. The church at Dubhdoire was founded about the same time as the monastery on *Inisdadromand*, and may have been in

* Smith's *Cork*, vol. i, page 281.

† O'Curry's *Extracts from Betham Mss.*, vol. v., R. Irish Academy.

connection with it, as the places are not far apart. Another church in Clare, farther north than Doora, namely, *Kilfinora*, the cathedral church of the ancient see of that name, was, I surmise, also founded originally by St. Brendan, in one of his early missionary visits to that district, though it may have been afterwards dedicated to St. Fiachna, or Fachanan, who was a special friend of St. Brendan's, as I will show further on, and who may have been associated with him in some of his missionary labours in north Clare. I am disposed to attribute this foundation to St. Brendan, from its name—*Kilfinoora*—meaning the church or cell of *Finabhar* ("Bright Gleam"), which, as I explained before, gave the name to a townland and to an ancient church in Kerry, probably borrowed from an *alias* name of Brendan. Whatever may be thought of this explanation of the name of this venerable church of *Kilfinora*—and I am not aware that any better one has been suggested—we certainly have some vestiges of St. Brendan's visits to the neighbourhood of that church in the magnificent well or rush of water, near Lisdoonvarna, a few miles from Kilfinora, which at some early period was dedicated to the saint, and still bears his name. This "Brendan's Well" and "Brendan's Bridge," which spans the fine stream of purest water issuing therefrom, remind us that the "name and fame" of the great Voyager, St. Brendan, were familiar as household words within the borders of ancient Kilfinora; and perhaps this fine stream, springing from Brendan's well, and wending its course through the curious gullies of that district, was one of the "fifty streams," of which the legend recorded in the text tells, that shared in Brendan's blessing, and thus "abounded in fish."

Of the after history of the monastery of Inisdadroman

there is no vestige in our Annals or ancient records. as far as I can discover; but from the fervour of its early members, amongst whom those "seven great saints," whose relics were enshrined on the island, lived and died, and the signal success of their missionary labours under St. Brendan's guidance, as indicated above, we may surmise that it continued to flourish long after St. Brendan's time, and for many centuries was a centre of religious life and literary culture to many districts of Munster, bordering on the Shannon. We read in the Life of St. Senan, that before he founded his great monastery and school at Iniscathy, he founded a religious house at *Inismore*, which is the large island in the Fergus estuary of the Shannon, now called Canon Island, not far from *Inis-da-droman* of St. Brendan's foundation. Those religious houses were probably still flourishing when the Danes, in one of their earliest descents upon our western coasts, swept up the Shannon, and, after ravaging the islands and coasts along the river, established themselves in Limerick. From this vantage-ground they frequently made excursions to plunder the "sacred isles," that were so numerous in the Shannon, above as well as below Limerick; and they not only plundered them, but seized permanent possession of many of them. Among other "sacred isles" of which the Danes had thus taken possession were *Iniscathy*, *Inismore*, and *Inisdadroman*, and here in their sore straits, after their great defeat by Mahoun, the brother of Brian Boromha, towards the end of the tenth century, when the power of the Danes of Limerick was completely broken, they took refuge, "entrenching themselves in Scattery Island as their headquarters, concealing their women and children in the smaller and more remote islands."* Thither the vengeance of Brian,

* "Wars of the Gaedhill with the Gaill," cxxxvi.

for the murder of his brother Mahoun, pursued them, and the O'Donnells of Corcabaiscin (West Clare), by his orders, attacked *Iniscathy*, slew the leaders of the Danes there, plundered that island, as well as *Inismore* and *Inisdadroman*, and other islands of the "harbour," * in which were the women and children of the foreigners, and in which they found a "great spoil of gold, silver, and wealth of various kinds." This was surely a righteous retribution for the ravages and sacrileges those "foreigners," wrought upon the sacred shrines and inhabitants of those islands for many years; and if any of the inmates of the religious houses there still survived, they may have rejoiced that "God had indeed arisen, and that his enemies were scattered."

The monastery had been destroyed long before this, and remained ruined and desolate for many years; but upon its site, or near it, was afterwards erected a mediæval parish church, the remains of which are noticed in the Ordnance Survey letter referred to in a previous page.† Of this church we find a record in the "Taxation" of the diocese of Killaloe (1301-7) as follows:—"Church of Inisdadruma (Island in the Fergus). Valor 10/." It now belongs to the parish of Killadysert, barony of Clonderalaw.]

XIII.—St. Brendan miraculously Frees the Town of Bri-uys, in Kerry, from a Pest of Insects.

Once upon a time, St. Brendan, when on a journey in the plain of West Munster (Kerry), came to the town or stronghold of *Bri-uys*, in the district of Cliath, over

* The Lower Shannon was called the harbour of Limerick.

† See page 187

against the "Hill of the Swine," and tarried there one night. The inhabitants made a bitter complaint to him of the pest of insects with which the place was infested beyond measure. Then the saint prayed to the Almighty God that the inhabitants of that town might be freed from this pest which was so hurtful to them, and at his prayer the pest at once abated, and soon afterwards ceased altogether; so that from that day to this none of these insects can live in that town.

[The plain referred to in the text was the south plain of Kerry (*Magh Deisceart*), of which Rathass, near Tralee, was the centre, separated from the north plain (*Magh Tuaisceart*, whence Rathoo) by a range of low hills, starting from near Fenit on the west, and running eastward through the heart of ancient Kerry into *Slieveluachra*, near Brosna. From this range, near its rise on the west, was thrown out like a spur a short hillock which terminates abruptly over the south plain, within a few miles of Tralee. On the brow of this hillock was *Bri-uys* (the hill of the fawn), now called *Knockanuish*, a word of the same meaning, on the site of which can be easily traced at present the ambits of three large forts, or cathairs, quite close to each other on the plateau which overhangs the plain, on which lay the *regio*, or district of Cliath, with the "Hill of the Swine" (now *Knocknamucaligh*) on the other side. This "regio Cliath" is referred to by St. Aengus Cele-De, in his tract "On the Mothers of Irish Saints," as *Altraighe Cliath*, within which lived *Mor*, the sister of St. David of Menevia, and her husband, *End or Erc*, who were the parents of three great Kerry saints—

namely, SS. Sedna, Gobban, and Eltin. This would show that the "district of Cliath" was that portion of the south plain which lay around Tralee, and extended westwards towards Knock-anuish and the Spa, for that was the *Altraighe*, the sept land of the Ua Alta, from whom St. Brendan sprung. Here, therefore, the saint was on his journey, when he tarried for the night at Bri-uys, where the inhabitants had reason to complain of the pest, from which he charitably relieved them. It is interesting and edifying to note that the saint, notwithstanding his many missionary labours throughout Munster at this period, and the care and superintendence of so many religious houses elsewhere, had found time to visit his spiritual children in Kerry, and probably he was on his way to his monasteries at Ardfert and West Corcaguiney on this occasion.]

XIV.—One of St. Brendan's Monks through Obedience exposes Himself to Death.

One day St. Brendan sailed to the above-mentioned island, *Da Dromand*, and left his boat at the shore, in charge of a young monk. When the sea rose very high, the brother of this monk said to St. Brendan: "Holy father, the tide is running very strongly, and is taking away the boat from the shore; it will soon drown my brother, and he will perish." Whereupon St. Brendan, moved to impatience, replied: "Do you love this brother more than I do? If you think so, and desire to show more compassion for him than I have, go to him now, and die in his stead." The brother went at once to the place of danger, in a spirit of obedience, and suddenly the sea rose up about him on every side, and he was drowned; but the young monk, his brother, was saved, for the sea was like a wall about him, as it had been to Moses in the Red Sea. Subsequently St. Brendan conceived a great fear of the Lord, on account of the death of this monk, judging himself responsible for it, and he asked the advice of saintly men on the subject. Their advice was that he should go to his foster-mother, St. Ita, who was inspired by God with a prophetic spirit, and she would declare to him what he ought to do. St. Ita then advised him to go on a pilgrimage for some time, to atone for his fault regarding this brother's death, and to preach the Gospel elsewhere, so as to lead other souls to Christ.

[There is no trace of this gruesome story of the monk going to his death through obedience to a hasty command of St. Brendan's in the Latin Life of the saint, as we find it in the *Codex Salmanticensis*, where it tells of his mission to Britain. This Life, after recounting in the terms I quoted above, the extraordinary success of the saint's missionary labours in Munster, after founding the monastery at *Inis-da-dromand*, immediately adds that "he (Brendan) by the advice of his foster-mother, St. Ita, went forth into Britain, with a holy company of disciples, in order that he may win unto the Lord foreign peoples also." The whole story, circumstantial as it is, was probably an afterthought of some of his admirers who wished to give the merit of a penitential pilgrimage to his missionary journeys in Britain; and, perhaps, to show the special tenderness of the conscience of the saint, who sought to expiate even an involuntary fault by a severe and laborious penance. We are told that religious writers often have a curious instinct to throw "double shades of darkness" upon some passages in the lives of the saints they write about, "in order to bring out more brightly the lights of the after picture." Hence may have come this strange passage in Brendan's Life, which is quite analogous to the story of St. Columba's "quarrel with King Diarmuid," as the cause of his exile from Ireland, which has been pronounced by good authority to be "an ill-constructed and inconsistent fable."

It is much to be regretted that of this period of St. Brendan's life, which was occupied in his missionary labours and journeys "in many parts of Munster," after his return from his famous voyages, until his mission to Britain, we have very meagre notice in his Latin Life, nor can the deficiency be supplied from any other source that I have access to. He was then in the vigour of his manhood, approaching his fortieth year, when he returned from his voyages, soon after A.D. 520, and he must have spent many years in the great work of establishing and consolidating the many religious houses he founded at that time. It was the golden prime of religious zeal and fervour among the holy men and women who then laboured for the sanctification of the tribes and the peoples of Munster. In the lives of some of those saints, who were contemporaries of St. Brendan, and who were fellow-workers of his in those apostolic labours, we meet an occasional reference to him. We are told that St. Fachtna (or Fachanan) of *Ross-ailithir*, who, like St. Brendan, had been fostered and trained to a holy life by St. Ita of Killeedy, was a special friend of his, and when he established his church and monastic school at Ross, about A.D. 530, St. Brendan became one of the earliest and most distinguished professors there, and by his great name contributed much to the *éclat* the school at Ross had attained, even in St. Fachtna's lifetime.

The relations of St. Brendan with St. Senan were also very cordial and intimate. When this great saint had founded his first monastery in Munster, at Iniscarra, on the River Lee, within a few miles of Cork, we read that a ship arrived at that port in which, among other pilgrims to Ireland, "there were fifty religious Romans, who had come through a desire of a more penitential life and of the study of the Scriptures, then flourishing in the Irish monastic schools, and who wished to place themselves under the guidance of holy men, who were famed for the sanctity of their lives and the observance of religious discipline." This happened about the time that Brendan was assisting St. Fachtna in establishing his great school at Ross; and when St. Senan took charge of ten of those fifty pilgrims to the shrines of holiness and sacred learning in Ireland, we are told that St. Brendan received another ten of them into his monasteries, while the remainder were sent to three other famous schools in other parts of Ireland. Soon after St. Senan founded another monastery at *Inismore*, in the estuary of the Shannon, as I have stated above, to which he may have been attracted by its proximity to St. Brendan's foundation on the neighbouring island of *Dadromand*, and where he may have cultivated more intimate relations with his saintly friend.

When St. Senan had founded his greatest church and monastic school at Iniscathy, lower down in the Shannon, we are told in his Life that he was visited there by St. Brendan and St. Kieran of Clonmacnoise, who had chosen him as their *anmchara*, or spiritual director; on which occasion, when the supply of food in the house was not abundant, a grand feast was miraculously provided for his visitors.

It was probably at this period that St. Brendan founded a church not far from Lorrha, in North Tipperary, where St. Ruadhan afterwards founded his famous monastery; of which we have some notice in the Life of this saint in the *Codex Salmanticensis*, already referred to. It is as follows:—"St. Brendan Mac Ua Alta had fixed a house for himself in a place called *Tulach-Brendan*, not far from St. Ruadhan's monastery, and the sound of the bell from one house used to be heard at the other. When Brendan learned this, he said: 'St. Ruadhan and I ought not to dwell so close to each other. I will therefore withdraw, and leave this place to St. Ruadhan;' and Brendan went away from that district, and afterwards founded his city of Clonfert. Then St. Ruadhan blessed him for this, and prophesied that the city he founded would be no less great and powerful than his own at Lorrha."

This story suggests very friendly relations between those saints, of which we will give some other indications later on.]

XV.—St. Brendan goes on a Pilgrimage to Britain. He Visits St. Gildas.

Soon after St. Brendan set sail on his pilgrimage to Britain, and went to visit the most holy senior, Gildas, a very wise man who dwelt there, the fame of whose sanctity was very great. Before the saint had arrived at the monastery, St. Gildas told his monks to prepare a repast for certain zealous labourers in the Lord's vineyard who would be their guests on that day, assuring them that they should then see a second St. Peter the

Apostle, again in the flesh in the person of this father, who was a tireless worker for the Lord, but whose virtue and power with God he wished to put to some trial, in order that he may know that the fault on account of which he came hither had been already pardoned by God. Then he directed the door porter to secure the outer door with iron bolts until it was opened by the divine power.

It was during the winter season, in the third year of his pilgrimage, that St. Brendan arrived at the monastery, and snow had fallen copiously so as to cover the ground, but none of it fell on St. Brendan or his disciples while they waited before the barred door. The door porter, noticing this from within, calls out to them: "Come in at once, and let your own merits open the door unto you." Whereupon St. Brendan directed his disciple Talmach* to open the door for them in the name of Christ; and when he, in obedience, put forth his hand towards the door, the bolts at once flew back, and were no longer visible. They then entered, and went towards the church of the monastery, the doors of which were closed against them in like manner; but St. Brendan knowing that this was done as a trial of his virtue, only placed his hand on the folding door, and said: "Oh, church of Christ, my true mother, open unto me;" instantly the seals or locks were broken, and the church lay open before

* Colgan has a notice of this disciple of St. Brendan's at February 26th. *Acta SS. Hib.*, page 414. He probably was the same Talmach who afterwards became a disciple of St. Finbarr's, of whom it is stated in the life of that saint, chap. x., that "Talmach gave his church to God and to Barre," when he was, no doubt, very advanced in life.

them, when they went at once into the choir. Here St. Gildas had a missal written in Greek characters, and this was placed on the altar for use at Mass. Then the sacristan said to St. Brendan, by order of St. Gildas: "Man of God, our father abbot commands you to offer the holy sacrifice; here is the altar prepared, and a missal in Greek letters, in which you are to read the Mass, as our abbot does." When St. Brendan opened the missal he prayed: "Grant unto me, O Lord Jesus, a knowledge of those unknown letters, as Thou hast by Thy power opened these doors that were barred against us." Truly all things are possible to the true believer, for St. Brendan knew at once those Greek characters as well as he did the Latin ones he had learned from his infancy.

He then proceeded to say Mass, and St. Gildas himself and all his monks came to the church to receive Holy Communion from his hands; but St. Gildas saw the real flesh of Christ on the patena, and the real precious blood in the chalice; and alarmed at this vision, he said: "Why have I brought this judgment of the Lord upon myself by making trial of your virtue, O man of God?" Then St. Brendan told him that his prayer would guard him from any punishment, especially as his trial of the pilgrims of Christ should now cease. St. Brendan then offered a prayer, and the body of Christ appeared in its usual species on the patena, and the precious blood in the species of wine in the chalice; whereupon all the holy men received Holy Communion and made fervent thanksgiving. St. Brendan remained at the monastery three days and nights.

[The date of St. Brendan's mission or pilgrimage to Britain is a matter for conjecture, but we will not be far astray in placing it about A.D. 540, thus allowing fifteen years or more for the period of his apostolic labours throughout Munster, of which we catch some shadowy glimpses in those few meagre notices I have given above. We have no account of his journey to Britain, nor of his peregrinations there, until he arrived at the monastery of St. Gildas, as stated in the text, which gives so curious and interesting a description of his reception. St. Gildas, surnamed the Wise (*Sapientissimus* in the text), was one of the most illustrious saints of Cymric Britain or Wales, who co-operated with St. Patrick and his successors in the work of evangelizing and sanctifying their Celtic brethren in Ireland. Many such devoted missionaries came over with St. Patrick himself, and laboured under his guidance in that holy work during his life, and after his death the supply of such zealous helpers from Wales was more abundant still, for many holy priests and laymen sought refuge in Ireland from the ruin and devastation wrought upon their country by the invading hordes of pagan Saxons, who were then ravaging with fire and sword the length and breadth of ancient Britain.

The historian of that period gives us a mournful picture of the terrible thoroughness of this onslaught on the Catholic faith, and on the homes of the Britons. "It was in vain that some sought shelter within their churches, for the rage of the invaders seemed to have burned most fiercely against the clergy; the priests were slain at the altar, the churches fired, and the people who sought refuge there were driven by the flames to fling themselves on a ring of pitiless steel that hemmed them in on every side." No wonder that from this ruthless havoc bands of fugitives came pouring into the shores of Ireland in a constant stream for some generations after St. Patrick's time: "Hoary priests and consecrated virgins and tender children: ecclesiastics bearing the relics of the saints; women flying from worse than death;" all claimed and received from their Irish brethren in the faith the welcome and solace they needed so sorely, while their presence brought with it a rich harvest of religion and culture to the people who hospitably sheltered and befriended them.

Among those refugee ecclesiastics whose visit to our shores was so fruitful of blessings, was probably St. Gildas the Wise. He became a distinguished teacher in the great school of Armagh soon after St. Patrick's death, and continued to govern it as rector with great success for many years. He is supposed to have returned to Wales soon after the death of his brother, Howel, a local dynast there, who was slain by the famed King Arthur early in the sixth century. He afterwards wrote a book on the *Destruction of Britain*, which is still extant, and which shows that he must have been a learned divine of great holiness of life, as well as a man of general culture, eminently qualified to preside over and direct the great school at Armagh. King Arthur is said to have expressed his regret for the murder of his brother, and to have sought pardon and reconciliation with him, which the saint granted, at the instance of an assembly of bishops and other clergy, who met on the occasion, and who imposed a suitable penance on the king for his crime.

In his book on the *Destruction of Britain*, St. Gildas gives a deplorable account of the moral and religious condition of his native Wales, reduced to the last extremity by domestic tyrants, as much as by its foreign foes, at the time he wrote, probably about A.D. 535. He lashes those local tyrants with fierce invective, and charges them with the crimes of perjury, robbery, adultery, and murder, declaring that their crying iniquities had brought down upon their country the vengeance of God, in the frightful scourge of the Saxon invasion. He addresses the clergy also in very severe language, and denounces woe, like another Jeremias, upon those faithless pastors, who, by truckling to those tyrants, sold their priesthood and betrayed their flocks.

During his stay in Wales St. Gildas was in frequent and most friendly intercourse with St Cadoc (Latinized Docus), who founded the great monastery and school of Lancarvan, over which he presided. At his request St. Gildas resumed his office of teaching, and directed the school at Lancarvan for one year. Soon after these two holy men fled away from the crowds of visitors and students that were attracted by their great repute for holiness and learning, and sought "deserts in the sea" in the islands of *Ronech* and *Echni*, in the Bristol Channel, where they may without distraction from the outer world, apply themselves to prayer and study.

We read in Ree's *Lives of Cambro-British Saints*, that "when St. Gildas dwelt in the island of Echni, devoutly serving God, he wrote a missal-book, and presented it to St. Cadoc, when he became his confessor; therefore that book was called the Gospel of St. Gildas." This story is very interesting, taken in connection with the "missal in Greek letters," set before St. Brendan by St. Gildas, as we read in our text, and it may serve to explain an obscure allusion to the "*Ritus celebrandi missam*," which we are told that "Irish saints of the second order received from the British saints, David and Gildas and Cadoc." This may mean that those Cambrian saints were all, like

St. Gildas, industrious copyists of the missal, and presented many copies of it to their contemporary Irish saints for use in Ireland.

St. Gildas and St. Cadoc were not long left in peace to enjoy the delights of heavenly solitude in those islands, for a band of pirates from the Orkneys swept down upon them, and plundered their little cells, making captives of some of their disciples. The saints escaped with their lives, and St. Gildas, after spending some time at the great monastery of Glastonbury, left his native Britain and migrated to Armoric Gaul, or lesser Britain as it was called, now Brittany, whither immense numbers of the ancient Britons had already taken refuge from their Saxon relentless enemies. This occurred, according to Mabillon, in A.D. 538. Here St. Gildas soon founded a monastery and school at a place called Rhuys,* a promontory overhanging the sea of Morbihan, and it was at this monastery, most probably, that St. Brendan visited him and received the singular welcome detailed in our text.

Here we are told that it was "after three years on his pilgrimage" St. Brendan, arrived at the monastery, but we have no intimation of where or how the saint had passed those years, and we are left very much to conjecture. We must suppose that after he had left Ireland he landed in Cymric Britain, or Wales, and that he soon after visited there the great saints who

* This is the peninsula of *St. Gildas de Rhuys*, which is surmounted by the largest tumulus in Brittany. Here Abélard, of mediæval notoriety, spent some years of his restless life in a monastery, which has long ceased to exist, but the site of which is still pointed out. He had sought in this "end of the earth," as he termed the place, to hide his shame; and, perhaps, atone for his guilt, but even here he could not rest in quiet or live in safety; but was still, as he tells in his Life, "driven about as a wanderer and a fugitive, as if the curse of Cain were upon me."—Weld's *Vacation in Brittany.*

were conspicuous for their holy and apostolic lives at that time. Among these St. David of *Kilmuine* (Menevia) held a foremost place, and for this reason may have been the first to receive a visit from St. Brendan. For this there may have been another reason also. We know that in St. Brendan's native *Altraighe*, in West Kerry, a sister of St. David's, *Mor*, the mother of three Kerry saints, was settled in marriage with a local chief named *End*, whose *Cathair* of *Cathair-einde* (now *Cahirina*) stood in the western suburb of the present Tralee, and that she resided there at the time that St. Brendan was making his missionary journeys to and fro in that district. The saint must have therefore known this saintly sister of St. David very well, and through her may have contracted a special friendship with that saint. In this case he would be sure to pay an early visit to *Kilmuine*, and spend some time in the society of the holy founder, and in co-operation with him in his apostolic labours. Thus may have passed a portion of the first "three years of his pilgrimage."

We have more distinct warrant for the association of our saint with another illustrious contemporary saint in Wales, viz., St. Cadoc of Lancarvan, mentioned above. In a Life of this saint we read that after he had founded his house at Lancarvan, one of the great centres of the monastic life in Cambro-Britain, and established around it various priories, each under the rule of its prior, he went on a pilgrimage to Ireland and remained three years in a famous monastery in Munster, where monastic discipline was very exact. "On his return to Wales he brought back with him several Irish monks and many British priests, who desired to become members of his community." In the copy I write this from, "the famous monastery" is stated to be that of Lismore, but if this meant the foundation of St. Carthage-Mochuda at Lismore, it would be a gross anachronism, for that great monastery was not founded for fully a century after the most probable date of St. Cadoc's visit to Ireland. This took place soon after the saint's expulsion, by the Orkney pirates, from his island-retreat in the Bristol Channel, and about the time of his friend St. Gildas's migration to Brittany; that is, about A.D. 538. This Munster monastery was therefore in existence before that date, and may have been one of those founded by St. Brendan himself, and which was then "famous for the strictness of its monastic discipline." However that may be, St. Brendan's visit to Wales coincides very closely, with this pilgrimage of St. Cadoc, and with his return home, with "several Irish monks and British priests," whom he had recruited in Ireland for his great monastery at Lancarvan; and who can tell but that St. Brendan himself and "the holy company of disciples" that accompanied him to Wales, may have furnished some of those Irish monks, who wished to join the saintly community of St. Cadoc, and who left their homes for distant Wales, under the guidance of St. Brendan, going forth on his pilgrimage at the same time? It is worthy of note, in this connection, that we have an account of St. Brendan's presence and residence in St. Cadoc's monastery, soon after this date, from which we may infer that he became a member of the community and assumed office there, probably as prior of one of those attached priories referred to above, before he left Wales to visit St. Gildas in Brittany. This account is given in the Life of St. Machutus—or St. Malo—by Bili—who is said to have been born near Lancarvan, and to have been educated there by St. Brendan, who is, in this Life, always called the "Master," in all the incidents and adventures recorded in that curious Breton legend. We will treat of this, after the next chapter, in which the miracles of St. Brendan are related.]

XVI. St. Brendan performs a great Miracle at the request of St. Gildas.

When these days had passed, the venerable St. Gildas said to St. Brendan: "There are in the wilderness hard-by very powerful wild beasts that frequently attack the people about here, and often beset even this city of ours; now God has vouchsafed to you the power to expel those beasts from amongst men, that by so great a miracle wrought here by you, through the divine grace, you may surely know that the fault which led to your pilgrimage has been pardoned by God." Then St. Brendan went forth into the wilderness, taking with him the aforementioned disciple, Talmach, while a number of men on horse-back followed, and looked on at a distance, desiring to see the issue. When they came to the lair of the wild beasts, they found the dam, with her young ones, asleep in the noontide sun; and holy Talmach went to rouse her up. Whereupon she uttered a loud roar, on hearing which all the other wild beasts rushed towards her. Then St. Brendan said to them: "Follow us now very gently, with all your cubs;" and while all who were looking on, expecting their instant death, they saw the wild beasts following them like domestic dogs, from which, however, the men on horse-back fled away in great trepidation; but St. Gildas, when he saw them so tame, even at the gates of the city, gave thanks to God for His wonderful works. Then St. Brendan commanded the wild beasts to go back again into the wilderness, and never more to harm anyone; and men know not what became of them, for they have not since been seen up to the present day. After this the venerable St. Gildas said to St. Brendan: "Accept me now, father, as a disciple of yours, and become the patron of this city and people." But St. Brendan replied: "Here I must not tarry, for my resurrection shall be in Ireland." Then St. Brendan, having received the blessings of St. Gildas and all his monks, as well as those of the inhabitants of the city, and having bestowed his blessing upon them in return, took his departure from the place, and in another district in Brittany he founded soon after a monastery, named *Ailech*. In another place, also, in Britain, in the district of *Heth*, he established a church, and a town around it, and there the holy father performed great miracles. Subsequently he sailed back to Ireland.

[The version of this story in the Life of Brendan in the *Codex Salmanticensis*, gives the *finale* somewhat differently: "Brendan ordered the wild beasts to go gently with him, and thenceforth to watch over the flocks of the district; whereupon they followed him like so many house-dogs, and having laid aside all their natural ferocity, they performed the duties of shepherds for the citizens. When St. Gildas had witnessed this and other like miracles wrought by Brendan, he offered to him his city, and himself as an obedient subject of his; but Brendan replied: "What is the world to me, or what care I for it all? (*Quid mihi, inquit, et mundo*) ?"

In this wonderful tale we have the only account now accessible of the life and work of St. Brendan during his stay among the Britons or Bretons, except what is added about his foundation of a monastic house at *Aleth*, and of a church in the district of *Heth*, both places said to be in Britain or Brittany. The period of his stay there was probably more than seven years, and during that time he, no doubt, laboured zealously and fruitfully in promoting the glory of God and the salvation of souls in many parts of Wales as well as Brittany. Hence St. Gildas directs his monks to prepare to welcome him as "a second St. Peter," so full was he of Apostolic zeal, and as a tireless worker for the Lord (*pater laboriosus*).

There was a wide field for the exercise of such laborious zeal in the moral and religious condition of the sorely afflicted Britons at that period, which St. Gildas deplores and denounces in his book on the *Destruction of Britain*, to which I referred before;* and we may well believe that St. Brendan and the fervent band of disciples who accompanied him on his mission to Britain devoted themselves to the arduous task of reviving the faith and reforming the morals of those people. Among the causes that produced this decay of religion and this depravation of morals, was the tyranny and cruel oppression, as well as the scandalous lives of their native princes, whose iniquities St. Gildas inveighs against so vehemently as more than sufficient to merit their terrible chastisements at the hands of their Saxon invaders. In his "Querulous Epistle," which forms the second part of his *Destruction of Britain*, he denounces by name five of those domestic

* *Supra*, page 201.

tyrants, and after specifying some of their infamous crimes, he compares them to various wild beasts which preyed upon the people; one he called "the panther," another the "lion's cub," another "the insular dragon," and so on. It is not surprising to learn, as we are told, that the saint had to seek refuge in Armoric Gaul, or Brittany, from the vengeance of those tyrants whose wrath he had thus incurred. St. Brendan's mission in Wales commenced soon after, and very probably the field of his missionary labours extended to the districts and peoples ruled by those wicked princes. He had need of all the Apostolic zeal and courage of "another St. Peter," to preach to and attempt the conversion of such monsters of iniquity and impiety; but we may be sure that the daring voyager, who braved all the dangers and terrors of the trackless ocean, the *mare tenebrosum*, in quest of the "Land of Promise of the Saints," or "of strange peoples to be won to Christ," would not shrink even from so desperate a task. We may, therefore, hope that he did essay the work of converting these human "beasts of prey," and more—that he effected the conversion and reformation of at least some of them; for I surmise that his success in thus morally taming those wild beasts is figured under the wonderful tale of his controlling and subduing the powerful beasts of the wilderness at the instance of St. Gildas; and that by the story of his changing those ravening "beasts of prey" into "guardians and shepherds of the flock," as we have it in the Life from the *Codex Salmanticensis*, is conveyed in allegory the effect of St. Brendan's mission upon some of those princes, whereby they were converted into the "guardians and shepherds" of their people, a miracle of divine power and grace more signal even than the saint's mastery of the "wild beasts of the wilderness."

In the Life of St. Machutus, or Malo, there are many references to St. Brendan's stay in Wales and Brittany. The earliest Life now extant of this saint was written about the middle of the ninth century by Bili, deacon of the church of *Aleth*, in Brittany, who tells us that when writing he had at hand another Life of the saint by an anonymous author, "who composed it many years before he (Bili) was born, as a faithful relation of what he had heard and learned from wise men who preceded him." This ancient Life had, it seems, been corrupted by many interpolations, which Bili proposed to eliminate in his edition of it. From all this we can infer that this earliest Life of St. Machutus was composed in the eighth century, not long after the probable date of the first Irish version of the Brendan Legend, many of the incidents of which it appears to have borrowed and adapted in a notable manner.

Machutus, the child of a local dynast, was born in Monmouthshire about A.D. 520, was baptized at the neighbouring monastery of Lancarvan, and became a pupil and disciple of St. Brendan's, when he visited there. The Life tells that soon after St. Brendan was seized with an ardent desire to travel in quest of the island *Yma* (meaning in Breton or Cymric the "Isle of the Just" or Blessed), and urged his pupil Machutus to accompany him, which he readily consented to do in the words of the Scripture text: "Master, I will follow Thee whithersoever Thou goest." St. Brendan had a strong and large vessel built, and prepared for a long voyage, he himself, his pupil, St. Machutus, and no less than nine hundred and three companions embarking. The voyage lasts for seven years, but the incidents of the last year only are related, and in all these Machutus fills the principal *role*. In the seventh year they discovered the island of the Giant Mildu, whom they restore to life and baptize. They learn from him the whereabouts of the island *Yma*, of which they were in quest, for he had once seen it; but he told them that it was completely surrounded by a golden wall of great height. This giant, being of preternatural stature, offers to draw their ship to that island by wading through the sea; but while he was doing this a great storm arose, and by the force of the waves the anchor cable by which he drew the vessel snapped, and they were fain to return to the giant's island, from which they soon after resolved to go back to their own country. On their voyage the crew suffered intense thirst, which Machutus assuaged in a miraculous manner. This occurred on Easter Eve, and it was on the next day, Easter Sunday, that the celebration of Mass by Machutus on the whale's back took place, as is related in the extract from this Life, already given in my "Note on Irish Life" (page 89, *supra*).

The voyagers returned home without having found the island *Yma*, just as in the Irish version, Brendan returns after his five years' voyage, having failed in his quest of the Land of Promise of the Saints; but Machutus is resolved again to seek out the wonderful secrets of the ocean, urged by the words of the same text quoted in the Irish version: "He who hath left house or brethren or sisters . . . or land for My Name's sake, shall receive an hundredfold, and shall possess life everlasting."

To a second voyage the parents of Machutus object, and his master, St. Brendan, is also unwilling to bless the enterprise; but the holy youth pleaded so earnestly, that his parents at length consent, and they and Brendan accompany him to the sea-shore, where a masted ship is found prepared by no human hands, and where he is favoured with a vision of Christ Himself, who, finding his motives pure and holy, blesses him, and foretells a prosperous voyage.

The accounts of this second voyage vary somewhat in the versions of the Life. In one, it is told that his vessel soon arrived at the *Island of September*, in front of the present St. Malo, whereon he found a hermit named Festivus, who had been warned in a dream of his visit, and under whose instruction he chose to remain. Thus ended the voyage. In another account we are told that in this second voyage "Brendan and Machutus had traversed the Orkneys and the northern islands of Scotland before they returned home." From this we may infer that St. Brendan had, after his visit to Wales, visited and evangelized some of the islands of Scotland. Hence in the *Calendar* * of David Camerarius, he is described as the apostle of the Orkneys and the Scottish Isles: "*Maii* 16 *die—Sanctus Brendanus, abbas, apostolus Orcadum et Scoticarum Insularum.*"

It was probably during this mission that the saint founded the church in the district of Heth, where he, as the text relates, "performed great miracles." This is supposed to be the island of *Tir-eeth* ("Land of Eth or Heth"), a large island off the coast of Argyle, Scotland. There are many other places among the isles, as well as on the mainland of Scotland, where the memory of St. Brendan was preserved in veneration. Canon O'Hanlon, in his Life of St. Brendan, May 16th (*Lives of Irish Saints*), thus notices some of those places: "Kilbrennan (Church of Brendan) in Mull; St. Brengan's chapel in St. Kilda; he was patron of Boyndie and Birnie; he was venerated at Cullen, at Dumbarney, and at Balbirnie; St. Brenghan's fair was

* Published in 1631, and dedicated to King Charles I.

held at Kilbar, in Ayrshire, and at Banff; the island of Bute got its name from a little cell erected there by St. Brendan, which in Gaelic was called *bothe*, and he was honoured as patron of this royal island; St. Brendan's haven at Innerbondy belonged to Arbroath abbey; the Church of Eassie, in Forfarshire, was dedicated to him, and several other churches in Scotland rejoiced in him as their patron." Memorials such as these, so wide-spread and enduring, indicate that the mission of St. Brendan to Scotland and the Isles must have been of some duration; but we have no means of ascertaining the time it occupied. It must have taken place before the saint's return to Ireland from his pilgrimage to Britain; that is, about A.D. 550; and, therefore, nearly twenty years before St. Columba prosecuted his mission of evangelizing those same islands of northern Scotland, which St. Brendan had traversed in his missionary journeys. He may, therefore, be justly honoured in the *Calendar* of the Scottish Church as the "Apostle of the Orkneys and the Isles of Scotland."

Ailech, where the text states he founded a monastery in Britain or Brittany, was, no doubt, the ancient *Alectum* or *Aleth* in Brittany, not far from the present St. Malo. It was a place of some importance, even before St. Brendan's time, being the chief city of an ancient Gaulish tribe, and afterwards the residence of a Roman prefect, and the seat of a military division under the empire. It was situated on a massive bluff at the mouth of the river Rance; on the other side was the precipitous rock on which St. Malo was built. Here St. Machutus, as his Life tells, found St. Aaron, a holy hermit, who had a cell upon this rock, and died there in 543, leaving St. Machutus or Malo to succeed him. Thence he passed over to Aleth, where St. Brendan had founded the monastery; and there he laboured as a holy and zealous preacher of the Gospel for some years, when he was consecrated first bishop of the ancient see of Aleth, which five centuries afterwards was transferred to St. Malo, where his relics were preserved, and to which he had given his name.

"In the seaward front of St. Malo, high above the highest tides, tower up from the deep sea great masses of storm-beaten rocks, like advanced posts, some of which have been utilized for purposes of fortification. One of the largest of these, *Cézembre*, which has almost the proportions of an island, has been so utilized, and on its craggy slope can still be distinguished the ruins of the hermit cell of St. Brendan, in strange contrast to the gleam of the cannon of the battery that crowns its rugged summit."* This was the Island of September, on which St. Machutus is said to have found the hermit Festivus, as related above, under whose instruction he remained for so long a time. Of St. Malo's residence there we have no further trace; but the existence of this ancient cell, dedicated to St. Brendan, indicates that saint's connection with the place, and very likely this weird rock in the sea was chosen by him as a solitary retreat from his neighbouring monastery at *Aleth*, to which he resorted occasionally.

Another interesting memorial of St. Brendan's visit to Britain, similar to that on the *Isle de Cézembre*, was the little oratory that still bears his name, which he built on the bold crag that overhangs the junction of the river Avon with the Severn, in the Bristol Channel, where its remains are still visible, to remind the Bristol mariners that once upon a time the great sailor-saint, Brendan, had blessed the seaward approach to their city of Bristol.]

* *Month*, Oct., 1881, art. "St. Malo."

XVII.—St. Brendan commends the Patronage of St. Brigid.

One day that St. Brendan was on his voyages on the ocean, he saw two monsters of the deep in dreadful conflict, one of them sometimes pursuing the other with great fury. The monster that was pursued, when it was nearly overtaken and vanquished by the other, cried out, in a human voice, in Brendan's hearing: "I commend myself to the protection of St. Patrick, the Chief-Bishop of the Irish." The other monster then shouted, also in human voice: "his protection will now avail you nothing." The monster pursued again cried out: "I commend myself to the protection of St. Brendan, here present;" and then its pursuer said: "Neither will his protection save you now." At last the monster that was pursued cried out: "I commend myself to the protection of the most holy virgin Brigid." Whereupon the monster in pursuit at once withdrew, saying that it dare not pursue further the monster that invoked the protection of St. Brigid; and thus the wretched creature escaped unharmed.

Then St. Brendan composed a hymn in praise of St. Brigid, for the greater glory of God; and when he returned to Ireland, he went to visit that saint; and having told her about those monsters, he asked her why such monsters of the deep had more fear of her than of other saints. The holy virgin replied by a question: "How often do you fix your attention upon God?" St. Brendan answered: "At every seventh step I take, or sooner, I have God in my thoughts; but sometimes I think of God alone for a long space of time." St. Brigid then said: "You therefore think of wordly things sometimes, and upon God at other times; for my part, since I first applied my mind to God, I have never for a moment diverted my attention from Him; the more constantly one fixes the attention of his mind and the love of his heart upon God, so much the more do the animals stand in fear of him." At this sentiment of the holy virgin Brigid, St. Brendan was greatly edified, and having received her blessing, and giving his in return, he proceeded on his way.

[In Note * (24) on Irish Life, I have given the version of this story from the Life of St. Brigid, where I observed that if the story was more than a pious allegory, and if such an interview took place between those saints, it must have occurred before A.D. 524—the year of St. Brigid's death. I know no reason to question the fact of the saints having met after St. Brendan's famous voyages, which, most probably, ended some time before that date; and there are some reasons why St. Brendan should visit, on such an occasion, his friend St. Brigid, who was the special and intimate friend of his patron St. Erc, whom she had accompanied into Kerry, and "near whose dwelling by the sea," at Kerry-Head, she had fixed her little convent "for many years," during St. Brendan's youthful pupilage under the holy Bishop, when she must have had many opportunities of knowing and loving the youthful saint. When St. Brigid left her convent over the Shannon, near Kerry-Head, she went

* Page 85, *supra*.

as her Life tells, into Connaught, and resided on the plain of Aei, "where she founded cells and convents round about." She had, no doubt, brought some of her Kerry nuns with her on this mission, and one of these, we may believe, was the holy religious, St. Caoilin,* the illustrious Kerry saint, who welcomed and protected her "Kerry cousins," the *Ciarraidhe-Aei*, who migrated to this plain of Aei, some years afterwards. Within this great plain St. Brendan received his "Religious Rule" from the angel, and there also he performed the signal miracle recorded in the Irish Life. During this first visit of St. Brendan to the plain of Aei—which took place not long after the date of St. Brigid's mission there, he must have come to know some of her convents and her religious, and very probably renewed the friendly relations of his youth with the saint herself. We have, therefore, some reasons to think that those saints may have had some such spiritual colloquy as is narrated in the text.

The insertion of the story here is somewhat out of chronological order, but it comes in seasonably to furnish an interesting and edifying explanation of the wonderful dominion over the "wild beasts of the wilderness," exercised by St. Brendan, as related in the previous chapter, and which the Creator has often vouchsafed to such eminent saints as he was, in proportion to the degree of their love of God, and the holiness and innocence of their lives. The great truth has been many times illustrated in the history of such servants of God, that in the words of St. Brigid:† "The more constantly and sincerely one fixes the attention of his mind and the love of his heart upon God,

* See "Notes on Irish Life," page 69, *supra*.

† The Four Masters in A.D. 525, refer to this interview between Saints Brendan and Brigid.

so much the more does the brute creation stand in awe of him."

The "Hymn of praise of St. Brigid," which the text tells us was composed by St. Brendan, is the ancient Irish hymn or poem in the *Liber Hymnorum*, beginning,

> "*Brigit be bhithmhaith, bruth ordhai oibhlech;*"

which is attributed to various authors, in the preface to it in the oldest MSS.; among others to St. Columba, and to St. Brendan. It consists of three quatrains; the English of the first, Dr. Whitly Stokes gives as follows:—*

> "Brigid, excellent woman, a flame golden, delightful,
> May she, the sun dazzling, splendid, guide us to the eternal kingdom!
> May Brigid save us over the throngs of demons!
> May she repel from us the attacks of all disease!"

XVIII.—St. Brendan erects a Cell in Inis-meic-Ichuind. The King of Connaught makes a Gift of the Island to him.

St. Brendan then came to the country of Connaught, and went into an island called in Irish *Inis-meicIchuind*, where horses of the king were on pasture. Here the saint when building an oratory, set the king's horses to draw materials. The holy bishop *Moenu* was there with St. Brendan at the time. When the King Aedh, son of Eathach Tirmcarna, heard of this, he declared in his wrath that he would surely put to death the person who had done him so great a wrong. In his rage he hastened to the island, but when he was preparing to

* Lives of Saints from *Book of Lismore*, page 199.

cross over in a boat, a violent storm suddenly arose, which agitated the waters of the lake from its depths for the space of three days, during which the king had to await a calm. On the night of the third day the Lord appeared to him in a dream, and said to him: "Take care that you do no harm to My servant Brendan: otherwise you will soon meet your death." When the storm subsided, the king made a gift of the island, together with the horses, to St. Brendan, for ever.

[St Brendan had now completed his pilgrimage in Britain, and returned to Ireland about A.D. 550. He had been absent on that mission perhaps ten years, and we should expect that after his return he would make an early and anxious visitation of his various monasteries throughout Munster, and especially of his earliest foundations in West Munster or in his native Kerry. He, no doubt, visited his dear friend and foster-mother, St. Ita, at her convent of Killeedy, and gave her, for her edification and "mental recreation," an account of his missionary labours and peregrinations among the Britons, as he had years before, on his return from his famous voyages, entertained her "with the wonders he had seen on the ocean." It would appear that on his return to Ireland certain disciples and friends from Britain accompanied him, and among these was, probably, "the son of a king of Britain," whom St. Brendan had brought with him, and placed for a time in his monastery in the Lower Shannon at *Inis-da-dromand.* Regarding this king's son, we have an extraordinary tale in the Life of St. Ruadhan, in the *Codex Salmanticensis*, as follows :—

"On a certain occasion the boat of Brendan was sunk to the bottom of the sea in the Lower Shannon (*Mare Luiemnech* in the text), and the son of the King of Britain was at the time asleep in the prow of the boat, and went to the bottom with it. Then Brendan told his monks to go at once to St. Ruadhan, for to him had God granted the power to raise their boat from the depths of the sea, and to restore to life the king's son that was drowned in it. They went accordingly to St. Ruadhan, and he came with them at once to the place where the boat had sunk, and when he had offered a prayer the boat instantly rose to the surface with the king's son in it alive and safe; whereupon he told them that St. Ruadhan had placed his cowl around his head, so that he felt not the water."

It is not stated whether St. Brendan was present on this occasion; very probably he was not; and when the story reached him at a distance, he directed his monks to call in their saintly neighbour, St. Ruadhan, from Lorrha, on the other side of the Shannon, to perform the needful miracle for his special friend, St. Brendan.

Another disciple who accompanied our saint from Britain was "that monk who had come from his parents with him from Britain," of whose death and miraculous restoration to life we will read in a succeeding chapter of this Life, and whose name is stated in the Life of Brendan, from the *Codex Salmanticensis*, to be Senan, whom St. Brendan restored to life, "because he had promised his parents, when they committed their son to his care, that they would see him again safe and sound."

I cannot help thinking that St. Brendan about this period visited his proto-monastery at Ardfert, and remained there for some time, in loving intercourse with his spiritual children in that religious house, which was his earliest foundation, and in which he, no doubt, retained an affectionate interest amid all his missionary labours and solicitudes. Here he may have sought and taken some needful rest after his many wanderings by land and sea, and having now long passed his sixtieth year, it would be natural enough that he should say: "Here, among my first-born spiritual children, is my rest for ever and ever; here will I dwell, for I have chosen it." But this was not his choice, for he knew for many years that "the place of his resurrection" should be elsewhere. Hence he soon after turned his face once more to "the country of Connaught;" and for this new missionary toil he had, I believe, a special reason and attraction.

For some time before this period a remarkable migration of St. Brendan's countrymen, the *Ciarraidhe*, was in progress from the plains of their native Kerry to the wide and beautiful plains of Roscommon and Mayo, in Connaught. This migration commenced early in the reign of Aedh, son of Eochaidh Tirmcharna, probably before A.D. 550, under the conduct of a Kerry prince, Cairbre MacConuire, who, because of some intestine broils, of which neither history nor tradition tells, was driven into forced exile, with large numbers of his clan. John O'Donovan* gives an account of this migration from an ancient Gaelic MS. in the library of Trinity College, Dublin, which is very interesting :—

"When first did the Ciarriadhe come into Connaught? Not difficult. In the time of Aedh, son of Eochaidh

* *Book of Rights*, page 100, n. f.

Tirmcharna. Which of them came in first? Not difficult. *Coirbri MacConuire*, who came from the south of Munster, whence he had been expelled. He came with all his people to Aedh, son of Eochaidh Tirmcharna. Coirbri had a daughter famed for her beauty and accomplishments, and Aedh asked her of her father in marriage. After the marriage she came one time to visit her father, who showed great grief in her presence. She asked him whence his grief arose. "My being landless in exile," said he. Messengers came from the king for his wife, but she would not go to him until he should give a good tract of land to her father. "I will give him," said Aedh, "as much of the wooded lands to the west as he can pass round in one day, and St. Caeilin, the pious, shall be given as a guarantee for it." The tale goes on to say that Cairbre had made a wide circuit in his day's journey, to the great jealousy and vexation of King Aedh's subjects, who conspired to poison Cairbre in a draught of beer; but this was revealed to St. Caeilin, who indignantly demanded why the king had violated her guarantee by conniving at this intended murder. "I will violate thee," said she to Aedh, "as regards thy kingdom." The king submitted to her award of punishment for his share in the conspiracy, which was a singular one. "Because you sought to destroy Cairbre, in a drink of beer, may the King of Connaught meet decline or certain death, if ever he drink of the beer of the *Ciarraidhi*."* He then gave the saint the land on which her church of

* It would seem from this that the beer of the *Ciarraidhe* was remarkably good; whereas, in the judgment of this saint, the privation of it was condign penance for the crime of a king. Ancient Kerry was famous also for its mede or metheglin, for O'Heerin sings of the King of Kerry, as

The chief of the mede-abounding land
From Tralee to the fair-streamed Shannon.

Termon Mor or Termon Caeilinne was afterwards built.

The migration thus commenced continued for many years, so that three extensive colonies of the *Ciarraidhe* were settled in large districts of Roscommon and Mayo, respectively called the *Ciarraidhe-Aei*, the *Ciarraidhe Locha na n-Airneadh*, and the *Ciarraihde Airtich.* These emigrants mostly belonged to one of the principal branches of the *Ciarraidhe* to which the sept of Altraighe, St: Brendan's own sept, gave its kinglets or chiefs, as O'Heerin tells us :—

> All the Altraighe return
> Two kings of the Plain of Ciarraidhe,
> A tribe ever ready in a point of difficulty,
> *O'Neidhe* and the *Clann-Conaire.*
>
> *O'Donovan's Translation.*

The saint must have, therefore, as a loyal clansman, taken a special interest in the fortunes of the exiled members of *Clann-Conaire*, and we may well believe that this was a strong incentive for his second journey into Connaught, where he may minister to their spiritual wants, and, if necessary, protect and defend them, as St. Caeilin, the holy nun, had occasion to do, from harsh or unjust treatment from their new rulers.* Some of these exiles were near relations of St. Brendan, one of whom, Fintan, who is said to have been a son of a Kerry prince and a nephew of the saint's, had been received at the court of King Brudin, in North

* An instance of such treatment is given in the *Book of Rights :*

> From the Ciarraidhe heavy the tribute
> That is given to the King of Connaught.

On this O'Donovan notes "that the Kings of Connaught contrived to make the Ciarraidhe and other tribes who had migrated from Munster pay more than a rateable tribute for their territory." (*Book of Rights*, page 103, n. *g*.)

Connaught, as a soldier of fortune, from which he had to fly, and take refuge with St. Brendan, in his monastery at Inisquin, after his secret marriage with a niece of the king's; the firstborn of the marriage being the renowned St. Fursey, who was baptized by St. Brendan, and nurtured and instructed by him in his early youth.

In his journey to "the country of Connaught," the saint was accompanied by a younger brother of his, Faitleac,* and when he had founded what was probably his first monastery at Connaught, at *Cluaintuasceart*, within the present county of Roscommon, among the exiled *Ciarraidhe*, who had settled there; he, after some time, left that foundation in charge of his brother, Faitleac, as we read in MacFerbuis, that "Fergus MacRahilly made reverence to Faitleac MacFinlogh of Cluaintuascart, as successor to Brendan, for it was to him that Brendan left his monks." He then proceeded farther west, along the great plain of Aei, with which he was familiar in his early journeys in Connaught, before his priestly ordination, until he reached Lough Corrib; and here, upon the largest of the beautiful islands that stud that magnificent sheet of water, he founded another monastery. This island is named in our text *Inis-meic-ichuind* (the island of the son of *Ui-Cuin* or *O'Quin*), now known as Inchiquin or Inisquin; it lies about half a mile off the eastern shore of the lake, and is more than a mile and a-quarter in length, containing nearly two hundred and thirty acres. The date of this foundation was about 552, a few years after King Aedh MacEochaidh had begun to reign, and probably after his marriage with the daughter of the exile *Cairbre MacConuire* of the Ciarraidhe. He is stated to have been the eighth Christian king of

* See note 3 on *Irish Life*, page 35, *supra*.

Connaught reigning at the royal seat of Rath Croghan, in Roscommon, for twenty-five years, and to have been killed at the battle of Binne-Baghna, in A.D. 576 (*Annals of Ulster*), by the Ui-Briuin, some of his own tribesmen. He is mentioned in the *Annals of Ulster* at A.D. 561, as one of the allied chiefs who gained the victory at the famous battle of *Cuildreimhne* over the forces of the Ard-righ Diarmait MacCearbhail, who had put to death his son, Cornan, despite of the protection and intercession of St. Columba, with whom the young prince had taken refuge after an unpremeditated homicide he had committed at Tara during the public games. This death of Cornan is said to have occasioned that battle.

From the story given in our text, I would infer that St. Brendan, having at first obtained the consent of King Aedh for his foundation on the island of Inisquin, was proceeding with his holy work there, when hostile influences wrought a change in the royal mind, as in the case of the king's dealings with the exile, Cairbre of the *Ciarraidhe*, and urged him to withdraw his consent, and even "to declare in his wrath" that he would take summary vengeance on the saint for trespassing on his favourite horse pasturage. Fortunately, a storm arose to prevent him from immediate action and to give time for reflection, when calmer and wiser counsels prevailed, so that when the storm blew over (in the royal mind, as well as in the elements), "the king made a gift not only of the whole island, but of all the king's horses thereon to St. Brendan for ever."

In this holy work Bishop Moenniu, who was a near relative of his, was associated with our saint. It is said that he had accompanied him on his famous Atlantic voyages, as one of the chosen clerics or priests from his West Kerry monasteries, and that he was his companion also during his pilgrimage and missionary journeys in Britain. We have no account when or where he was consecrated bishop. It was at some date probably before he joined St. Brendan at Inisquin, and if he had spent any time in his native Kerry, after his return from Britain, as I believe St. Brendan had done, he may have there received episcopal consecration from some of the bishops * who had assumed jurisdiction in Kerry after the death of St. Erc, the foster-father of St. Brendan. The name has taken various forms in our early records, but that form we have in our text is probably as early and authentic as any of the others.

The first part of the name Mo-ennu, is the term of endearment *Mo* (my) prefixed to the names of so many of our early Irish saints, in the language of their devout clients; and, taking this away, we have the proper name *Ennu*, in the genitive case Ennean, as the name of this holy bishop. This was probably the name of the founder of the ancient church of Killeiny, near Castlegregory, barony of Corcaguiney, which has been sometimes accredited to St. Enda of Arann, because of the similarity of the name, and for no other reason that I have heard, but which more probably was a foundation of this St. Ennu, or Mo-ennu, who was a companion and fellow-labourer of St. Brendan's in so many of his missionary enterprises at home in Kerry as well as in foreign countries.

When St. Brendan founded his great church and monastery at Clonfert, in A.D. 560, he was selected by the saint to preside over them as bishop, and if he outlived his master, to succeed him as bishop-abbot. After

* See note 3, "Irish Life," pages 34, 35, *ante*.

governing Clonfert for many years with a great repute for learning and sanctity, and with great prudence and success, he died there on March 1st, A.D. 571, or 572, on which day his festival is noted in the calendars of Irish saints.]

XIX.—St. Brendan Restores to Life one of the Religious of Inis-da-dromand.

About this time St. Brendan sent five monks into his monastery on this island that they may remain in that community; but one day, the demon sowing strife between them, one stealthily wounded in the head another monk, who was a senior. When this brother died, some of the monks went in haste to St. Brendan, and told him what had happened. The holy father said to them: " Go back at once, and tell your wounded brother to awake from his sleep, for his Abbot Brendan was calling him." They returned and addressed these words to their deceased brother, and he instantly arose, and went towards St. Brendan, carrying still in his head the iron weapon with which he was wounded.

When St. Brendan saw him he said: "Dear brother, do you desire to remain still in this life, or do you prefer to go now to heaven?" The brother joyfully chose to depart at once to Christ, and so he died in peace. He was buried in the island of *Inisquin*, and his grave there is called in Irish *Lebayd in tollcynd* (" the bed of the wounded head "), and is held in great honour.

[From this extraordinary tale we may infer that St. Brendan, during his second mission in Connaught, and after founding some monastic houses there, retained still control and jurisdiction over his earlier foundations in Munster, as well as in Kerry, and that he exercised this jurisdiction occasionally by transferring monks from one house to another, according to the requirements of monastic discipline, or the interests of the communities or of individual members thereof. The story also reminds us that sometimes, even in well-regulated and fervent communities, "the demon will sow strife" among the members, leading to the commission of great crimes, just as we read in the "Voyage,"* of the unhappy brother among the companions of the saint, who was "a son of perdition," and who, for his evil life, "was doomed to the worst of all deaths, eternal death in hell."

We can also infer from the story that St. Brendan was habitually resident for some time in his monastery on Inisquin, for thither the account of the brother's death was brought to him, and there the re-awakened and risen brother found him, and, in reply to his question, made choice of a present holy death and immediate union with Christ in heaven in preference to a longer life. The grave in which he was buried on the island, called in Irish *Lebayd in tollcynd* (the earthly bed or grave of the man of the wounded head), must have been known to exist, and to be called by that name at the time this Latin Life was written, for it is stated to be still "held in great honour," though no trace probably remains for many centuries of this honoured grave, or of its suggestive name, in connection with the site of this island monastery, which is still used as a burial-ground.]

* See chapter xii. of the "Voyage," p. 162, *supra.*

XX.—St. Brendan Restores to Liberty a Man sorely distressed in Captivity.

One day St. Brendan went ashore from this island to the neighbouring mainland, and he met there an unhappy man, who, with tears, cast himself at his feet, saying: "Take pity on me, oh! holy father, for I have been most cruelly reduced to slavery by my lord the king." St. Brendan, knowing his great misery, turned up the earth with his staff, and took therefrom a lump of gold, which he gave to the man, cautioning him to tell no one, but to give this gold to the king, who would then emancipate him and his children. Nevertheless, he informed the king how he had got the gold, and then the king, when he heard of the miracle, said: "This gold is the gift of Christ, and it is not my right, but that of His servants, to keep it. I will, therefore, grant you and your posterity liberty gratuitously; you are now free to go whither you will." The man soon after returned to St. Brendan with the gold he gave him, giving thanks to God for his freedom.

[From this interesting tale we may learn that in St. Brendan's time, and under the Christian kings of Connaught, there were persons and families reduced to bondage, and living as slaves or serfs under the dominion of their masters. These were a numerous class in Ireland in pre-Christian times; and we have it on good authority* that the territory of Luighne, or Gaileanga, in North Connaught, was occupied by an enslaved tribe

* See O'Flaherty's *Ogygia*, c. 69.

of the Firbolgs, called "Gaileans," and "Damnonians," down to the third century of the Christian era, when they were dispossessed by a Munster prince, Cormac Gaileang, and dispersed through the surrounding districts. Those bore the brand of serfdom wherever they passed, and transmitted the inheritance of bondage to their descendants for many generations. Hence there can be no doubt that in Connaught, as well as in many other parts of Ireland, in pre-Christian times, personal slavery was not uncommon, and had become hereditary in many families. But when the light of the Christian faith was diffused over the land, and when the benign and civilizing influences of religion were applied to work a salutary change in the morals, as well as in the social relations of the people, this unhappy condition of personal and hereditary bondage was gradually disappearing, though exceptional cases of the kind, such as that of this "unhappy serf," who appealed to St. Brendan for charitable deliverance from his cruel bondage, must have occurred for some generations after the establishment of Christianity in Ireland.]

XXI.—St. Brendan Founds his great Monastery at Clonfert. One of its Religious is Restored to Life.

St. Brendan was seventy-seven years old when he founded his monastery and city of Clonfert; and while he tarried there, a certain monk, who had come away with the saint from his parents in Britain, died in the monastery. On the third day after his death, St. Brendan said to the holy Bishop Moenniu: "Place my staff on the body of the deceased brother." When the bishop had laid the staff on the body, already for three days cold in death, the deceased brother at once arose from the dead, and being restored to perfect health, was sent back, much strengthened in faith, to his own country of Britain

---

[The date indicated here for the foundation of Clonfert is A.D. 560, for St. Brendan having been born in A.D. 483, would be seventy-seven years old at that date. The annals of Innisfallen assign the date of the foundation to the very day of the famous battle of Cuildreimhne, which occurred in A.D. 561. Referring to King Diarmait's defeat in that battle, those annals record: *Diarmait vero fugit, et in eo die Cluainferta-Brenainn fundata est, angelo imperante.* The annals of Ulster also note the foundation at two different years, so that it must have been considered by our ancient annalists as an event of great importance. The reference to it in the Life of Brendan, from the *Codex Salmanticensis*, is interesting, as it furnishes the key to the allusion in the annals of Innisfallen to the "orders of the angel" (*angelo imperante*) for this foundation "Some time afterwards St. Brendan said to the brethren: 'We must go into the country of the Hy-Maine (*Mananeorum regiones*, in the text), for that land hath need of us, and there perhaps shall our relics repose. I have heard its angel waging battle in my name, and we must therefore lend him assistance, for our Redeemer's sake.' On that year the kings of the northern parts of Ireland and Aedh. King of Connaught, with all their forces, gave battle to Diarmait, King of Ireland, at a place called *Cuildremhne*, and won the victory. Then the man of God, Brendan, went forth into the land of Hy-Maine, and there founded his famous monastery of Clonfert, saying: 'Here is my rest; here will I dwell for ever.' In that place he became the father of many servants of God, and thence he diffused the light of life and virtue all round."

I have already* referred to the monk, the subject of this tale, who had accompanied St. Brendan from Britain, and whom the saint restored to life, "because he had promised his parents in Britain that they should again see their dear son safe and sound." His name, according to the version of the story in the *Codex Salmanticensis*, was Senanus or Senan.]

XXII.—St. Ita on Christmas Night receives the Holy Communion from St. Brendan.

St. Ita, the foster mother of St. Brendan, on a Christmas night, said in her heart: "Would that I could on this blessed night, receive the Holy Communion from the hands of my foster-son, most holy Brendan." When the holy virgin, full of faith, rose during the night to celebrate the vigil of the festival in her convent, she was taken up by an angel, like another holy Habacuc, and borne away to the city of Clonfert-Brendan. There St. Brendan, foreseeing in spirit her visit to him, went forth to meet her in the porch of his church, bearing the Blessed Sacrament; and the saint of God, having alighted on the earth, received the Holy Communion from the hand of St. Brendan, with fervent thanksgiving to Christ. When the saints had imparted blessings mutually, the holy virgin was again borne away by the angel to her own convent. The distance from St. Ita's

* See page 220, *supra*.

convent, Cluaincredail, in Munster, to the city of Clonfert-Brendan in Connaught, was a three days' journey, over which the saint was taken away and brought back by the angel in one hour's time.

[This story of St. Ita's receiving Holy Communion from St. Brendan at Clonfert is not given in the Life of that holy virgin, published by Colgan, in *Acta SS. Hiberniae;* but a very similar one is found in that Life, which may have suggested the curious tale related in our text. "On a great festival, St. Ita besought the Almighty God to grant her, as a special favour, that she might on that day receive the Holy Communion from the hands of a certain holy priest. Through the divine bounty, she was immediately conducted to the city and the church of Clonmacnoise, where, being at a great distance from her convent, Cluain Creadail, she had the happiness, as she had desired, of receiving Holy Communion, which was administered to her by a venerable priest. No one had seen her on her journey to Clonmacnoise, nor when returning thence, nor did anyone witness her reception of the Holy Sacrament on the occasion; but after she had arrived at her convent on the same day, an angel revealed to the aged holy priest all that happened."

At the time that St. Brendan founded Clonfert, viz., A.D. 560, St. Ita must have attained a great age, probably of more than ninety years, and she could scarcely make a visit to Clonfert at that period of her life, even to enjoy the much-desired happiness of receiving Holy Communion from the hands of her dear foster-son, St. Brendan, by the ordinary mode of travelling. Hence if she did make this visit in the body, and not merely in the spirit, or in an ecstatic vision, such as she may have been favoured with often during her life, the ministry of an angel to enable her to accomplish it was very appropriate.

St. Brendan had sometimes, as his Lives tell us, visited this saintly nun at her convent, and held many spiritual colloquys with her. Of one of these we have some notice in the Life of St. Ita, referred to above. We are told that on one occasion of this kind, "St. Brendan asked St. Ita, what were the three acts of virtue most pleasing in the sight of God. The saint replied: 'The confident resignation of a pure heart to God; a simple religious life; magnanimity with charity—these three good works are most agreeable to the Lord.' Then, being asked what were the three things most displeasing to God, she answered: 'A countenance hating mankind; a depraved affection in the heart; an absorbing love of riches—these three things are very displeasing in God's sight.' Whereupon St. Brendan and those who were present admired the wisdom of the holy virgin, and gave glory to God, who seemed to have spoken through the lips of His gifted servant."

Another story regarding the kindly relations between these two great saints, that we find in the Life of St. Ita, may be given here, as it speaks eloquently of some of their characteristic virtues.

A spiritual child of St. Ita, in whom the saint took a special interest, yielded to temptation, and fell away from virtue, becoming an outcast and a wanderer; until at length she seems to have lost her faith and sold herself into the servitude of a cruel task-master in Connaught, who is said to have been a magician. The loving heart of St. Ita yearned for the conversion of her fallen child, and she prayed earnestly for her. After some years, she discovered her miserable condition, and it was revealed to her that if the unhappy one were again restored to liberty, she would do penance, and atone for her past crimes. But her task-master would not set his captive free, and then St. Ita had recourse to her friend St. Brendan, and entreated him to use his great influence with the King of Connaught to procure the liberty of this wretched vassal. He at once complied, and soon succeeded in rescuing the poor creature, and sending her back to St. Ita, who received her with tender compassion, even with joy, as the Life relates, and gave her the opportunity of performing condign penance, in the practice of which she persevered to the end of her life.]

XXIII.—A Miracle of the Holy Virgin St. Chiar.

In the district of *Muscry-tire*, in the province of Munster, a flame with a pestilent stench burst forth from the earth, which the inhabitants endeavoured to extinguish with water, but in vain. St. Brendan having come to the place, saw that the land was being burned up by those flames, which were rising still higher, and he said to the people: "Unhappy men, you see here a fire from hell issuing out of the earth." They implored his aid, and he said to them: "Make a three days' fast, and I will earnestly pray to God for you." When they had fasted three days, the saint bade them go to *St. Chiar*, a holy virgin, to whom God had granted the power to extinguish this fire, by her holy prayers. When St. Chiar had prayed to God against the fire, the flames were at once and completely extinguished, so that they never more appeared in the district.

[There were no less than six territories in Munster, known as *Muscraidhe*, or the Sept-lands, according to John O'Donovan,* of the descendants of Cairbre Musc, son of Conaire Mor, monarch of Ireland, in the beginning of the third century. *Muscraidhe-tire* of our text was the district now comprised in the baronies of Upper and Lower Ormond, in North Tipperary, and within this district was the church of St. Ciar or Chiar, now called Kilkeary, which is near the town of Nenagh. St. Brendan's visits to this district must have been frequent from an early period of his missionary career in Munster. We have already seen† that before he went on his pilgrimage to Britain he had founded a monastery at a place called Tulach-Brendan, not far from Lorrha, where St. Ruadhan had his church, and therefore probably within this district of *Muscraidhe-tire*, through which he frequently passed on his journeys to his house at Tulach-Brendan, which lay on the northern side of it. When on one of these journeys, the incidents that are related in the text may have come under the saint's notice, and he may, when appealed to by the people, in their alarm and distress at such an occurrence, have recommended them to fast, and to seek the prayers of their local saint—the holy virgin *Chiar*, in order to obtain relief. This was the saint to whom the ancient church of Kilkeary was dedicated, and from whom it had its name. There are many virgin-saints of that name on the calendars of our early Irish saints, but which of these was the patroness of Kilkeary ancient church in Upper Ormond, or which of them it was whose miraculous power St. Brendan recommended on this occasion, it is now impossible to determine.]

* *Book of Rights*, page 42, n.

† Page 197, *supra*.

XXIV.—St. Brendan Visits the Saints of Meath.

Once upon a time, St. Brendan went to visit the saints who dwelt in the territory of Meath. At that time *Diarmait MacCearbhail,* who then reigned at Tara, as monarch of Ireland, had a vision in a dream, in which he saw two angels taking the royal collar of gold from his neck, and giving it to a man whom he knew not. On the following day St. Brendan came to visit the king, who, when he saw the saint, told his courtiers that this was the man to whom he saw his royal collar given in his vision. Whereupon his wise men declared to the king that his vision meant that hitherto sovereign rule in Ireland belonged alone to the kings thereof, but that henceforward it should be shared with the saints of Ireland, and that the saint now present, Brendan, should have extensive jurisdiction throughout the land. When St. Brendan heard of this vision, and of its interpretation by the wise men, he said that thus it would come to pass that all good things will be given in this life, as well as in the life to come, to those who truly serve God, according to the text: "Seek first the kingdom of God, and His justice, and all other things shall be added unto you." (St. Matthew, vi. 33.) And King Diarmait rendered great honour to St. Brendan, for he was a righteous and Christian king.

[Diarmait MacCearbhail, who was monarch of Ireland when this visit of St. Brendan to his saintly brethren in Meath is said to have occurred, began his inauspicious reign in "Tara of the Kings" about A.D. 544, on the tragic death of the Ard-Righ, *Tuathal Maelgarbh*, who was slain in the midst of his soldiers, by the foster-brother of Diarmait, at the forfeit of his own life; and after a troubled reign of about twenty years, was himself assassinated in A.D. 565, by *Aedh Dubh*, King of Dalaradia. There can be no doubt that St. Brendan had often in the course of his missionary peregrinations visited the holy places and the holy men who dwelt in Royal Meath, from the time of his earliest pilgrimage among the saints of Erin, when he first went forth, by the advice of his foster-father, St. Erc, "to learn and to write down all the rules and customs of the saints" in many parts of Ireland, in which were, no doubt, included the early saints of Meath. When the renowned St. Finnian founded his monastery and famous school at Clonard, in Meath, about 530, St. Brendan is said to have been for some time a disciple of his, like so many of the illustrious saints who were his contemporaries—for St. Finnian of Clonard was specially honoured with the title of "Tutor of the saints of Ireland;" and among his celebrated pupils at this famous school were the two Kierans (viz., of Clonmacnoise and of Saighir), the two Brendans (viz., of Ardfert and of Birr), the two Columbas (viz., Columbcille and Columb MacCrimhthain), SS. Lasserian, Canice of Kilkenny, Ruadhan of Lorrha, and other great saints, who were designated among "the twelve apostles" of the Church of Ireland at that time. At what particular period of St. Brendan's life he received those lessons of holiness and learning at the feet of St. Finnian of Clonard, we have no means of ascertaining; but we may reasonably surmise that it was soon after the foundation of the School of Clonard, in 530—while St. Brendan was still engaged in his missionary labours in Munster, before his pilgrimage to Britain, which took place soon after that date. It would be interesting to know how far St. Brendan was influenced to undertake his great missionary enterprises in Britain by his intercourse with, and by the advice of St. Finnian at Clonard, who had devoted many years of his own early missionary life to work for the sanctification of the Britons in Wales, under the guidance of the renowned Saints David of Menevia and Cadoc of Lancarvan, with whom St. Brendan afterwards laboured so fruitfully in the same missionary field. We may well suppose that among the lessons of wisdom imbibed at Clonard by St. Brendan, were the special results of the missionary experiences of St. Finnian among those Britons for whom he was soon to labour on a similar mission. When St. Brendan returned from Britain, the great school of Clonard was still flourishing under the personal superintendence of St Finnian, and we may believe that while our saint was preparing for his second course of missionary labours in Connaught, before 550, he visited his friend and tutor, at Clonard, more than once, when he had opportunities of meeting again, and renewing an early friendship with many of the "saints of Meath." It is probably one of these visits that is commemorated in our text—which may have taken place before the death of St. Finnian, in 552—and, therefore, early in the reign of Diarmait MacCearbhail, before that king had entered into any of those unhappy conflicts with some of the saints of that period, which ended so disastrously for himself and his dynasty.

At this period, the relations of King Diarmait with the prominent saints with whom he came in contact were kindly and generous, as far as we know. He had been a liberal benefactor to St. Kieran of Clonmacnoise, when he made his great foundation there, and until the death of that saint, some years afterwards. He had given the site and large endowments to St. Columba for his great monastery at *Ceanlios*, or Kells, within royal Meath, and about the same time we read that he allowed Bishop Maighnean, the founder of Kilmainham, near Dublin, and of Kilmainhambeg in Meath, to address several sermons to himself and his court at Tara, with such effect that many of his courtiers renounced the world, and entered religious houses; and the king himself made his confessions (*Coibsena*, in Irish text) to the holy bishop, and bestowed abundant arms upon him and his companions.*

At this period of his history, King Diarmait was very probably "a righteous and Christian monarch," as our text declares him to have been, who rendered due honour to all other saints, as well as to St. Brendan, on proper occasions. But a change seems to have come over his spirit and dispositions in that respect in the course of his reign; and perhaps we have in the curious story of his dream, narrated in the text, an inkling of the motives and influences that brought about that change. He saw in his dream the collar of gold, the emblem of his royal power, taken from his neck by angels, and given to one whom he afterwards recognised to be his visitor, St. Brendan; and then his "wise men," probably some Druids, whom the king is stated to have often employed as his soothsayers towards the close of his reign, interpreted his dream to mean that his sovereign power would pass from him to the saints of Ireland, who should henceforth be the supreme rulers of the land. No wonder that King Diarmait, who was very tenacious of his royal authority, and very jealous of any interference with his

* O'Curry's *Manners and Customs*, vol. i., p. ccxi., note.

sovereign rights from any quarter, should, on hearing this interpretation of his vision, grow somewhat apprehensive of the ever-increasing influence of the illustrious saints of his time, and begin to resent their claims for certain privileges, such as that of "sanctuary," as an infringement of his royal power. Hence may have come his arbitrary and insolent treatment of the great St. Columba, from whose protecting arms he tore, with every mark of indignity, Cornan, the son of the King of Connaught, who had taken sanctuary with the saint, after the commission of an unpremeditated crime, for which, however, the king put him to death without mercy. This cruel violation of St. Columba's privilege of sanctuary by the death of this Connaught prince, is said to have occasioned the war against King Diarmait which ended so disastrously for him in the battle of *Cuild-remhne*, in the present county of Sligo, wherein three thousand of the king's troops were slain, and his power was almost completely broken. This is said to have occurred on the very day on which St. Brendan founded his great church and city of Clonfert, in the territory of Hy-Maine, in the south-east of the present county of Galway. Within this territory, ruled as its chief at that time Aedh Guairè, who was a special friend of St. Brendan's, whose foundation at Clonfert he liberally patronized. This chief, a few years afterwards, grievously offended King Diarmait MacCearbhail by illusing and, on some provocation, slaying one of the royal heralds who had come to him with the king's commission to collect certain royal tributes from his territory. Guairè, to escape the vengeance of Diarmait, fled for protection to his cousin, the Bishop Senach, residing in Lower Ormond, on the other side of the Shannon; but the bishop, not deeming the fugitive sufficiently safe from the power of the king, under his own protection, had him conveyed without loss of time to the more sacred and secure sanctuary of the celebrated St. Ruadhan of Lorrha, in that district, who is said to have been the uncle of Aedh Guairè. The king discovered the place of his retreat, and came from Tara, with a strong force, to Lorrha to demand from St. Ruadhan the delivery of Guairè into his hands. This the saint peremptorily refused; whereupon the king took him by force, in violation of the privilege of the saintly sanctuary, and dragged him off, a prisoner, to Tara, to be punished for his crime. Thither St. Ruadhan closely followed, accompanied by St. Brendan, as the special friend of Guairè, the princely benefactor of his church at Clonfert; and by Bishop Senach, with whom he had at first taken refuge. Those saints, "with their clerics, and their bells, and their croziers," pleaded hard for mercy for the criminal, but the king obdurately refused to release his prisoner, even though all the courtiers and chiefs who were present joined with the bishops in asking his pardon. Then, as the story runs in the *Annals of Clonmacnoise*, "St. Ruadhan and the bishop who was with him took their bells that they had, which they rung hardly, and they cursed the king and the place, and prayed God that no king or queen would or could ever dwell in Tara, and that it should be waste for ever, without court or palace; and so it fell out accordingly." In the following year, the king was murdered, in consequence, it was believed, of his insults to St. Ruadhan, and after him no king or queen ever reigned again in Tara.]

XXV.—St. Brendan explains to his Brethren how intolerable are the Pains of Hell.

One day when St. Brendan was on a journey, a great storm of hail and snow arose upon him and his companions on the way. Some of the brethren said to St. Brendan: "Holy father, the cold in the infernal regions is not more intense than this we feel now." "You speak like ignorant rustics," rejoined the saint. "We have seen Judas, the betrayer of our Lord, in a dreadful sea, on the Lord's day, wailing and lamenting, seated on a rugged and slimy rock, which was now submerged by the waves and again emerged from them somewhat. Against the rock there rushed a fiery wave from the east, and a wave of icy coldness from the west alternately, which drenched Judas in a frightful manner; and yet this grievous punishment seemed to him a relief from pain, for thus the mercy of God granted this place to him on the Sundays as some ease amidst his torments. What, therefore, must be the torments suffered in hell itself?" When the brethren heard this, they besought the Almighty God to take pity on their manifold miseries.

[Here we have a very early version, perhaps the earliest germ, of the interesting legend of St. Brendan's interview with Judas Iscariot during his voyage in the northern seas, which is told so dramatically in the twelfth chapter of the "Voyage," * and in the poem of

* See pp. 162-168, *supra*.

Mathew Arnold appended to that chapter. The "moral" of the tale, as we have it in this primeval version, was plainly to impress upon all the unspeakable intensity of the torments of the reprobate in hell, by a comparison or contrast with Judas's grievous sufferings on that rock in the ocean, which were a mitigation of, and a respite from, his far more dreadful torments in hell, granted to him, through the mercy of God, in honour of the Lord's day. In later versions, the "moral" is pointed somewhat differently, and the respite of Judas is attributed to the mercy of God remembering on his behalf, even amidst his justly-merited torments in hell, some "small fragments of goodness" he had shown during his life; as Mathew Arnold beautifully expresses it:

> That germ of kindness, in the womb
> Of mercy caught, did not expire;
> Outlives my guilt, outlives my doom,
> And friends me in the pit of fire.*

It may seem difficult to reconcile this "moral" with the principles o sound theology, especially with that text of the prophet: "If the just man turn himself away from his justice, and work iniquity, . . . all his justices which he hath done shall not be remembered." † But the sentiment may, however, be quite orthodox, if applied, with some scope for poetic license, to the awarding of the final doom of the reprobate, while mercy may still temper justice, and each one shall be judged "according to his works, be the same good or evil."

In the early English prose version of this tale, given in the *Golden Legend* of Wynkyn de Worde,‡ the details

* See page 167, *supra.*

† Ezechiel xviii. 24.

‡ See Appendix, *postea.*

of Judas's "fragments of goodness" vary from those set down in our Latin version; the "prongs" or "tongs" are changed into "ox-tongues"—which, the *Golden Legend* makes Judas tell: "I gave some time to two preestes to pray for me. I bought them with mine owne money; and therefore they ease me, because the fysshes of the sea gnaw on them and spare me."

This version has been followed by Mr. Sebastian Evans in his poem on St. Brendan, from which I insert those stanzas:—

And Judas answered: "By Christ's dear grace,
This day am I loosed from mine own due place
With Herod and Pilate and Caiaphas;

"For He whom the gates of the hells obey,
Each winter hath granted me here to stay
From Christmas Eve for a night and a day.

"And this is my paradise, here alone
To sit with my cloth and tongues and stone,
The sole three things in the world mine own.

"This cloth I bought from the Lord's privy purse,
But gave to a leper. It hath this curse,
That it beats on my skin, but it saves from worse.

"These tongues I gave to the poor for meat,
In the name of Christ—and the fish that eat
Thereon as they list, forbear my feet.

"This stone I found by a road where it lay,
And set for a step in a miry way;
Therefore sit I on stone, not ice, this day!"]

XXVI.—St. Brendan exhorts his Brethren to confide in the Providence of God.

On another day, when Brendan was travelling through a forest, a violent storm was raging, and by the force of the gale trees were blown down on every side as he and his companions journeyed on. One of the brethren said to the others: "We are in great danger from those falling trees." Then Brendan told them: "One night, while all our crew were asleep in the boat on the wide ocean, I alone remained awake, and we came to an island which had many openings through it. It was supported on four great legs over the sea, and between those legs our boat passed under the island, and thus we sailed right through, while the island stood above us. Be it known to you, therefore, brethren, that God, who sustains that island over the sea in that manner, and who allowed us to sail in safety under it, can save us without hurt from the danger of those falling trees." On hearing this example the brethren grew strong in their confidence in Christ.

[Among the "Wonders of the Ocean" recounted in the tenth chapter of the "Voyage of St. Brendan," * one of the most marvellous is that "chrystal column in the sea" with its "rare canopy of silvery sheen," which the saint saw at some distance from him, "on the day on which three Masses had been said" (Christmas Day). This was, no doubt, an iceberg, and the descrip-

* See page 158, *supra.*

tion of it given by the ancient story-teller in the text of the "Voyage" is very interesting, and though the phrases may not be quite scientific, they are very graphic and fairly accurate. Here, in the above text, we have a still more primitive account of this same phenomenon, given in what must have been an archaic tradition of one of St. Brendan's instructions to his religious, the "moral" of which he pointed by an allusion to his wonderful passage through "the island supported over the sea on four great legs," in which guise we may still recognise the primeval story of the iceberg.

Those references to incidents of the "Voyage of St. Brendan," which the fragments of early tradition, such as we find here in this Latin Life, ascribe to the saint himself in his moral discourses to his brethren, would show how widespread and enduring was the popular belief in the reality of the great voyage, and of many of its legendary incidents. It may not be out of place to set down here some similar allusions to the voyages of our saint, taken from the Lives of some of his saintly contemporaries.

In the Life of St. Abban, the great Leinster saint, in the *Codex Salmanticensis*, we read that he made special friendship and brotherhood with St. Brendan, and "that soon after the latter's seven years' pilgrimage on the ocean, he paid him a special visit, of which St. Brendan being apprised by an angel, went forth to meet him, and welcomed him with great joy. Then he related at large to his visitor all the wonderful things he had seen on the ocean; and when the saints had thus spent some days in mutual solace, and having established lasting brotherhood between themselves and their successors, St. Abban returned to his own monastery."

In the Life of St. Flannan, Patron of Killaloe, in

the same *Codex Salmanticensis*, St. Molua relates a prediction of St. Brendan's, regarding the birth of St. Flannan. St. Molua, who had founded the ancient Church of Killaloe, desired, in his old age, to have St. Flannan, the son of the King of Thomond, Theodoric or Turlough, appointed as his successor; and he addressed the assembled prelates of the clergy and the chiefs of the territory, in presence of King Theodoric, as follows:—"The time is now come when I must, according to the prophecy of St. Brendan, retire and give place to this holy youth whom God has chosen; for among the many marvellous things the holy father Brendan had seen and related during his voyage to the islands of the ocean, being full of the Holy Spirit as he always was, he predicted *that on the banks of the Shannon there would arise, like the Star from Jacob, one of the royal blood, who should smite and put to flight the princes and the rulers of darkness.*"

In the Life of St. Fintan Munnu, son of Tulcan, also in the *Codex Salmanticensis*, there is related a curious vision the saint is said to have had, in which he saw the "Land of Promise of the Saints," and places therein marked out for himself and St. Colombcille on one side, and places for St. Brendan and St. Canice on the other side, not far away. This vision was told only after the death of St. Fintan by a holy hermit, who stated he heard it from the saint himself.]

XXVII.—St. Brendan Saves the Province of Connaught from an Invasion.

Once upon a time the King of Munster came into Connaught, with a large army, to lay waste that country. St. Brendan, then very old, at the entreaty of the men of Connaught, went out to meet the Munstermen, and besought them to make peace, but these men in their pride would grant neither peace nor truce to the saint. But when they were proceeding to ravage the country, they were for a whole day kept moving round in a circle at one place, and could make no advance. Then they felt that a miracle had been wrought against them, and, being seized with fear, they decided to return to their own country. Thus through the power of God, they went home empty-handed; for who can resist the will of the Almighty ?

When St. Brendan was returning from these men, there was brought to him on the way a boy who was dumb from his birth; and the man of God having blessed his tongue, the boy at once spoke distinctly, and all who were present gave glory to God.

[This incident must have occurred some years after the foundation of Clonfert, when St. Brendan was a very old man (*Senex*, in the Latin text), probably on the verge of his ninetieth year. The loving trust and profound veneration which he had won from the people of Connaught by the extraordinary holiness of his life, and the untiring labours of his apostolic ministry amongst them for so many years, induced them, with their King Aedh MacEochaidh at their head, to entreat the interposition of the saint, as peace-maker between them and their Munster invaders. He went forth on his mission of charity, and, like another St. Leo, stood bravely between his people and their relentless enemies, whom he, with a power and success no less than those of the great Leo himself, deterred and turned back from the havoc they sought to bring on his country. There is no record, as far as I can discover, in our ancient annals, of any such invasion as this of the Munstermen into Connaught, occurring about the date; but the early records of that time are very meagre, and there can be no doubt that many intestine broils and local wars and conflicts such as this were carried on then, as well as at other periods of Irish history, of which no account has come down to our times.]

XXVIII.—St. Brendan Visits his Sister, St. Briga, and makes Arrangements for his Interment in Clonfert.

St. Brendan, when very old, went to visit his sister, St. Bryg, who, under his direction, was governing a convent of nuns at Eanach-duin (now Annadown), in the province of Connaught and in the district of the Hy-Bruin. While he was biding there, on a Sunday after he had offered the Holy Sacrifice of the Body and Blood of Christ, the venerable saint said to his sister and to the brethren who were with him: "My very dear friends, on this day the Lord my God summons me to life eternal, and I adjure you, in the name of Christ, to do exactly what I now tell you, if you would have my blessing. Conceal my death here, until my body has been carried to my city of Clonfert, for there I have chosen the place of my resurrection. If the people here about come to know of my death amongst them, they will surely bury me here against my wishes. You will therefore act in this manner; place my corpse in a waggon, and cover it over carefully with other things. You will send only one brother in charge of the waggon, who will tell all who ask him that he is carrying the goods of St. Brendan, to his own city of Clonfert. All who may meet him will then let him pass, except one man, a soldier, named Curryn, blind of the left eye. This man will not believe the words of the brother, but, more cunning than others, will sharply question him as to what he was carrying so secretly, and will closely search the waggon. When he finds and recognises my body, he will in a terrible voice order the brother to leave amongst them the saint of God; and addressing me he will cry out: 'Here in our country you will be buried with all honour, so that your resurrection may be amongst us, O man of God.'

"Then the brother shall look into a trench beside him, and seeing there a lump of pure gold, shall offer it to this soldier, saying: 'Take this gold given by God, and let me freely go my way.' This the man will refuse, and then the brother shall promise: 'You will have the chief power in your tribe, and your descendants after you, if you allow me to pass on.' But the man, not trusting this promise, will still prevent a passage; and then the brother shall declare to him: 'You will not have eternal life, unless you permit the saint of God to be borne to that place where he ordered his burial; and a sure sign I give you of the truth of what I say, when I tell you the thought of your heart when you met me, was to usurp the chieftaincy of your tribe by murdering members of your own family.' When the man will thus learn from another the secret thoughts of his heart, and will know thereby that what was promised would surely come to pass, he will allow the brother to proceed in peace with my body, who will thereupon earnestly bless him, and go on his way rejoicing."

When his sister and the brethren heard this adjuration, and this prediction of what was to happen, they promised the holy father that they would do what he had commanded.

[Eanach-duin ("the marsh or moor of the fort"), latterly called Annaghdown, was situated on the eastern shore of Lough Corrib, some distance from Inisquin to the south, on the north side of a rocky inlet of the lake, into which a small stream flows. Here can be seen at present a picturesque group of interesting ruins, consisting of the extensive remains of an abbey and monastery, of a nunnery, and of other ecclesiastical buildings; while on the other side of the stream there are still remaining a tall square castle, in fine preservation, and the walls of the bishop's residence, with the enclosed holy wells of St. Brendan, and of St. Cormac beside them. We have no account of the exact date when St. Brendan founded the convent at Eanach-duin, over which he placed his fondly-loved sister, St. Bryg, to govern a community of nuns. It was probably not long after the foundation of his island monastery on Inisquin, on which occasion, as we have seen above (page 225, *supra*), he received from King Aodh MacEochaidh a grant of the whole island. While the saint, with his monks, was working zealously, from this house on Inisquin, to instruct and reclaim the wild and half-pagan tribes that dwelt on the borders of Lough

Corrib, he must have felt how much the success of those apostolic labours would be promoted by the co-operation of a community of nuns in edifying and educating the people of the district. Hence, we may surmise, St. Brendan called to his aid his holy sister, St. Bryg, from the convent in Kerry—or perhaps from one of those nunneries on the great plain of Aei (Co. Roscommon), founded by St. Brigid soon after her sojourn in Kerry, where she had been for years a professed nun, and placed her in charge, under his direction, of this convent of nuns at Eanach-duin, on the shores of Lough Corrib.

Until this reference to St. Bryg, we find no mention of her intercourse or sisterly relations with St. Brendan, in any Life or story of the saint that is now accessible, except the interesting allusion in the Irish Life,* to her companionship with him in his early youth, when he was under the pupilage of Bishop Erc, which tells us: "At this time there lived with him, Bryg, who was an own sister of his; and great was his affection for her, as the attendance of the angels about her was visible to him." St. Bryg then had been the playmate and child-nurse † of the youthful Brendan, and during all the years that had passed from that time until she took charge of his nunnery at Eanach-duin, the "great affection" of their youthful relations, no doubt, continued to grow in strength and fervour. Hence we may well believe that when "King Aodh MacEochaidh," as the *Book of Ballymote* tells, "gave Eanach-duin to God and Brendan," for the purpose of founding a convent of nuns there, St. Bryg promptly complied with the invitation of her saintly brother, to govern the community under his guidance.

* See page 13, *supra*.

† She was probably some years his junior as she survived him.

It was probably while St. Brendan lived at and worked his holy mission from Inisquin, that he sought out a deeper solitude, wherein to refresh his spirit, by a closer union with God in prayer and contemplation—one of those "deserts in the sea," which had, all his life long, so many attractions for him. On the extreme west of Erris, off the coast of Mayo, lies the island of Inis-gluair or Inishgloria, on which there are still remains of an oratory and cell, said to have been founded by the saint, and which yet bear his name. Another such "desert in the sea" he resorted to also, off the coast of Connemara, on an island called Inisnee, at the mouth of the Owanmore or Ballinahinch river, on which there are the ruins of an ancient oratory dedicated to St. Brendan.

When our saint had founded his great church and monastery at Clonfert, he seems to have committed the government of that house and school to his special friend, Bishop Moennean, and to have still abided frequently at his island monastery of Inisquin. Here he was training to holiness many fervent disciples, among others St. Meldan, who is said to have succeeded him in the abbacy of Inisquin after his death, and to have rendered that house even more famous than it was under the rule of St. Brendan, about A.D. 580. Into the little *hospice* attached to this monastery St. Brendan received his nephew, Fintan, the West Kerry prince, and his wife, the beautiful Gelgeis, when, after their secret marriage, they fled from the wrath of the royal father of the latter; and here, about 570, was born the child who afterwards became the renowned St. Fursey, having received his earliest nurture and education from St. Brendan himself, and later on from St. Meldan, and probably also from another saintly disciple of St. Brendan, named Beoan. St. Fursey in after life venerated those two saints in a special manner, and in the accounts he gave of those wonderful visions which made his name so famous, he represents St. Meldan and St. Beoan as appearing to him in angelic forms, among the celestial spirits who had been communing with him, and as addressing him in lengthened discourses full of heavenly knowledge and wisdom; after which they directed him to return again to the earth, and to announce to the world what he had seen and heard in his ecstatic visions. Many years afterwards when St. Fursey proceeded on his apostolic missions to England and to France, he carried away with him the relics of those saintly disciples of St. Brendan—St. Meldan and St. Beoan whom he loved and venerated as his holy patrons.

Though St. Brendan devoted much of his time and zealous labours to his house on Inisquin, we must believe that he frequently visited his church and school at Clonfert, and took an earnest part in the ministrations and apostolic works of the community there. In the beautiful legend of the angel's visit to him in the form of a bird (given at p. 270, *postea*) we get an interesting glimpse of the saint's fervent ministrations on some of those visits. He tells us, in that legend, how it happened that he could not listen to earthly music after hearing the heavenly strains from the angel: "One day, just seven years ago, as I was in this church (of Clonfert) after preaching here, and after Mass, all the clergy having gone to their refection, I was left alone here, and having made a visit to the Body of Christ, a great longing for my Lord seized me, and a trembling and an awe came upon me; then I saw a radiant bird, which perched on the altar." St. Brendan gives this account to the "student-harper," who found him in the same church "on Easter Sunday, seven years before his death, after he had celebrated the Divine

Office, preached and said Mass;" when, as a special privilege, he was permitted to play on his harp "three lively strains" for the aged saint. If these circumstantial accounts of St. Brendan's ministrations on Sundays, at his church of Clonfert, be not all pure fancy, which we have no reason to believe they are, we have here an edifying picture of a "tireless worker for God," the *pater laboriosus*, as St. Gildas styled him in his middle life during his mission in Britain, persevering to extreme old age in the laborious works of his apostolic ministry.

All this time St. Brendan maintained friendly relations with many of the illustrious saints who were his contemporaries, and with some of them he seems to have been on terms of special intimacy, such as St. Ruadhan of Lorrha, as we have seen in some instances referred to in previous pages, and also St. Canice of Kilkenny and Aghaboe. This great saint, though born in Glengiven (county Derry), according to the more reliable pedigrees, came from the same Kerry stock as St. Brendan himself, being descended from Alt, the *Stipes* of the *Altraighe*, in the fifth remove. We read in the Life of St. Canice, that in his youth he lived some years in Wales at the monastery of Lancarvan under St. Cadoc, by whom he was being educated. Here he very probably met St. Brendan, who tarried there about the same time, and the friendship then commenced was renewed and improved when St. Canice returned to Ireland. Soon after the foundation of the Church of Clonfert, St. Brendan employed artificers to make a gold chalice for the use of the altar there. The supply of gold material not being sufficient, St. Brendan sent to his friend, St. Canice, for some of the precious metal, "because," as the story tells, "on account of his frequent visits to Britain, he was likely to have it."

However, he had none to give on this occasion, and he was so grieved and ashamed at refusing any such favour to St. Brendan, that he produced the needful quantity of the purest gold by an extraordinary miracle, and sent it to his friend, who had the gold chalice finished with this material, which chalice, as the Life of St. Canice, in the *Codex Salmanticensis,* assures us, "remains to the present day." *

About this time, as we read in Adamnan's Life of St. Columba; † "four great holy founders of monasteries came from Ireland to visit St. Columba in the island of Hinba." These were St. Comgall, founder of the great monastery and school at Benchor (Bangor, *hodie)* on the southern shore of Belfast Lough; St. Canice, founder of Aghaboe and Kilkenny; St. Cormac Ua Liathain, a favourite disciple of St. Columba's, whom he had appointed abbot of his great foundation at Durrow (county Westmeath), when he was leaving Ireland for Iona; and St. Brendan of Clonfert, the greatest "founder of monasteries" of them all. These holy men invited their host, St. Columba, to celebrate

* Another indication of the special friendship of St. Brendan and St. Canice we find in a curious *Scholium* in the *Feilire* of St. Aengus, appended to Brendan's festival, at May 16th :—

Acnta Choinnig, is Barrai ocus Brenaind diblinaib, Cipè sarages nec dibh, fertai in trir oca digail ; that is, in literal English : "The alliance of Canice, and Finnbarr, and Brendan with each other ; whoever outrages any of them, the miraculous powers of the three will avenge it."

This alliance must refer as much to the successors and the "families" of these saints as to themselves ; indeed, in the case of St. Finnbarr of Cork, he was not of the age to make such an alliance with St. Brendan, who died when Finnbarr was very young ; but the relations of his great school at Cork, with the successors of Brendan at Clonfert, notably with St. Cummian Fada, fourth bishop of Clonfert, who was educated at St. Finnbarr's famous school, were very friendly.

† L. iii., c. xvii.

Holy Mass in their presence; and then, as Adamnan relates: "During the celebration of the Holy Sacrifice of the Mass, St. Brendan Mac Ua Alti saw, as he told Comgall and Cannech afterwards, a ball of fire, like a comet, burning very brightly on the head of Columba the whole time he stood before the altar offering the Holy Sacrifice."

This notable reunion of these illustrious saints took place on the island of Hinba,* where St. Columba founded an oratory or cell, some time after his establishment at Iona, and whither he retired occasionally for closer and less distracted communion with God than he found possible at his greater church and monastery there. Adamnan relates, circumstantially, several of those retreats of Columba to this island, and the wonderful manifestations of the Divine favours and the communications of the Holy Spirit made to him there on such occasions.

On this occasion of the visit of St. Brendan and his saintly companions to the island, St. Columba was probably engaged in one of those spiritual retreats, and the globe of fire which St. Brendan was permitted to behold flaming over his head during the celebration of the Holy Mass, was, no doubt, a meet emblem of the fulness and fervour with which the Spirit of God communicated His graces to the ardent soul of the saint while celebrating the divine mysteries.

St. Brendan was several years older than the other saints who were present. He was then, probably, far beyond his eightieth year, for the incident must have occurred some years after the founding of the monastery at Iona by Columba, in A.D. 565, when St. Brendan had already passed that great age. It is hard to think

* Not surely identified; it lay not far from Iona.

that the venerable patriarch would, at such a period of his life, have travelled from the shores of Lough Corrib or from Clonfert, hard by the Shannon, over land and sea, to distant Iona or Hinba, for the mere purpose of a friendly visit to St. Columba, and we may well believe that the arduous journey had a much higher and holier purpose. We have already seen * that St. Brendan had laboured long and successfully in an apostolic mission in North Britain and the Isles, of what was afterwards called Scotland, more than twenty years before Columba had set foot on Iona or commenced his first mission amongst his kinsmen, the Albanian Scots; and we may surmise that even amid the cares and duties of his arduous ministry in Ireland during all those years, our saint did not lose sight of, nor a loving interest in, the fruits of his apostolic labours among the Orkneys and the Isles, of which he has been since honoured as the apostle. He very probably visited the scenes of those early labours from time to time, in order to preserve and promote the growth of the seed of Christian faith and morality that he had sown; and perhaps it was in the course of one of those tours of visitation, which he continued to make even in his extreme old age, that the incidental visit to Columba on the island of Hinba took place. Here he found the great saint who was destined to be his worthy successor in the apostolate of that land and of those isles wherein he himself had laboured so zealously; and it may have been that, though, like the high priest of old, he was then the "lamp of God about to be extinguished," he saw in the vision of the "globe of fire, blazing like a comet, over the head of Columba," the augury and the consoling assurance that this new apostle of the Northern Picts and of the

* See page 213, *ante*.

Orkneys and the Isles, as Columba has been justly styled, was raised up and specially blessed by God to carry on, with more signal success and more glorious results, the apostolic work he had himself commenced many years before.

If St. Brendan thus evinced a paternal interest in the fruits of his early missions in North Britain by those kindly visits to the scenes of his labours there, we must believe that he failed not to make similar visits occasionally to those religious foundations throughout Munster, and especially those in and near his native district in West Kerry, which were the earliest, and therefore probably the dearest, objects of his holy zeal and solicitude. It would be strange, indeed, that the venerable father should favour his spiritual children in the islands of Bute and Kilbrandon and Tirree, and many other islands on the coasts of North Britain, with those paternal visits, and omit similar tokens of an affectionate interest in the holy communities at Inis-da-droman, on the Shannon, and at Ardfert, his first love, and at the other monasteries of West Kerry, who all venerated him as their founder and their holy patron. He therefore visited all those houses from time to time, probably to the latest period of his life; and perhaps it was on one of the latest of those visitation tours among his West Kerry foundations, that the incident occurred to him that is related in the interesting story * of the "Holy Well of Brendan's Anointing," where he is said to have sailed in his *currach*, from one of his oratories on the Blasquet Islands, across Dingle Bay, to visit the little monastery of his disciple St. Beoan, in the Glen (bar. of Iveragh),

* See page 278, *postea*.

the remains of which are still known as *Kilbeoanigh* (the cell or church of St. Beoan).

While we contemplate the venerable patriarch thus visiting his spiritual children in his numerous religious houses in Ireland and Scotland, we may feel how justly Adamnan ranks him among "the great holy founders of monasteries," and we may well apply to him the praises bestowed by* St. Bernard upon another of them, St. Comgall of Bangor: "He was the parent of many thousand saints, and the head of many religious establishments, that were holy and fruitful in saints. . . . Indeed, the spiritual children of this holy man had so multiplied throughout the whole of Ireland and Scotland, that in them would seem to have been verified the words of the Psalmist: '*Thou hast visited the earth, and hast plentifully watered it; thou hast many ways enriched it. The river of God is filled with water; fill up plentifully the streams thereof and multiply its fruits.*" (Ps. lxiv.)

Occupied to the last with devoted and fruitful labours and journeyings by land and sea, for the glory of God and the salvation of souls, such as the scant materials at hand enabled me to shadow forth dimly in the preceding pages, our saint attained the patriarchal age of ninety-four years, and the period had at length arrived, when, like another great patriarch of monks, St. Anthony, he should feel and say: "I, as it is written, go the way of my fathers, for I perceive I am called by the Lord." St. Athanasius, in his *Life of St. Anthony*,† tells how the saint, when he knew his death was approaching, withdrew, for some time, from all his outer monasteries, "into the inner mountain," where he loved to dwell, and there retaining with him only

* *Life of St. Malachy*, c. vi. † § 90.

the two ascetics who had ministered to him for some years on account of his age, he gave them strict charge and directions about the burial of his body in the earth where no one may know the place except themselves, and then prepared to die.

In like manner, St. Brendan, knowing the hour was approaching when he should depart this life, withdrew from all his other religious houses and retired to the convent of his beloved sister, at Eanach-duin, and retaining with him there a few of his brethren, to whom he gave those minute directions regarding the disposal of his body, and its sure burial "in the place of his resurrection" in the sacred soil of Clonfert-Brendan, which are detailed in our text so dramatically, he foretold to his sister the time of his death, as we read in his Life in the *Codex Salmanticensis* more at ength. Here we are told: "The blessed soldier of Christ, Brendan, knowing that his death was approaching, came to visit his own sister, the holy virgin Bryg. Among many other things, he foretold to her the place of her resurrection in these words: 'Not here, but in your own country of the *Tragei* * will your resurrection be. Proceed thither, therefore, for the people there will obtain God's mercy through you; there you will find a house of monks, not of nuns; but God is now calling me to Himself, out of the prison of this body.' Whereupon his sister, in great grief, said to him: 'Beloved father, your death shall be death to us all, for if in your absence during life, it was hard to live without you, what must it be when you are dead?' Then Brendan said to her: 'On the third day from this I will go the way of my fathers.'"]

* Probably the people who dwelt near the shore (*Traig*, in Irish) of Tralee Bay, where St. Bryg was born.

XXIX.—Death of St. Brendan in his Ninety-fourth Year.

Soon after this St. Brendan gave his blessing to his sister and to the brethren, and, proceeding to the convent, passed beyond the threshold. Here, raising his eyes to heaven, he said: "Into Thy hands, O Lord, I commend my soul; save me, O Lord, my God;" and then the aged most holy Brendan gave forth his soul to God, on Sunday, the 17th of the calends of June (May 16th), having completed the ninety-third year of his age.

His corpse was afterwards placed in a waggon, and one brother was sent in charge of it, as the saint had directed, and everything occurred on the journey as he had foretold before he died. A great multitude of holy men assembled from all quarters on the occasion, and his blessed body that had been borne, in the manner related, from the convent of Eanach-duin to his own city of Clonfert—a three days' journey, was buried in the place of honour, with all glory and reverence; with psalmody and spiritual canticles; our Lord Jesus Christ reigning over heaven and earth, and all creatures, in union with the Father and Holy Spirit, for ever and ever. Amen.

Here ends the Life of St. Brendan, abbot and confessor.

[In the *Codex Salmanticensis* there are some pathetic touches added in the account of the death scene of our saint: "On the Lord's day, after offering the Holy Sacrifice of the altar, St. Brendan said to those about him: 'Commend to God in your prayers my departure from this life.' Whereupon his sister, Bryg, said to him: 'Dear father, what have you to fear?' '*I fear*, said he, '*as I pass away all alone, and as the journey is darksome; I fear the unknown region, the presence of the King, the sentence of the Judge.*'" He then directed the brethren to remove his body secretly to Clonfert, lest, if this were done openly, it would be detained by the people on the way. Having afterwards given to all a last embrace, and imparted to his sister loving messages for all absent friends, he passed to his eternal rest in the ninety-sixth year of his age." Here the age of St. Brendan is set down as two years more than what is stated in our text, but according to the best authorities he was born in 483 (probably in March or April), and died on the 16th of May, A.D. 577, when he had well entered on his ninety-fourth year. His festival is marked in all our ancient martyrologies and calendars at the 16th May, which is stated to have been the day of his death; thus in the *Feilire* or Festology of St. Aengus Cele-De, we have on that day an entry signifying:—

> "The summons of Brendan of Cluain
> Into the victorious eternal life;"

and the gloss adds: "*i.e.*, the calling of Brendan of Clonfert to the kingdom of God."

What a beautiful and holy death was this of our saint on that Sunday in May, when in the arms of his saintly sister Bryg, the "child-nurse of his early youth," surrounded by her community of holy nuns, and by the brethren whom he specially loved, and whom he chose among all his spiritual sons, to minister to him the last offices and the last consolations of religion—after having just before said his last Mass, and having received the all-atoning Victim in the Holy Sacrifice for the last time, he gave forth his blessed soul in peace and holy joy to the Divine Master whom he had served so faithfully and so zealously during his long life. In a *Lectio Brevis** (Lesson) for his Office, in some ancient MSS. we read of the vision of this holy death, with which St. Columba was favoured in Iona: "On a certain day, while St. Columba was abiding in Iona, he called very early in the morning for his attendant, Diarmuidh, and gave him these orders: 'Let the sacred mysteries of the Eucharist be quickly prepared, for this is the *natalis* (birthday) of blessed Brendan.' 'Wherefore,' said the attendant, 'do you order such solemnities for the Mass to-day, as no messenger has come from Ireland with tidings of the death of that holy man?' 'Go,' said Columba, 'and do what I order, in accordance with the vision I have had; last night I saw the heavens suddenly opening, and choirs of angels descending to meet the soul of the blessed Brendan, and so great and incomparable was the brightness, that for a while it illumined all the world within my view. For then his soul was borne upwards by the ministry of the angels, in exultant procession, before the throne of the Divine Majesty, where it is now crowned with the brightest laurel-wreath of a glorious reward.'"

After his saintly death his sacred remains, in compliance with his directions, were removed to Clonfert, and many precautions, such as our text describes, were necessary in order to avoid or disarm the opposition of the tribesmen round about Eanachduin to the removal of his body for interment elsewhere. These were the *Hy-Bruin-Seola*, who, no doubt, loved and venerated him much after the many years of his holy life and

* Cardinal Moran's *Acta Sti. Brendani*, p. 140.

labours amongst them, and who would, therefore, desire earnestly to secure his burial in their midst. They were also a sturdy and rather unmanageable race, of whom "the one-eyed soldier, Curryn," referred to in our text, was a fair specimen; and within the year on which St. Brendan died, they provoked the wrath of King Aedh MacEochaidh, who "had given Eanachduin to God and Brendan," by some rebellious conduct, and on his going with a strong force to chastise them, they rose against him in full strength, and in a conflict that ensued, they slew him on the battle-field. It must have been, therefore, a service of some difficulty and danger to bear away the venerable remains of St. Brendan through their district to distant Clonfert for burial amongst another people; but the saint's minute instructions to his loving sister, Bryg, were faithfully carried out, and the humble waggon laden with Brendan's "goods and chattels" was suffered to pass on "to his own city of Clonfert," which was reached after a journey of three days. Here amidst the tribesmen of the Hy-Maine, there was no occasion for concealment, and "a great multitude of holy men assembled from all quarters" to do him honour; and we may well believe that the honours paid to him by prelates and clergy, and chieftians and people at Clonfert, were no less signal and prolonged than those accorded to St. Senan, on a like occasion, at Iniscathy, a few years before. The Life of this great saint tells us: "When the monks of Iniscathy, accompanied by Bishops Erc, Mola, and other prelates, brought the blessed remains of St. Senan from the nunnery where they first lay after his death, to his island monastery, it was unanimously resolved that the body of the saint would not be committed to the earth until all the prelates and clergy of the neighbouring churches, the heads of religious houses, and the chiefs of the surrounding countries had assembled to celebrate the obsequies of the holy man, and for a whole week the days and nights were passed around his bier, in the chanting of sacred canticles, and in the performance of religious rites."

No record remains to us of any such lengthened celebration before St. Brendan was interred "in the place of honour" at Clonfert; but the fact would serve to explain why the festival of the saint was set down in many later catalogues of Irish saints on May 26th—which may have been the day of his burial, ten days after his death, thus allowing three days for the journey from Eanachduin, and a full week for his obsequies at Clonfert, in "all glory and reverence," as our text has it.

At last the great voyager and the greater apostolic missionary, "the tireless worker for God" by land and sea, St. Brendan, is laid to his eternal rest, beside his life-long friend and zealous co-operator, the abbot-bishop who ruled, as his vicar, over his church and school at Clonfert for many years, St. Moennean, who had died six years before him, and his immediate successor, chosen by himself, St. Fintan Corach ("the chorister," so called because he was famed as a master of psalmody), assumed the government of the house, and the custody of the venerable relics of his saintly predecessors. These were indeed a precious dowry, a rich inheritance for that church of Clonfert—the latest off-spring of Brendan's apostolic zeal, the spiritual child begotten in his old age, which therefore received a "Benjamin's portion" in those venerated relics, like the latest born of the patriarch of old. There is no reason to doubt that the possession of those relics enhanced the celebrity of that church, and increased its attractions for pilgrims to its sacred shrines, and for scholars to its famous schools during many centuries, and contributed, in no small degree, to make that "little oasis" amid the moory reaches along the banks of the Shannon, as Clonfert has been called, a centre of religious life, and a much-frequented home of learning for many generations.

"*Defunctus adhuc loquitur;*" the venerable patriarch had passed to his rest—his relics were honoured by his devout votaries—but his spirit still lived and worked among his numerous spiritual children in the many religious foundations he had made; and not only his spirit of exalted virtue and holy zeal survived amongst them, but also his "*virtus,*" his "miraculous powers," were still exercised for the edification and advantage of many of those who for long years honoured him as their glorious patron in heaven. It was the remarkable frequency of the display of this "virtus Brendani" in the miracles wrought through his intercession at Clonfert-Brendan, his latest spiritual child, and at Ardfert-Brendan, his earliest begotten—as well authenticated traditions testify*—that furnished the *rationale* of the names they bore and still bear in our Irish language; for *virtus Brendani* became "*firt* or *fert-Brenain,*" or later, "*feart Brenain,*" in the mouths of the Irish children of St. Brendan.†

* I can certify to the existence of such traditions among old people at Ardfert, regarding many extraordinary miracles said to have been wrought there in past times, through the intercession of our patron saint. We have, in the published MSS. of the great Franciscan, Father Luke Wadding, an account of what he calls the "latest miracle at Ardfert, which had the fame, as well as the name of miracles." He tells how some iconoclast soldiers, who garrisoned Ardfert Abbey under one of Queen Elizabeth's captains, in 1580, lost their lives in attempting to dislodge, from its pedestal on the gable of the Abbey, a beautiful statue of the Blessed Virgin "through the miraculous power of St. Brendan."

† See note, page 115, *ante*.

I have already applied to him the words of St. Bernard, uttered in praise of one of his saintly contemporaries: "He was the parent of many thousand saints." These words were true of him during his life—they are more signally true of him and of his myriad spiritual children since his death, even in those three ancient dioceses that paid him special honour as their holy patron, Eanachduin (Annaghdown), Clonfert, and Ardfert-Brendan, for many centuries. As the learned Coadjutor Bishop of Clonfert has written *—and with his eloquent words I will conclude this portion of *Brendaniana*:—"St. Brendan has now many thousand spiritual children in Kerry and Galway who revere his memory as a precious inheritance and a bright example. The ancient cathedrals of Clonfert and Ardfert have been seized by the stranger, and are desolate or decaying. Inishgloria and Inisquin are waste and silent solitudes; Annaghdown and Inish-da-druim are in ruins; yet the tree of Christian faith and virtue, which Brendan planted, flourishes like the palm-tree by the waters, producing each year richer and more abundant fruits." *Sic floreat et vigeat in perpetuum! Amen.*]

* *Irish Schools and Scholars*, page 221.

LEGENDS OF ST. BRENDAN.

I.—THE LEGEND OF ST. BRENDAN, THE YOUNG HARPER, AND THE ANGEL.

(From *Book of Lismore.*)

ONCE when Brendan Mac Ua Alta was in Clonfert, on Easter-day, seven years before his death, he celebrated the Divine Office in the church, preached, and said Mass. When midday came the monks proceed to their refection. There was a young cleric amongst them in the refectory, having his harp to play for them, and they gave him their blessing.

"It would be sweet and pleasant to me now," said this cleric, "were Brendan here, that I might play three lively tunes for him." "He would not allow you approach him," say the monks, "for it is now seven years since Brendan made merry, or listened to any worldly music; for he has two balls of wax, tied together with a string, lying ready on his book; and when he hears such music he puts the balls into his ears."

"I will, however, go," says the young cleric, "to play for him." He goes off with his harp tuned. "Open," said the cleric. "Who is this?" said Brendan. "A clerical student come to play the harp for thee." "Play outside the church," said Brendan. "If it be not disagreeable to thee, I would thank thee to let me into the church to play for a while." Brendan then opens the door, and the cleric produces his harp; when Brendan at once places the two waxen balls in his ears. "I do not like," said the student, "to make music for thee unless thou takest the wax out of thine ears." "It shall be done," said Brendan. Then he placed the balls on his book, and the student plays three lively strains for him. "A blessing on thee, O student, with thy music," said Brendan, "and Heaven's melody for it hereafter!"

Then Brendan puts the balls again into his ears, for he wished not to listen to any more music. "Why dost thou not listen to the music?" said the young cleric; "is it because it seems bad to thee?" "Not so," said Brendan; "but thus it happened, one day, just seven years ago, as I was in this church, after preaching here, and after Mass, all the clergy had gone to their refection. I was left here alone, and having made a visit to the Body of Christ, a great longing for my Lord seized me. As I remained here, a trembling and awe came upon me, and at the window I saw a radiant bird, which then perched on the altar. I could not look on it, because of the sunlike radiance around it. "A blessing on thee, and do thou bless us, O cleric," said the bird. "May God bless thee," said Brendan. "Who art thou?" "The Angel Michael," said the bird, "come to commune with thee." "We give thanks to God for this communing; and wherefore hast thou come?" "To bless thee," said the bird, "and to make music for thee from thy Lord." "Great is thy welcome to me," said Brendan. "Then the bird places its beak beside its wing, and I remained listening to it from one canonical hour to another, and then it bade me farewell."

Then Brendan places a stole on my neck, and asks me, "Is that melodious to thee, O student?" "I give my word, before God," said Brendan, "that after that melody, no melody of the world's music seems sweeter to me than the placing of this stole over thy neck, and little profit do I deem the hearing thereof. Take my blessing, O student, and may Heaven be thine, because of thy music," said Brendan.

[John O'Donovan refers to this interesting legend, in a note to his *Four Masters*, Anno 553; and he says that in O'Clery's *Irish Calendar* is told the story of the visit of St. Michael Archangel to St. Brendan, after Mass and sermon, in the Church of Clonfert, in the shape of a beautiful bird, who continued to sing heavenly music for him during twenty-four hours; after which the saint could never enjoy, and never condescended to listen to, any earthly music, except one Easter Sunday, when he permitted a student of his people to play for him on his harp. He endured his music with difficulty, and after a while giving his blessing, he put the balls of wax into his ears, which he always did when he came within hearing of earthly music, thus shutting out all human melody, which was discord to him, and admitting only the harmonies of angels.

On this O'Donovan remarks that, if the story be not all pure fiction, "it might be inferred from it that St. Brendan had a most exquisite ear for music."

Was it St. Brendan's "exquisite ear" and love of heavenly music that led him to select for his immediate successor in the Church of Clonfert St. Fintan, surnamed Corach, or the Melodious, who was famed in his time as an excellent psalm-singer and choir master, as St. Ængus Cele-De tells us? This St. Fintan was of the Corcaguiney race, and related to St. Brendan's mother, St. Cair, or Cara; he may have been, in fact, the "young student" harper who was making his studies then in the school of Clonfert, and who, because he was of the saint's own "people" or family; ventured to ask, and obtained, the privilege of playing to him on his harp, notwithstanding St. Brendan's known repugnance to such earthly strains. St. Fintan Corach survived St. Brendan about thirty years, and was succeeded in Clonfert by Senach Garbh and Colman son of Comgall, immediately, who were also very probably of the same race, as St. Brendan, the founder of the church, according to the established rule by which the Comarb, or successor, was chosen from the kin or the tribe of the founder of the church or abbey, when a suitable subject thus qualified was available. This succession in Clonfert is thus given in the *Feilire* of St. Ængus :—

> "Fintan the Melodious, Senach the Rough,
> Colman, son of Comgall, the Guileless,
> Three great (spiritual) kings, with warfare of valour,
> One after the other in the Abbey of (Clonfert)." *]

II.—The Legend of the Three Students who went on a Pilgrimage.

(From *Book of Lismore.*)

Three young clerics, of the men of Ireland, went on their pilgrimage, and fervently and heartily they went.

* See Dr. Healy's *Irish Schools and Scholars.*

They took no provision with them to sea, only three cakes. "I will bring the little cat," says one of them.

When they reached the main sea—"Let us," said they, "in Christ's name, cast away our oars into the sea, and throw ourselves on the mercy of our Lord." This was done.

Not long afterwards they arrived, under Christ's protection, at a beautiful island, where there was abundance of firewood and water. "Let us," said they, "build a church in the midst of our island;" and they built one. The little cat goes away from them, and brings back a real salmon, and thus procures three salmon every twenty-four hours for them. "Oh! God," said they, "our pilgrimage is now no pilgrimage at all after this fashion, for we have brought abundant provisions in bringing our little cat to feed us, and it is sad to eat of his fishing. We will not, therefore, partake of the cat's providing." Wherefore they remained twenty-four hours without food, until there came a message from Christ that there was on the altar half a wheaten cake and a piece of fish for each man. "Well then," said they, "let each of us announce his work for Him who sends this food."

"I will sing, first," says one of them, "the thrice fifty psalms every day together with the canonical office and mass."

"I will sing," says another, "the thrice fifty long prayers with the canonical hours and mass every day."

"I will sing," said the third, "thrice fifty *Hymnum dicats** every day, with celebrating canonical hours and mass."

* St. Hilary's hymn in praise of Christ.

This is practised for a long space of time, and at length one of the students died. His requiem was sung by the others, and he was buried. The survivors divide between them the duty-prayers of their deceased comrade, who had the thrice fifty psalms, and say them every day.

Soon after another died, and was buried by his comrade, who took upon himself all the duty-prayers of the deceased, which was a heavy burthen upon him the sole survivor.

Under this he murmured. "Of a truth," says he, "their Lord hath a greater love for the two deceased than He hath for me. He has taken them unto Himself, and He hath left me here."

An angel visits him. "Thy Lord is angry with thee," saith the angel, "because of thy murmuring; for thou wilt not be without mercy from Him." "Why then," said he, "does He not suffer me to die like my comrades?" "The choice was thine," saith the angel, "when you divided the duty-prayers between you three; the man who chose the thrice fifty psalms was to have a short life here, and was taken first; the man who chose the thrice fifty prayers neither adds to or takes from his life here; but for you who chose the thrice fifty *Hymnum dicats*, there is long life here and the kingdom of heaven hereafter."

"A blessing on the Lord from whom thou hast come. I am very thankful to Him."

So he dwelt on his island till he was aged and withered, and till Brendan came from the sea to him; and Brendan blessed him, and gave him the Viaticum and all the sacraments, and so he went to heaven. And a watch of angels is always over their resting-place in the island.

[The Irish text of this ancient legend is given by Dr. Whitley Stokes, in his Preface to his *Lives of Saints from the Book of Lismore,* with an English translation; and he tells us "that the legend is also found in the *Book of Leinster,* whence it has been published, with a French translation and notes, by M. Henri Gaidoz, in *Mélusine.* The language of the Irish text seems very archaic and difficult to translate, perhaps even more so than that of the very analogous legend that we find in the Irish version of the voyage of Brendan, as given in the "*Betha Brenainn,*" *Book of Lismore.* This legend tells that when St. Brendan, towards the close of his seven years' quest of the "Land of Promise of the Saints," was approaching a small, delightful, beautiful island, where there was abundance of excellent fish, and wherein there was "a church built of stone, and a penitent white-faced old man praying therein;" his vessel was pursued by a monstrous sea cat, which swam after it from this island, and threatened to devour the saint and his companions. They all prayed to the Lord earnestly for deliverance, and suddenly there arose from the depths of the sea "a huge sea-whale, between them and the monstrous sea-cat." Between those a fierce combat ensued, till each of them drowned the other, and neither was seen any more. Then Brendan and his people render thanks to God, and, returning to the island, are welcomed joyously by the venerable old man, who salutes them in a poem of six quatrains, given in the Irish text, but which Dr. W. Stokes does not translate into English, awaiting, as he says, a second copy yet to be found.

He tells them that " he was of the men of Ireland, and that there were twelve of them who went on their pilgrimage, bringing with them this sea-cat, like a little bird, that was very dear to them. Afterwards it grew greatly in size, but never did hurt to any of them. Eleven of those who came on their pilgrimage hither are now dead, and I am here alone, entreating thee to administer unto me Christ's Body and His Blood, that I may then depart to heaven." Then he reveals to St. Brendan the land he was seeking, even the Land of Promise, and, having received the Holy Viaticum, died, and was buried on the island, along with his brethren, " with honour, and great reverence, and with psalms and hymns, in the name of the Father, and the Son, and the Holy Ghost."

Such is the form of the legend in the *Betha Brenainn*, and it seems to have grown out of that of the " Three Students," who brought their " little cat " with them on their pilgrimage, which was so expert in catching salmon for them. In the later form this " little cat " becomes the monster sea-cat, " like a young ox or a three-year-old horse, overgrown by feeding on the fish of the sea and the island ;" and the three pilgrims are increased to twelve. of whom the survivor greets St. Brendan and his people.

This later version must have been current and popular in Ireland before the close of the eighth century, for in the litanies of St. Aengus Cele-De, which are believed to have been composed before 790, there is an invocation of the twelve pilgrims referred to in this legend :—

" *In da aílíther dec, día n-airnaich Brenaind in oen fer in-innis in caitt í m-bethu, hos omnes invoco.*" (" The twelve pilgrims, of whom Brendan found the sole survivor in the Island of the Cat—all these I invoke.")

In those litanies of St. Aengus there is another invocation, which would indicate that some version of the voyage of St. Brendan, similar to that we have in the *Book of Lismore*, if not absolutely the same, was well known to the faithful in Ireland at the time St. Aengus composed those litanies for their devout use. The saint invokes:—"*In t-ancara for rainic Brenain ar a cind i tír tharngire; cus na h'uili noemaib torcratar in huibh insib ind ociain—hos omnes invoco.*" ("The anchorite whom Brendan met in the Land of Promise, with all the saints who perished in the Isles of the Ocean—all these I invoke."]

III.—The Holy Well of Brendan's Anointing.

(*From Local Tradition in the Island of Valentia.*)

One day, when St. Brendan was sailing in his *currach* (coracle) from one of his oratories on the Blasquet Islands, across Dingle Bay, to visit the little monastery of St. Beoanigh at the Glen, in the parish of Killemlagh, barony of Iveragh, he was suddenly hailed, as he drew near the northern coast of *Ilaun Dairbhre*, or Valentia Island, by a man standing on one of the headlands there, who made signals to him to come on shore without delay. The saint at once turned his little boat towards the land, and put into a narrow creek, where he found a landing-place like that he came to on the first island he reached on his great* "Voyage," "where the rocks stood on every side, of wonderful steepness, like a

* *Supra*, page 121.

wall." Here he drew up his boat, and ascended the frowning cliff by means of steps, which are to this day as firmly and safely set on the face of it, as if carved out by the hand of man. Having learned from the stranger that there were two persons, lying at the point of death, some distance inland, who had not received the last Sacraments, he followed his guide, who led him into the thick of a forest—which is now-a-days an extensive bog, called Emlagh, in the town-land of Coorha-beg, and here he discovered two men who were dying, and who had earnestly desired and prayed to die in the Christian faith, but who had not been baptized, nor received any religious instruction for want of opportunity. The strange guide then disappeared, and St. Brendan having instructed the dying men, administered to them the Sacraments of Baptism and Extreme Unction, and in a short time afterwards they died holy and happy deaths. They were buried where they died, and two pillar-stones, which must have been brought from afar, mark the spot where they were laid at rest. The well from which the saint had procured the water for their baptism, and which flows near the place of their burial, is known and recognised as a holy well, still called by Irish-speaking people—*Tobar olla Brenainn* (the Well of St. Brendan's Anointing). It is much frequented by pious pilgrims, who perform certain devotions there, and many miraculous cures are popularly believed to have been granted to such devotions. The "round," as the devout practice is called, consists in repeating certain prayers, when going along by four large stones, sunk in the earth, in the form of a cross; and it appears that each of those stones is a rude cross of a very ancient type, which is partially covered by the boggy soil.

The little creek, near the present Colloo Head, by which St. Brendan landed on the island, received from him a special blessing on the occasion, as the tradition tells, so that ever after it abounded in shoals of excellent fish, and became the favourite fishing-ground of the islanders, until, within the memory of some now living in the neighbourhood, the great supply of fish there proved for many too strong a temptation to profane the Lord's day, and led to Sabbath-breaking and neglect of Mass by the fishermen, which brought on the waters of the creek the curse of barrenness, which clings to them at the present day.

[The present Parish Priest of Valentia, from whom I received this interesting tradition, informs me that he had heard a different account of how St. Brendan was summoned by his mysterious guide to administer the Sacraments at this holy well; but the version given above seems to have been more generally current in the locality. The existence of other forms of the tradition would show that it was an ancient one, and had come down through various and independent channels. The remains of "the little monastery of St. Beoanigh," which St. Brendan is said to have been visiting on this occasion, still exist in the Glen, but in the last stage of ruin and desolation. It had been a very interesting specimen of the earliest of our Irish monastic establishments of which we have any remains now existing.

When I saw the place nearly forty years ago, the ruins of nine bee-hive cells could be traced, clustered around what had been a larger building in the centre, probably the oratory, of which only a small portion of a side-wall was visible. Enclosing the whole, which covered about a quarter of an acre of land, were the remains of a rudely-built *cashel*, or stone fence, which had been in many places levelled with the ground. Beside the enclosure there gushes forth from the living rock of the mountain, that here rises abruptly over the site, a copious stream of limpid water, which is called St. Beoanigh's Well,* and all around for some distance are traces of ancient graves and burial cists, with a few pillar-stones still erect beside them, within which, no doubt, many of the early monks who worked and prayed in those dismantled cells and oratories were laid at rest, and where also the forefathers of many a neighbouring hamlet sleep their last sleep. The place is known as *Killabeonigh* (church or cell of St. Beoanigh), and gives its name to a large townland which comprises nearly the whole of the "Glen" within which lay the ancient monastery. This Glen, so called *par excellence*, consists of a cluster of mountain valleys, radiating towards the north and west from the shore of St. Finan's Bay, on the south, and shut in and sheltered by lofty hills that rise precipitously over them; and in these vallies can still be traced unmistakable vestiges of very early as well as later Christian settlements within them. Not far from the venerable monastic *laura* at *Kilabeonigh* there are remains of an oratory of the earliest type, which is very much dilapidated; and in one of the valleys trending to the north-west, called *Coom-anaspuig* (mountain-valley of the bishop), there stands an ancient oratory, one of

* This well is marked on Ordnance Survey Maps, but not the ancient *laura*.

the finest and most perfect of its kind that remains in Kerry, being somewhat larger than the remarkable one at Gallerus, barony of Corcaguiney, perhaps better finished, and very well preserved. On the eastern side of the Glen we find the ruins of two mediæval parochial churches, one of them some centuries older than the other, and of a better style of masonry, but neither showing any architectural features worthy of note. The existence of those monastic and ecclesiastical remains within the ambit of the Glen, plainly indicates that the place had been a centre of religious life and light from the earliest ages of the faith in Kerry; and surely the situation was well chosen for such a purpose, by the pioneers of the primeval religious foundations there, for it would be difficult to find anywhere in Ireland a more secure retreat from the outer world, or a dwelling of more sunny aspect or more charming prospect towards the sea, than is to be found in the bosom of this beautiful Glen of Iveragh. From every side can be seen the bold and picturesque cliffs and headlands that surround St. Finan's Bay, on the east and on the west; while not far out in the offing, fully in view, tower up grandly the Greater and Lesser Skelligs, like two mighty ships sailing along majestically, "with every shred of canvas set," towards which the favourite port of departure, as well as the landing-place on return, for all pilgrim visitors, from time immemorial, was the *caladh*, or the narrow creek that runs from St. Finan's Bay into the centre of the Glen.

The earliest religious foundation there was apparently the little monastery of St. Beoanigh, and, judging from its present remains, we can scarcely entertain a doubt that this was founded, and the group of humble cells and the rudely-built oratory were erected about the time of St. Brendan, by St. Beonigh, one of his disciples, and probably the same saint whose name we find as "Beoanus" in the Latin Lives of St. Fursey, in connection with the wonderful visions of that renowned saint. The founder of Killabeoanigh had very probably come from one of St. Brendan's West Kerry monasteries, and having, like his great patriarch, as the Valentia tradition relates, "crossed Dingle Bay in his currach" with some of his brother monks, in quest of a suitable place for a new foundation, amidst the hills of Iveragh, and having rounded Bray Head and Canduff on that coast, came within view of the Glen, and chose within its bosom the delightful situation for the little monastery with which his name is associated.

If this conjecture regarding the founder of Killabeoanigh be well grounded, as I believe it is, it would explain the kindly interest shown by St. Brendan in his visits, of which tradition tells, to the new foundation of his spiritual children there; and it would serve to identify St. Beoanigh of the Glen with the St. Beoanus of the "Visions of St. Fursey," and to throw some light on obscure passages in the early Life of the latter saint. As I have stated in a previous page, St. Fursey was born in A.D. 570, a few years before the death of St. Brendan, near the island-monastery of Inisquin, whither his father, Fintan, the West Kerry prince, had fled for protection to that saint, who is said to have been his uncle, from the vengeance of Aedh Find, King of North Connaught, after his secret marriage with his daughter, the beautiful Gelgeis. Soon after, through the good offices of St. Brendan, the offended father forgave the refugees, and Fintan and his wife took up their residence on the adjoining mainland at a place called Ard-Fintan to the present day, where other children were born to them, among whom were probably Ultan and Foilan, the saintly brothers of St. Fursey and his companions in many of his apostolic missions in his latter life. Here, in the course of some years, news was brought to Fintan, that his father, Finlogh, who was king in West Kerry, had died, and that the chiefs of the tribe had elected him to succeed his royal father. He therefore returned to his native district, bringing his children, Fursey and the others, with him, and resided in the royal mansion, one of those great *cathairs*, in Corcaguiney, some of which are grand and imposing even in their ruins at the present day. Here he sought out the holiest and most learned teachers for his children, and got them educated in religious knowledge and trained to piety by some bishops who dwelt within his territory.* Under those instructors, Fursey soon made great progress in learning and piety, but when he reached a mature age, he desired to devote himself entirely to the study of the Holy Scriptures and to the practice of Christian perfection; and for this purpose "he left his country and the home of his parents," as his old Life relates, "and repaired to a distant part of Ireland;" probably the monastery of Inisquin, where St. Meldan, the friend of his childhood, was abbot. After some years devoted here to study and to the discipline of the religious life, he founded a monastery on the adjacent mainland, at a place then called *Rathmuighe*, but afterwards known as Kilursa (Church of Fursey), which gives name to a large parish on the borders of Lough Corrib. To provide suitable subjects for his new monastery, he resolved to return to the country of his parents, West Kerry, in order to invite and induce some of his relatives and friends there, of whose virtues and

* See Dr. Lanigan's *Ecclesiastical History*, vol. ii., chap. xvi., pp. 449-454.

fitness for the monastic state he had previous cognizance, to join his new community. When on this mission, he had arrived near the mansion of his father, he was seized with a sudden illness of an extraordinary nature, and having been conveyed unconscious to a house beside the way, he lay for several hours, it was supposed, at the point of death. It was during this seizure, and the recurrence of the same afterwards, that he had those wonderful visions that have made his name so famous, and the detailed accounts of which, furnished by himself at various times and to different persons during his after life, were written down at some length before the time of Venerable Bede, for he refers to them with respect in his *Ecclesiastical History*, and became so celebrated and universally known in mediæval Europe, that it is said they furnished Dante with the ideas of the future state and the plan and scenes of his sublime poem, the *Divina Commedia.*

In one of those visions, he saw, after a variety of most wonderful spiritual manifestations, the Bishops Beoanus and Meldanus, who are said to have been then dead, issuing from the inner courts of heaven, in the guise of angels of dazzling brightness; and he heard them addressing to him lengthened instructions replete with heavenly wisdom, which are given in some detail in the written accounts of the visions.* In those accounts the chief part of such discourses is attributed to St. Beoanus, regarding whom Dr. Lanigan says he can find nothing certain, but that his repute for sanctity was equally great with that of St. Meldan; and he supposes that he belonged to some part of Connaught, though the particular place he does not know.

* An interesting account of those visions is given by Canon O'Hanlon, in his Life of St. Fursey, Jan. 16.—*Lives of Irish Saints*, vol. i.

I have given here what Dr. Lanigan claims to be "the most correct account of St. Fursey's younger days that he was able to collect from the old Acts of his life;" and though it has occupied more space than perhaps ought to have been devoted to it in a volume of *Brendaniana*, my readers will, I hope, excuse the trespass, because of the interesting information it supplies or suggests regarding the relations of so renowned a saint with the holy men of his time in West Kerry. We learn from it that certain bishops took part in his education there from his youth to early manhood, and it clearly implies that those bishops were residents in the district. Who were the bishops who thus instructed and trained to holiness the youthful Fursey? I think, without doing violence to the probabilities of the case, I may state that St. Beoanigh of the Glen was one of them. This saint, I believe, founded his monastery there about A.D. 560, when he was perhaps thirty years of age, and received soon after the paternal visit from St. Brendan of which the Valentia tradition speaks. Here he remained for some years, until he had placed the new establishment on a solid basis, and grounded its community in religious discipline. Then he may have returned to his old monastic home beside Brandon Hill, some time after the death of his holy patriarch, St. Brendan, in 577, and there received episcopal consecration, probably from Bishop Cuan or Mochua,* the founder of ancient Kilquane (Church of Cuan) in that district, who resided not far from that church at the episcopal seat of

* If the founder of this Kilquane were the founder of another Kilquane, in the parish of Ballymacelligott, as I believe he was, he was certainly a bishop, for the latter church was named, on the map of the Desmond confiscations accurately made in A.D. 1587—*Kileaspuig-Croin*, the Church of Bishop Cron, or Cronanus, a well-known *alias* of Cuan or Mochua.

Cathair-easpuig (Bishop's Fort), where the name survives, and the ruins of the ancient *cathair* are to be seen at the present day.

About this time Fintan had come with his family from the shores of Lough Corrib, to assume regal sway in West Kerry in succession to his deceased father, and soon after placed his first-born son, Fursey, under the care of the local bishops, whom I believe to have been no other than the Bishops Cuan and Beoanigh, "to be well educated and instructed in religious matters." Under the tutelage of those holy men the saintly youth remained for some years, until in early manhood he departed, as stated above, "from his country and his parents," probably about 592.

We are not to suppose that St. Beoanigh had forgotten or lost sight of his spiritual children in the Glen all this time, and we may well believe that he occasionally "crossed Dingle Bay in his currach" to visit them, especially after his consecration as bishop, and to perform all episcopal functions they may require. When he had advanced in age, those sea journeys were scarcely possible, and then he took up his residence permanently at *Coomaneaspuig* (Bishop's Mountain Valley), within the Glen, where his loving sons of the monastery built for his use the beautiful oratory, worthy of a bishop, that stands there still in marvellous preservation. Here he lived and laboured for God's glory and the sanctification of souls during many years, until at a venerable old age he died in the odour of sanctity, and was buried amid the tears and prayers of his spiritual children, at Killabeoanigh, within its little oratory, where his relics were enshrined, and whither numerous pilgrims have resorted from generation to generation, even to the present day, to honour his memory and to seek his intercession.

The death of St. Beoanigh most probably took place some years before the date generally assigned to the occurrence of St. Fursey's ecstatic seizures, during which he had those wonderful visions; that is, about A.D. 620. We may, therefore, believe that when the saint saw in ecstacy the glorified spirits of Bishops Beoanigh and Meldanus in angelic brightness, he had really before his mind's eye the saintly instructors of his youth and early manhood, St. Beoanigh of the Glen and St. Meldan of Inisquin, and that the wise and weighty lessons he had received from those holy teachers for many years, lived again in his memory so vividly during his illness, that he was able to recall and repeat them at great length after his recovery. He loved those saintly men during life, and he revered their memories after death so much that, when in after years he was leaving Ireland for his apostolic missions in England and France, he lovingly bore away with him, as his Life relates, relics of those saints, and preserved them in special veneration until his death.

The mission of St. Fursey to West Kerry, in quest of eligible subjects for his new monastery, was, no doubt, eminently successful; for, as he knew well from his early experiences there, the district was indeed a very fruitful field for such a harvest as he sought to garner within it, and had been blessed with a spiritual fecundity that bloomed beauteously in a profusion of the flowers and fruits of the religious life. The good seed that St. Brendan had sown amid the hills and vallies that cluster around the holy mountain that bears his name, had, in truth, fallen upon excellent soil, and "had brought forth fruit one hundred-fold;" so that even in the lifetime of the saint, and soon after his death, that country of West Corcaguiney became the home of multitudes of holy men and women, who, about the time of the visit of St. Fursey, were in the first fervour of their faith and love of God. The fame of this religious fervour spread abroad, even unto the most distant parts of Ireland, and attracted to the district devout pilgrims from various directions, who resorted to it as "the refuge of the penitent or the school of the saint." Among those pilgrims, one of the most illustrious was Melchedair MacRonan, the grandson of the King of *Uladh* (now county Antrim), who came from the remotest north of Ireland to dwell among the saints of West Kerry, as the ancient chronicler* has it: "*for bru an mara, fri cnoic mBrenain aniar*" (on the brink of the sea near Brandon Hill on the west). Here this holy man lived and laboured in God's service for many years, until his saintly death, of which we have record in the *Martyrology of Donegal*, on May 14th, A.D. 636; and local tradition loves to tell how he drew many souls to Christ, and baptized his converts in the holy well beside the ancient oratory, still known as *Log Melchedair* (the pool of Melchedair), and how, when he had completed his beautiful oratory there, now, alas! in ruins, not far from the interesting remains of the fine Hiberno-Romanesque church, built many centuries later, he would invoke the special blessing of St. Brendan upon the work, by marshalling a grand procession of all the saints within the district in a solemn pilgrimage to the oratory on Brandon Hill, there to celebrate a High Mass of thanksgiving in honour of the glorious patriarch, who had reached his heavenly crown many years before.

The assembly of the saints was so numerous that they were able to realize the words of the prophet;† for, in their grand procession, "a path and a way was there, and it was called the holy way;" and this way, for

* In the *Book of Ballymote*.

† Isaias xxxv.

the seven miles of the pilgrimage from the oratory of St. Melchedair to St. Brendan's oratory, on Brandon-Hill, is still well defined and known as the "Pathway of the Saints." The story I have related in a previous page (*supra*, p. 78) relying on local tradition, about the extraordinary length of this procession, will not be considered an extravagant improbability, when we are reminded of the multiplicity of the early Christian remains of various religious foundations that still exist in that district. A gentleman,* who knew the locality well, and took an enlightened interest in its archæology, made out about fifty years ago a list of what he called "the principal remains of antiquity" within its borders, and he challenged any district of its extent in Ireland to show "so many and such a variety of ancient remains, and in such a fine state of preservation as are to be found there." I need not give the whole list, as he made it out, but I may mention some of the early Christian remains: twenty-one churches in ruins, and nine church sites; fifteen oratories; nine penitential stations; forty *calluraghs* ("calvaries," early Christian cemeteries); two hundred and eighteen *cloghauns*, or bee-hive cells and houses; twelve large stone crosses; fifty-four monumental pillars, most of them bearing Ogham inscriptions; and sixty-six holy wells, many of them bearing the name of a saint. Besides these, which existed fifty years ago, how many fine relics of the faith and piety of the early Christian population there must have perished utterly during the many centuries that have since elapsed.

It is, therefore, no exaggeration to state that soon after St. Brendan's time this whole district, the field of

* Mr. R. Hitchcock, in a paper in *Kilkenny Archæological Journal*, vol. i.

his earliest missionary labours, and the scene of some of his first monastic foundations, was in truth a "land of saints;" a veritable Thebaid amid the hills of West Kerry, to which may be well applied the praises bestowed by St. Athanasius, in his *Life of St. Anthony*, on the Thebaid of Egypt, during the lifetime of that saint:—"Among the mountains there were monasteries, as if tabernacles, filled with divine choirs, singing, studying, fasting, praying, exulting in the hope of things to come, and working for alms-deeds, having love and harmony one towards another. And truly, it was given one there to see a peculiar country of piety and righteousness; a multitude of ascetics, whose one feeling was towards holiness. So that a stranger, seeing those monasteries and their order, would be led to cry out: 'How beauteous are thy homes, O Jacob, and thy tabernacles, O Israel; as shady groves, as a garden on a river, as tents which the Lord has pitched, and as cedars by the waters.' "—§ 44.]

IV.—The Island of St. Brendan.

(Abridged from Washington Irving's "Columbus.")

One of the most singular geographical illusions on record is that which, for a long while, haunted the imaginations of the inhabitants of the Canaries. They fancied they beheld a mountainous island, of about ninety leagues in length, lying far to the Westward. It was only seen at intervals, though in perfectly clear and serene weather. To some it seemed one hundred leagues distant, to others forty, to others only fifteen or eighteen.

On attempting to reach it, however, it somehow or

other eluded the search, and was nowhere to be found. Still there were so many persons of credibility who concurred in testifying to their having seen it, and the testimony of the inhabitants of different islands agreed so well as to its form and position, that its existence was generally believed; and geographers inserted it in their maps. It is laid down on the globe of Martin Behem, projected in 1492, as delineated by M. De Murr, and it will be found in most of the maps of the time of Columbus, placed commonly about 200 leagues west of the Canaries. During the time that Columbus was making his proposition to the court of Portugal, an inhabitant of the Canaries applied to King John II. for a vessel to go in search of the island. The name of St. Brendan was from time immemorial given to this imaginary island, for when the rumour circulated of such a place being seen from the Canaries, which always eluded the search, the legends of St. Brendan were revived, and applied to this unapproachable land. Some have maintained that it was known to the ancients, and was the same mentioned by Ptolemy among the Fortunate or Canary Islands, by the name of *Aprositus*, a Greek word signifying inaccessible; and which, according to Friar Diego Philippo, in his book on the Incarnation of Christ, shows that it possessed the same quality in ancient times of deluding the eye, and of being unattainable to the feet of mortals. But whatever belief the ancients may have had on the subject, it is certain that it took a strong hold on the faith of the moderns, during the prevalent rage for discovery, long after the time of Columbus.

It was repeatedly seen, and by various persons at a time, always in the same place and in the same form. In 1526, an expedition set off from the Canaries in quest of it, commanded by Fernando de Troya and Fernando Alvares. They cruised in the wonted direction, but in vain; and their failure ought to have undeceived the public. "The phantasm of the island, however," says Viera, "had such a secret enchantment for all who beheld it, that the public preferred doubting the good conduct of the explorers rather than their own senses." In 1570 the appearances were so repeated and clear, that there was an universal fever of curiosity awakened among the people of the Canaries, and it was determined to send forth another expedition. That they might not appear to act upon light grounds, an exact investigation was previously made of all the persons of talent and credibility who had seen those apparitions of land, or who had other proofs of its existence.

Alonzo de Espinosa, governor of the island of Ferro, accordingly made a report, in which more than one hundred witnesses, several of them persons of the highest respectability, deposed that they had beheld the unknown island about forty leagues to the north-west of Ferro; that they had contemplated it with calmness and certainty, and had seen the sun set behind one of its points. Testimonials of still greater force came from the islands of Palma and Teneriffe. There were certain Portuguese who affirmed that, being driven about by a tempest, they had come upon the island of St. Brendan. Pedro Vello, who was the pilot of the vessel, asserted that, having anchored in a bay, he landed with several of the crew. They drank fresh water in a brook, and beheld in the sand the print of footsteps, double the size of those of an ordinary man, and the distance between them was in proportion. Having seen much cattle and sheep grazing in the neighbourhood, two of their party, armed with lances, went into the woods in pursuit of them. The night was approaching, the heavens began to lour, and a harsh wind arose. The people on board the ship cried out that she was dragging her anchor, whereupon Vello entered the boat and hurried on board. In an instant they lost sight of land, being, as it were, swept away in the hurricane. When the storm had passed away, and the sea and the sky were again serene, they searched in vain for the island; not a trace of it was to be seen, and they had to pursue their voyage, lamenting the loss of their two companions who had been abandoned in the wood.

A learned licentiate, Pedro Ortiz de Funez, Inquisitor of the Grand Canary, while on a visit at Teneriffe, summoned several persons before him, who testified having seen the island. Among them was one Marcos Verde, a man well known in those parts. He stated that, in returning from Barbary, and arriving in the neighbourhood of the Canaries, he beheld land which, according to his maps and calculations, could not be any of the known islands. He concluded it to be the far-famed *St. Brendan.* Overjoyed at having discovered this land of mystery, he coasted along its spell-bound shores until he anchored in a beautiful harbour formed by the mouth of a mountain ravine. Here he landed with several of his crew. "It was now," he said, "the hour of the Ave-Maria, or of vespers; the sun being set, the shadows began to spread over the land. The navigators having separated, wandered about in different directions, until out of hearing of each other's shouts. Those on board, seeing the night approaching, made signals to summon back the wanderers to the ship. They reimbarked, intending to resume their investigations on the following day. Scarcely were they on board, however, when a whirlwind came rushing down the ravine with such violence as to drag the vessel from her anchor and hurry her out to sea; and they never saw anything more of this hidden and inhospitable island."

The mass of testimony collected by official authority, in 1570, seemed so satisfactory, that another expedition was fitted out in the same year in the island of Palma; but it was equally fruitless with the preceding, St. Brendan seeming disposed only to tantalize the world with distant and serene glimpses of his ideal paradise, or to reveal it amidst storms to tempest-tost mariners; but to hide it from all who diligently sought it. Still the people of Palma adhered to their favourite chimera. Thirty-four years afterwards, in 1605, they sent another ship on the quest, commanded by an accomplished pilot, accompanied by the Padre Lorenzo Pinedo, a holy Franciscan friar, skilled in natural science. St. Brendan, however, refused to reveal his island to either monk or mariner.

Upwards of a century now elapsed without any new

attempt to seek the fairy island. At length, in 1721, the public infatuation again rose to such a height, that another expedition was sent, commanded by Don Gaspar Domingues, a man of probity and talent. As this was an expedition of solemn and mysterious import, he had two holy friars as apostolic chaplains. They made sail from the island of Teneriffe towards the end of October, leaving the populace in an indescribable state of anxious curiosity. The ship, however, returned from its cruise as unsuccessful as all its predecessors.

Such are the principal facts existing relative to the island of St. Brendan. Its reality was for a long time a matter of firm belief. It was in vain that repeated voyages and investigations proved its non-existence: the public, after trying all kinds of sophistry, took refuge in the supernatural to defend their favourite chimera. They maintained that it was rendered inaccessible to mortals by divine providence, and they indulged in all kinds of extravagant fancies concerning it. Some confounded it with the fabled island of the Seven Cities,* where, in old times, seven bishops and their followers had taken refuge from the Moors; some

* Washington Irving, in his *Chronicles of Wolfert's Roost and other Papers*, gives a Portuguese legend of this "Island of the Seven Cities," in which he charmingly tells how "Don Fernando de Alma, a young cavalier of high standing at the Portuguese Court," fitted out, sometime in the fifteenth century, long before Columbus crossed the ocean, an expedition "to sail in quest of the sainted island," furnished with a special commission from the king, "constituting him governor of any country he might discover." The "young cavalier" discovered the island in due course, and the story relates his wonderful adventures therein, and his more wonderful departure therefrom; but the tale is too long for insertion here, especially as it bears a strong family likeness to the stories of the expeditions to the "Island of St. Brendan" told in the text.

of the Portuguese imagined it to be the abode of their lost king Sebastian; while the Spaniards pretended that Roderic, the last of their Gothic kings, had fled thither from the Moors after the disastrous battle of the Guadelete. Others suggested that it might be the seat of the terrestrial paradise; the place where Enoch and Elias remained in a state of blessedness until the final day; and that it was made at times apparent to the eyes, but invisible to the search of mortals. Poetry, it is said, has owed to this popular belief one of its beautiful fictions; and the garden of Armida, where Rinaldo was detained enchanted, and which Tasso places in one of the Canary Islands, has been identified with the imaginary St. Brendan.

The learned Father Feyjoo, in his *Theatro Critico*, has given a philosophical solution to this geographical problem. He attributes all these appearances, which have been so numerous and so well authenticated as not to admit of doubt, to certain atmospherical deceptions, like that of the *Fata Morgana*, seen at times in the Straits of Messina, where the city of Reggio and its surrounding country is reflected in the air above the neighbouring sea; a phenomenon which has likewise been witnessed in front of the city of Marseilles. As to the tales of the mariners who had landed on those forbidden shores, and been hurried from thence in whirlwinds and tempests, he considers them as mere fabrications.

As the populace, however, reluctantly give up anything that partakes of the marvellous and mysterious, and as the same atmospherical phenomena which first gave birth to the illusion may still continue, it is not improbable that a belief in the island of St. Brendan may still exist among the ignorant and credulous in the Canaries, and that they at times behold its fairy mountains rising above the distant horizon of the Atlantic.*

V.—Hy-Brazil, the Isle of the Blest.

It will be interesting and instructive to set down beside this account of the "Isle of St. Brendan" the favourite spectacular chimera of the inhabitants of the Canaries, some of the stories that have been told of similar atmospherical illusions, visible from the western coasts of Ireland, which induced among the inhabitants there a firm belief in the existence of the famed Hy-Brazil, at some leagues distance off our western shores.

Mr. James Hardiman † tells us:—"The inhabitants of the western coasts of Ireland think they frequently see emerging from the ocean certain 'happy islands,' which they suppose to be bound by some ancient power of enchantment. The belief in the existence of these *Miranda loca,* which Usher informs us were seen in the ocean by St. Brendan, seems in former times not to have been confined to the vulgar. In an unpublished MS. History of Ireland, written about 1630, now in the library of the Royal Irish Academy, we are gravely told that 'the *Tuathdedanans* coming in upon the *Firbolgs,* expelled them into the out islands which lay scattered

* *Life of Columbus,* Appendix No. xxiii.
† *Irish Minstrelsy,* vol. i., pp. 368-371.

on the north coasts, and they themselves were served in the same measure by the *Clanna Milidhes*;* but what became of the remainder of them, I cannot learne, unless they doe inhabitt an iland which lyeth far att sea, on the west of Connaught, and sometimes is perceived by the inhabitants of the *Oules* and *Iris*. It is also said to be sometime seene from St. Helen's Head, being the farthest west point of land beyond the haven of Calbeggs (Killibeggs), Co. Donegal. Likewise several seamen have discovered it att sea, as they sailed on the western coasts; one of whom, named Captain Rich, who lives about Dublin, of late years had a view of the land, and was so neere that he discovered a harbour, as he supposed by the two headlands at either side thereof, but could never make to land, although when he lost sight thereof in a mist which fell upon him, he held the same course several hours afterwards. In many old mapps (especially mapps of Europe, or of the world) you shall find this land by the name of *O'Brasile*, under the longitude of 03° 00′, and the latitude of 50° 20′. So that it may be, those famous enchanters, the *Tuathdedanans*, now inhabit there, and by their magic skill conceal their iland from forraeigners.'

"But the most complete account of this fanciful island is to be found in a letter from a gentleman in Derry, named William Hamilton, to his friend in England, printed in London, in A.D. 1675, in a pamphlet which is now so scarce, that I am induced to lay it entire before the reader. It is entitled, '*O'Brazile, or the*

* The Milesians, or descendants of Milesius.

Enchanted Island, being a perfect relation of the late discovery, and wonderful dis-inchantment of an island off the north of Ireland.' *

" HONORED COUSEN,

. . . In requital of your news concerning the well-deserved fatal end of that arch-pirate, Captain Cusacke, I shall acquaint you with a story no less true, but much more strange and wonderful, concerning the discovery of that long talk't-of island, *O'Brazile*, which you have often heard of. I know there are in the world many stories and romances, concerning enchanted islands, castles, towers, &c.; and that our king's dominions may be nothing inferiour to any other nation, we have had an enchanted island on the north of Ireland. When I went first into the kingdom of Ireland to live, and heard these stories, which were common in every one's mouth, about this island of *O'Brazile* (as they called it), which multitudes reported often to be seen upon the coast of Ulster, I look't upon it as a perfect romance, and many times laught the reporters to scorn; though many sober and religious persons would constantly affirm that in bright days (especially in summer time) they could perfectly see a very large absolute island; but after long looking at it, it would disappear. And sometimes one friend and neighbour would call another to behold it, until there would be a considerable number together, who could not be persuaded but that they perfectly saw it; some of them have made towards it with boats, but when they came to the place where they thought it was, they found nothing.

" I confess there were (in those days) two things

* As the whole is too long for insertion here, I will give a few extracts from the "curious narrative."

made me a little to wonder: firstly, how it came to be inserted into many of our maps, both ancient and modern, by the name of *O'Brazile;* and, secondly, what moved your cousin, who was a wise man and a great scholar, to put himself to the charges and trouble (in the late king's time) *to take out a patent for it, whenever it should be gained.* Since the happy restoration of his majesty that now reigns, many reports have been, that it had been dis-inchanted or taken; yea, at the time of the last parliament in Dublin (in the year 1663), one coming out of *Ulster*, assured the House of Commons (whereof he was a member) that the enchantment was broken and the island gained; but it proved not to be so. About two years after, a certain Quaker pretended that he had a revelation from heaven, that he was the man ordained to take it, and in order thereto he built a vessel; but what became of him or his enterprise, I never heard; it seems that the full time was not then come; but I am now sure that the time or enchantment is now out, and the island fully discovered or taken, 'in this manner.'"

He then goes on to relate at some length how "one Captain *John Nisbet,*" formerly of *Lisneskey*, Co. Fermanagh, but latterly "of *Killybegs*, Co. Dunnegal," discovered this mysterious island, "upon the 2nd of this instant March, 1674, after a most terrible thick mist of fog had cleared away," when he found himself upon a certain coast, close by the shore. Here the captain and some of the crew landed, and met with a variety of adventures that are related in detail, but which I need not repeat here. The correspondent winds up his relation by the assurance: "Dear Cousin, you need not be afraid to relate all this, for I assure you, beside the general discourse of the gentlemen in the country, I had it from Captain Nisbet's own mouth, since which several gentlemen have sent an express, with the true relation of it, under their hands and seals, to some eminent persons in Dublin.

"Your most affectionate Cousin,

"WM. HAMILTON.

"LONDONDERRY, *March* 14*th*, 1674."

It is very likely that the "learned Father Feyjoo," who pronounced so strongly upon "the mariners' tales" about the "Island of St. Brendan," as seen from the Canaries, would not be complimentary to Cousin Hamilton of Derry, for his "curious narrative" of the disenchantment of *O-Brazile* by the Killebegs captain and his ship's crew, and would not hesitate to declare his relation to be "a mere fabrication" *with a circumstance.* There can be no doubt that such atmospheric deceptions as led to the belief in the existence of this fanciful island of Hy-Brazail, were visible, not only from the shores of Western Donegal, but along the western coasts of Connaught and Munster whenever and wherever the conditions of sea and sky were favourable to their production; but the phenomena did not always assume the shape of an island, for they put on various appearances, which were sometimes very curious and fantastic. In O'Flaherty's *West Connaught* * we have an account of some strange atmospheric illusions occasionally visible from the Isles of Aran. "From those isles and the west continent often appears visible that enchanted island called O'Brasil,†

* Hardiman's edition, page 69.

† "The people of Aran say that O'Brasil appears but once every seven years."—Hardiman's Note, page 69.

and in Irish Beg-ara, or the Lesser Aran, set down in cards of navigation. Whether it be reall and firm land, kept hidden by speciall ordinance of God, as the terrestiall paradise, or else some illusion of airy clouds appearing on the surface of the sea, or the craft of evill spirits, is more than our judgments can sound out. There is, westward of Aran, a wild island of huge rocks (Skird Rocks) the receptacle of a deale of seales thereon yearly slaughtered. These rocks sometimes appear to be a great city far off, full of houses, castles, towers, and chimneys; sometimes full of blazing flames, smoak, and people running to and fro. Another day you would see nothing but a number of ships, with their sailes and riggings; then so many great stacks or reekes of corn and turf; and this not only on fair sun-shining days, whereby it might be thought the reflection of the sun-beams on the vapors rising about it had been the cause, but alsoe on dark and cloudy days."

Some years ago I got a description of phenomena similar to those visible from the Aran Islands from an intelligent man who lived near the Sandhills on the western coast of Ardfert parish, who had himself witnessed them a short time previously. He told me that about noon on a bright summer day he was doing some business on the sandhills near Ballinprior when, on looking seaward, his attention was suddenly arrested by an extraordinary spectacle, visible over the sea, apparently midways between Kerry Head and the outer Magheree Island, which, while he looked on for an hour or more assumed different aspects, sometimes like a large town with a number of spires and chimneys; then it seemed to be pasture land with cattle grazing about it; and again, some ships in full sail came into view. All at once the whole vanished from his sight, "like the baseless fabric of a vision, leaving not a wrack behind."

In connection with the view of *Hy-Brasail* from the Aran Isles, I will insert the fine poem of Gerald Griffin on the subject:—

HY-BRASAIL,* THE ISLE OF THE BLEST.

On the ocean that hollows the rocks where ye dwell,
A shadowy land has appeared, as they tell;
Men thought it a region of sunshine and rest,
And they called it *Hy-Brasail*, the isle of the blest.
From year unto year, on the ocean's blue rim,
The beautiful spectre showed lovely and dim;
The golden clouds curtained the deep where it lay,
And it looked like an Eden, away, far away!

A peasant who heard of the wonderful tale,
In the breeze of the Orient loosened his sail;
From Ara, the holy, he turned to the West,
For though Ara was holy, *Hy-Brasail* was blest.
He heard not the voices that called from the shore,
He heard not the rising wind's menacing roar;
Home, kindred, and safety, he left on that day,
And he sped to *Hy-Brasail*, away, far away.

Morn rose on the deep, and that shadowy isle,
O'er the faint rim of distance, reflected its smile;
Noon burned on the wave and that shadowy shore
Seemed lovelily distant, and faint as before;
Lone evening came down on the wanderer's track,
And to Ara again he looked timidly back;
Oh! far on the verge of the ocean it lay,
Yet the isle of the blest was away, far away!

* *Hy-Brasail*, not O'*Brasail*, is the correct form of the name, for the etymology plainly is *I*, or *Hy* (island), and *brath* (for ever) or *breadh* (happy)—*Saoghal* (life) = Isle of everlasting—or happy life, or "Isle of the Blest."

Rash dreamer, return! O, ye winds of the main,
Bear him back to his own peaceful Ara again;
Rash fool! for a vision of fanciful bliss,
To barter thy calm life of labour and peace.
The warning of reason was spoken in vain;
He never revisited Ara again!
Night fell on the deep, amidst tempest and spray,
And he died on the waters, away, far away!

Appendix.

EARLY ENGLISH METRICAL LIFE AND EARLY ENGLISH PROSE LIFE OF ST. BRENDAN.

Those interesting early English versions of the Brendan Voyages, were edited for the Percy Society, by Mr. Thomas Wright, F.S.A., who was its Secretary and Treasurer, and published, in 1844, by that Society in a volume of *Early English Poetry and Popular Literature of the Middle Ages*, which was the fourteenth volume of the series of the publications of the "Percy Society." Those publications are now exceedingly rare, and difficult to be obtained, being accessible only in some of our public libraries. I found the whole series, some years ago, in the Library of Trinity College, Dublin, where it is marked (B. MM. 14); and, desiring to re-publish those early English versions of the Brendan Legend, I asked permission to take a copy from which I could get them printed. I have to thank the Rev. Dr. S. Haughton, Senior Fellow, T.C.D., for his great kindness, in not only obtaining permission to have a copy made for me, but in getting the copy made by one of the regular copyists employed in the Library, and sent to me, at his own expense. I give not only the versions—Metrical and Prose—but also the valuable Preface and Notes of the Editor, Mr. Thomas Wright, which will add very much to the interest of this portion of "Brendaniana."

PREFACE.

One of the most remarkable and widely-spread legends o the Middle Ages, was that of St. Brendan. Almost all nations which lived near the sea have had their legendary navigators. St. Brandan was a Christian Ulysses, and his story had much the same influence on the Western Catholics as the *Odyssey* upon the Greeks. There are several remarkable points of similarity between St. Brendan and the Sinbad of the Arabian Nights, and at least one incident in the two narratives is identical—that of the disaster on the back of the great fish. How far the Christians of the West were acquainted with the story of Sinbad, it is difficult to say; but we have nearly conclusive reasons for believing that the legend of St. Brendan was known at an early period to the Arabs. Some of the Arabian geographers describe the "Island of Sheep," and the "Island of Birds," in the Western Ocean, in words which must have been taken from our Christian legend.

The legend of St. Brendan exercised an influence on geographical science down to a late period, and it entered as an important element into the feelings of the Spanish sailors when they went to the discovery of America. There are, indeed, some incidents in the legend which might be supposed to have arisen from the traditional stories of early adventurers (for such there were, without doubt), who had been accidentally or designedly carried far out in the extreme west. So late as the end of the sixteenth century, the Spaniards and Portuguese believed in the existence of the Isle of St. Brendan, situated in the direction of the Canaries, which was seen sometimes by accident, but which could never be found when sought for (*quando se busca no se halla*). This notion existed still later in Ireland. Several expeditions were fitted out by the Spaniards in search of this island; a king of Portugal is said to have made a conditional cession of it to another person, "when it should be found;" and when the crown of Portugal ceded its right over the Canaries to the Castilians, the treaty included the Island of St. Brendan, as the *island which had not been found.* There were many who believed that this isle of St. Brendan had served as the retreat of Don Rodrigo, when Spain was invaded by the Arabs, and at a later period of King Sebastian, after the fatal battle of Alcazar.

As far as I have been able to trace the history of the legend of St. Brendan, I am inclined to think that it first took the definite form in which it afterwards appeared, in the latter part of the eleventh century; at which time, probably, the Latin prose narrative was written; although I think M. Jubinal has somewhat overrated the antiquity of the manuscripts used for his edition. Metrical versions of the legend, in Latin and Anglo-Norman, appeared in England as early as the reign of Henry I., and are preserved in manuscripts in the British Museum; the Latin one in Ms. Cotton. Vepas. D. xi.; and the Anglo-Norman version, dedicated to Henry's queen, Aaliz, in Ms. Cotton. Vespas. B.X.

The MSS. of the prose Latin text are very numerous; it has been edited, with early French versions in prose and verse, by M. Achille Jubinal, in an interesting volume entitled, *La Legende Latine de S. Brandaines, avec une traduction inédite en prose et en poésie Romanes*, 8vo., Paris, 1836; to which I refer for further information on the subject, and for an account of the numerous other versions in almost every language of the West, several of which were printed in the earlier ages of typography.

The English metrical version of this legend, now printed for the first time, is extracted from the early metrical series of Saints' Lives, which is so frequently met with among English manuscripts, and which appears to have been composed towards the end of the thirteenth, or beginning of the fourteenth century The copy from which it is here printed (MS. Harl., No. 2277, fol. 41, V°.) is of the earlier part of the fourteenth century. This version is somewhat abridged from the Latin text, and differs so much from it in one or two circumstances, that it would appear to have been taken immediately from some other source. The English prose version is taken froṁ Wynkyn de Worde's edition of the *Golden Legend* (Lond. 1527), and may assist such of our readers as are less intimately acquainted with the language of the fourteenth century in understanding the metrical legend. I have never examined into the question of the immediate source of the Lives in the English *Golden Legend;* but there is such a close resemblance between the two versions here printed, not unfrequently approaching to an identity of words, that there can be little doubt of the one having been taken from the other. In the few hasty notes thrown together at the end, I have selected two or three various readings from a collation (made several years ago) of the text of the Harleian manuscripts, with a good copy of the *Metrical Saints' Lives* in the library of Trinity College, Cambridge. R. 3, 25.

THOMAS WRIGHT, F.R.S.

THE METRICAL LIFE OF ST. BRENDAN.

Seint Brendan the holi man was *ȝund of Irlande;
Monek he was of hard lyf, as ich understonde,
Of fasting, of penance y-nouȝ; abbod he was there
Of a thousend monekes that alle an under him were.
So that hit ful an a dai, as oure Loverdes wille was,
That Barint, another abbot, to him com bi cas;
Seint Brendan him bisoȝte anon that he scholde understonde,
And telle that he i-seȝ aboute in other londe.
This gode man, tho he hurde this, sikinges he makede
y-nowe,
And bigan to wepe in gret thoȝt, and ful adoun i-suoȝe.
Bituene his armes Seint Brendan this holi man up nom
And custe and cride on him forte that his wit aȝe com.
"Fader," he seide, "par charité, other red thu most take;
Hither thu com for oure solaz, and for such deol to make,
Tel ous what thu hast i-seȝe, as thu hast aboute i-wend
In the mochele see of occian, as oure Loverd the hath i-send."
Nou is the see of occian grettest and mest also,
For he goth the wordle aboute and alle othere goth therto.
So that Barint the olde man riȝt at his hurte grounde,
Wel wepinge began to telle what he er founde;
He seide, "Ich hadde a godsone, Mernoc was his name,
Monek he was as we beoth, and man of grete fame,
So that his hurte gan wende to a privei stede and stille,
Ther he miȝte alone beo to servi God at wille;
So that bi mi leve he wende and alone drouȝ
To an ylle that is in the see that is delitable y-nouȝ,
Biside the Montayne of Stones that couth is well wide.
So longe that this gode monek in this ylle gan abide,
That he had under him monekes meni on.
Anon tho ich i-hurde this, thider-ward ich gan gon,
So that in avisioun oure suete Loverd him kende,
That aȝe me, er ich come ther, threo journeyes he wende,
So that we dude ous in a schip, and evere est-ward we drowe
In the see of occian with turmentz y-nowe.

* This *digraph* means either *gh*, or *dh*, or *y*, according to *context*.

Toward than est so fur we wende, that we comme atte laste
In a stude suythe durc and clouden overcaste;
Al o tide of the dai we were in durchede.
Atte laste oure suete Loverd forthere ous gan lede,
So that we seȝe ane lond, thiderward oure schip drouȝ,
Briȝttere hit thoȝte than the sonne, joye there was y-nouȝ.
Of treon, of erbes, thikke hit stod biset in eche side;
Of preciose stones ek that briȝte schyneth wide;
Eche erbe was ful of floures, eche treo ful of frut,
Bote hit were in hevene nas nevere more dedut.
Therinne with joye y-nouȝ longe we'gonne wende;
Theȝ hit ous lute while thoȝe, we ne miȝte fynde non ende,
So that we come to a water cler and briȝt y-nouȝ,
That evene fram-ward than est to-ward thane west drouȝ.
We stode and bihulde aboute, for we ne miȝte over wende;
Ther com to ous a ȝung man suythe fair and hende,
He welcomede ous everechon miltheliche and suete,
And nemnede evereches oure name, and wel myldeliche ous
gan grete,
And seide, "ȝe miȝte wel Jhesu Crist wel faire thonki mid
riȝte,
That schoweth you his priveité and so moche of his miȝte.
This the londe that he wole ȝut er the worldes ende
His durlings an urthe ȝeve, and hider hi schulle wende;
This lond is half in this side, as ȝe seoth wel wide,
And biȝunde the water halfen—del al bi thother side.
That water ne mowe ȝe passi noȝt, that other del to i-seo,
Her ȝe habbeth al a ȝer meteles i-beo,
That ȝe ne ete ne drinke nȝot, ne slepe mid ȝoure eȝe;
Ne chile ne hete ne fonde ȝe noȝt, ne no nyȝt i-seȝe;
For this is Godes privé stede thurf him is al this liȝt,
Therefore hit worth her evre dai, and nevre more niȝt.
If man nadde aȝe Godes heste nothing mis-do,
Herinne hi hadde ȝut i-lyved and here ofspring also.
ȝe ne mote bileve her no leng, agen ye mote fare,
They hit ne thenche ȝou bote a while, ȝe habbeth i-beo her
ȝare."
That so he brouȝte ous in our schip, and faire his leve nom:
And tho we were ham-ward in the see, we nuste whar he
bicum.
Aȝe-ward we wende aȝen oure wille, that of-thoȝte ous sore
y-nouȝ,
Aȝen to this other monekes this schip wel evene drouȝ;

This monekes urne aȝen ous, tho hi ous miȝte i-seo,
And sori were and wrothe y-nouȝ that we hadde so long
i-beo.
We seide hem that we hadde i-beo in alle joye and feste,
Bifore the ȝates of Paradys, in the lond of biheste,
That oure suete Loverd hath bihote hem that he loveth her,
Ther is evere dai, and nevere niȝt, and evere liȝt suythe cler,
"Certes," quath this monekes, "this we mowe i-seo
Bi the suete smyl of you, that ȝe habbeth ther i-beo."

THO Seint Brendan i-hurde this, he thoȝte and stod
stille;
He wende about his monekes, and tuelve out he nom,
That he triste to mest of alle whan eni neode him com;
Thuse he nom in Consail, and in priveté sede,
"Siggeth what youre Consail is to do such a dede."
"Leove fader," quath this othere, "oure wille we habbeth
forsake,
Oure freond and al oure other god, and clanliche to the
i-take;
And whan all oure dede is on the, and thu wost that hit beo,
We schulle blitheliche with the wende Godes grace to seo."
So that hi faste fourti dawes, and gret penance dude also,
And bede ȝurne oure Loverdes grace thulke veyage to do.
Hi leten hem diȝte a gret schip, and above hit al bi-caste
With bole huden stronge y-nou y-nailed thereto faste,
And siththe i-piched al above, that the water ne come.
Hi wende to here bretheren, and wel faire here leve nome,
And siththe in oure Loverdes name to schipe wende anon;
Here bretheren that bihynde were sori were echon.
And tho hi were in the schip, after ther come go tuo,
And bede faste that hi moste thane wei mid hem go.
"ȝe mowe wel," quath Seint Brendan, "acȝoure on schal
atta ende
Repenti er he com aȝe, and al quic to helle wende."
Thider wende this holi man whoder oure Loverd hem sende,
And this tuei monekes that come last also with hem wende.

IN the grete see of occian forth hi rewe faste,
And triste al to oure Loverdes grace, and nothing nere
agaste.
The see drof here schip after wil, the wynd was gret y-nouȝ:

As the wynd hem drof est forth, wel evene the schip him drouȝ
Evene aȝe that the sonne ariseth a midsomers day :
Nou nuste non of hem whar he was, ne no lond he ne say.
Evene forth riȝt fourti dayes the wynd hem drof faste,
So that hi seȝe in the north side a gret ylle atte laste,
Of harde roche and gret y-nou, in the see wel heȝe ;
Threo dayes hi wende ther-aboute er hi mitȝe come ther neȝe.
A lute havene he fonde tho, a-lond hi wende there,
Hi wende a-lond as maskede men. hi nuste war hi were ;
Ther com go a wel fair hound, as hit were hem toslere ;
At Seint Brendanes fet he ful a-doun, and make de faire chere.
" Beau freres," quath Seint Brendan, " ȝe ne thore nothing drede ;
Ich wot this is a messager the riȝte wei ont to lede."
This hound ladde this holi man to an halle fair y-nouȝ,
Gret and stare and suythe noble, evene in he drouȝ.
This monekes fonde in this halle bord and cloth i-sprad,
And bred and fisch ther-uppe y-nouȝ, ther was non that nas glad.
Hi sete a-doun and ete faste, for hem luste wel ther-to ;
Beddes ther wer al ȝare y-maked, er here soper were i-do,
After here soper to bedde hi wende to resten hem as the wise.
Tho hi hadde alle i-slepe y-nouȝ, sone hi gonne arise,
And wende to here schip, as hi hadde er i-beo ;
In the see well longe hi were er hi miȝte lond i-seo.
Tho hi seȝe, as hi thother side, an ylle fair y-nouȝ,
Grene and wel fair lese, thider-ward here schip drouȝ.
Tho hi come on this faire lond, and bihulde about wide,
The faireste scheep that miȝte beo hi seȝe in eche side ;
A scheep was grettere than an oxe, whittere ne miȝte non beo,
Gret joye hi hadde in here hurte, that hi miȝte thus i-seo.
Ther com go a wel fair man, and grette hem with faire chere,
And seide, " ȝe beoth hider i-come ther ȝe nevere nere :
This is i-cliped the Lond of Scheep, for scheep wel faire her beoth,
Mochele and white and grete y-nouȝ, as ȝe al dai i-seoth ;
Fairere hi beoth than ȝoure scheep, grettere unyliche,
For marie weder is her y-nouȝ, and lese suythe riche,
Her nis nevere wynter non, for her nis non i-founde,
Achi eteth therbes nue as hi springeth of the g[ro]unde ;

Ne me negadereth noȝt of here mule, that hi schold the worse beo,
For this thing and meni other the bet hi mowe i-theo.
To a stede ȝe schulle hunne wende, thurf oure Loverdes grace,
That is Foweles Parays, a wel joyful place;
Ther ȝe shulle thus Ester beo, and this Witsonedai also.
Wendeth forth a Godes name, that this veyage were i-do!"

SEINT BRENDAN and his bretheren to schipe wende anon,
And rue forthe faste in the see, with tempest meni on,
So that hi seȝe in another side an ylle gret y-nouȝ;
Here schip thurf Godes grace thider-wardes drouȝ,
Tho hit cam almest ther-to, upe the roche hit gan ride,
That hit ne miȝte noȝt to the ylle come, ac bilevede biside.
This monekes wende up to this ylle, ac Seint Brendan noȝt;
This monekes gonne make here mete of that hi badde i-broȝt.
Hi makede fur, and soden hem fisch in a caudroun faste;
Er this fische were i-sode, somdel hi were agaste.
For tho this fur was thurf hot, the yle quakede anon,
And with gret eir hupte al up: this monekes dradde echon,
Hi bihulde hou the yle in the see wende faste,
And as a quic thing hupte up and doun, and that fur fram him caste.
He suam more than tuei myle while this fur i-laste.
The monekes i-seȝe the fur wel longe, and were sore agaste:
Hi cride ȝurne on Seint Brendan, what the wonder were.
"Beoth stille," quath this gode man, "for noȝt ȝe nabbe fere!
ȝe weneth that hit beo an yle, acȝe thencheth amis,
Hit is a fisch of this grete see, the gretteste that there is,
Jascom he is i-cleped, and fondeth niȝt and dai
To putte his tail in his mouth, ac for gretnisse he ne mai."
Forth hi rue in the see evene west wel faste
Threo dayes er hi seȝe lond, hi were somdel agaste;
Tho seȝen hi a wel fair lond, of floures thikke y-nouȝ.
Wel glade hi were tho hi seȝe that here schip thider drouȝ.
In this faire lond hi wende lengere than ich telle,
So that hi fonde in a place a suythe noble welle;
Bi the welle stode a treo, brod and round y-nouȝ,
Foweles white and faire y-nouȝ were in everech bouȝ,
That unethe eni leef hi miȝte theron i-seo,
Ther was joye and blisse y-nouȝ to lokie on suche o treo.

SEINT BRENDAN for joye wep, and sat a-doun a-kneo,
And bad oure Loverd schowi him what such a cas miȝte beo.
Tho fleȝ ther up a lute fowel, tho he gan to fleo,
As a fithele his wynges furde tho he to him-ward gan teo;
Murie instrument nevere nas that his wyngen were.
He bihuld Seint Brendan with wel faire chere.
"Ich hote," seide Seint Brendan, "if thu ert messager,
That thu sigge me what ert, and what ȝe doth her."
Theȝ hit thoȝte aȝe cunde, this fowel ansuerede anon,
"We were," he seide, "some tyme was, angeles in hevene echon;
As sone as we were y-maked, oure maister was to prout,
Lucefer, for his fairhede, that he fel sone out,
And mid him also meni on, as here dede was,
And we fulle also a-doun, ac for no synne hit nas,
Ac for nothing that we assentede to his foule unriȝt,
Bote soulement for to schewe oure Loverdes suete miȝte;
Ne we ne beoth her in pyne non, ac in joye y-nouȝ we beoth,
And somdel oure suete Loverdes miȝte we seoth,
And bi the woithe we fleoth, and by the lifte also,
As gode angles and lithere ek riȝt is for to do,
The gode to do men god, the lithere lithere makieth;
And sonedai, that is dai of rest, such forme we maketh,
The forme of suche white foweles as thu miȝt i-seo,
Honnreth God that ous makede her on this brode treo.
Tuelf month hit i-passed nou, that ȝe gunne out wende,
And all this six ȝer e schulle fare, er ȝe schulle bringe ȝoure wille to ende;
For whan ȝe habbeth i-wend sove ȝer oure Loverd wole ȝou sende
A siȝt that ȝe habbeth longe i-soȝt, anon after the sove ȝeres ende;
Eche ȝer ȝe schulle her mid ous holde Ester feste,
As ȝe nou doth, forte ȝe come to the lond of biheste."
Nou was hit an Esterdai that all this was i-do:
The fowel nom his leve of hem, and to his felawes wende tho.
The foweles tho hit eve was, bigonne here evesong;
Muriere song ne miȝte i-beo, theȝ God silf were among.
The monekes wende to bedde and slepe, the soper was i-do,
And tho hit was tyme of matyns hi arise ther-to.

The foweles sung ek here matyns wel riȝt tho hit was tyme,
And of the Sauter seide the vers, siththe al to prime,
And underne siththe and mid-dai, and afterwardes non,
And eche tyde songen of the dai as cristene men scholde don.
This monekes were in the lond eiȝte wyke also,
For to al the feste of Ester and of Witsonedai were i-do;
Tho com átte Trinité this gode man to hem ther,
That spac with hem in the Lond of Scheep, and ladde
about er.
He chargede here schip suythe wel mid mete and drinke
y-nouȝ,
And nom his leve wel hendeliche, and aȝe-ward drouȝ.
The seint Brendan was in his schip and his bretheren also,
This fowel that spac with hem er, wel sone com hem to.
He seide, "ȝe habbeth her with ous this heȝe feste i-beo,
Gret travayl ȝou is to come er ȝe eftsone lond i-seo;
ȝe schulleth after sove monthes, i-seo a wel fair yle,
That Abbey is i-cliped, that is hunne meni a myle.
ȝe schulleth beo mid holie men this mydewynter there,
ȝoure Ester ȝe schulle holde ther as ȝe dude to ȝere,
Upe the grete fisches rugge, ther thi monekes were in fere,
And ȝoure Ester mid ous riȝt as ȝe nou were.
Seint Brendan a Godes name, and his bretheren echon,
In the grete see of occian forth wende anon;
The wynde hem harlede up and doun in peryls meni on,
So weri hi were of here lyve, that hi muste whoder gon.
Four monthes hi were in the see, in this grete turment,
That hi ne seȝe nothing bote the see and the firmament;
Tho seȝen hi fur fram hem an ylle as hit were,
He cride ȝurne on Jhesu Crist that hi muste aryve there.
ȝut after than that Seint Brendan furst this yle i-seȝ,
In the see hi wende fourti dayes er hi miȝte come ter neȝ;
That hem thoȝte here lyf hem was loth, this monekes were
agaste,
Hi cride ȝurne on Jhesu Crist, and his help hede faste.
A lute havene suythe streit hi fonde atte laste,
Unethe here schip com ther neȝ, here ankre ther hi cast.
This monekes wende ther a-lond, wel longehem thoȝte er,
Hi wende and bihulde aboute, wel murie hem thoȝte ther,
So that hi seȝe tuei faire wellen, that on was suythe cler,
And thother wori and thikke y-nou; the monekes ȝeode ner,
To drinke of this faire wil; Seint Brende seide tho he hit i-seȝ,
"Withoute leve of other men ne come noȝt ther neȝ,

Of olde men that therinne beoth, for mid gode wille
Hi wolleth parti therof with ȝou, therfore beoth ȝut stille.'
A fair old man and suythe hor aȝen hem com gon,
He wolcomede hem fairė y-nouȝ, and Seint Brendan custe
anon.
He nom and ladde him bi the hond bi a fair wei,
Aboute into meni o stede, and siththe into an abbei.
Seint Brendan bihulde aboute, and eschte what hit were,
And what maner men were therinne, and ho wonede there;
Stille him was that olde man, and no ȝaf him non ansuere.
Tho seȝe hi come a fair covent, and a croice to-fore hem
bere,
With taperes in eche side, monekes hit were echon,
Revested in faire copes aȝen hem hi come anon,
With processioun fair y-nou; the Abbot bihynde cum,
And faire custe Seint Brendan and bi the hond him nom,
And ladde him and his monekes into a wel fair halle,
And sette hem a-doun a-renk, and wasche here fet alle.
Of the wori wel hi wasche here fet, that hi er i-seȝe;
Into the freitour hi hadde hem siththe and sette him ther
wed heȝe
I-melled with his owe Covent; tho hi were alle i-sete,
Ther com on and servede hem, and brouȝte hem alle mete;
A fair whit lof he sette, bituene tuo and tuo,
White mores as hit were of erbes bifore him sette also,
Suettere thing ne miȝte beo, hi ne knewe hit noȝt on,
Of the clere wel that hi seȝe er the monekes dronke echon.
"Beoth nou glade," the Abbot seide, "and drinketh nou
y-nouȝ,
In charité, of thulke water that ȝe wolde er with wouȝ;
Hit is betere dronke in charité, whan hit is ȝou i-brouȝt,
Than ȝe hit theofliche nome, as ȝe hadde er i-thoȝt
This bred that we eteth nou, we nuteth whanne hit is,
Ac a strong man hit bringeth ech dai to oure celer i-wis;
We nuteth noȝt bote thurf God whanneȝ hit is i-brouȝt
For ho so douteth Jhesu Crist, him ne failleth nouȝt.
Four and tuenti freres we beoth her, and whan we beoth
i-sete,
Tuelf suche loves eche dai he bringeth ous to mete;
And feste and everech holi day, and whan hit Sonedai is,
He bringith o us four and tuenti loves, and ech monek
haveth his,
That ech frere of that he leveth wite to his soper;

For ȝou hit is to-dai i-dubled, as ȝe seoth nou her
For oure covent nis noȝt her, for moche del is un-y-ete,
So that oure Loverd thurf His grace ech dai sendeth oure mete,
Siththe Seint Patrikes dai, and Seint Alvey also.
We habbeth i-beo her fourscore ȝer that noman ne com ous to;
Evereft oure Loverd thurf his grace i-fed ous hath echon.
This weder is murie evere ek, and sicknisse nis ther non.
And whan we schule do oure servise, oure Loverd tent oure liȝt,
And oure taperes ne beoth nothe lasse, theȝ hi berne day and nyȝt."
Hi arise up and to churche wende, tho hi hadde alle y-ete,
Tuelf other freres of the queor hi mette to-ward the mete.
"Hou is this?" quath Seint Brendan, "nere thuse noȝt with ous?"
"Leove fader," the Abbot seide, "hit mot nede beo thus:
Ther nulleth bote four and tuenti monekes in oure celle beo i-do,
And whan ȝe were ther with ous hi ne miȝte noȝt also;
The while we siggeth eve-song hi wolleth sitte and ete,
Here eve-song hi wolleth sigge whan we habbeth y-ete."

SEINT BRENDAN bihuld here fair weved, him thoȝte hit was al,
Weveth and caliz and cruetz, pur cler crestal;
Sove tapres in the queor ther were, and nomo,
And four and tuenti sigen ek, to whan hi scholde go;
For ther were four and tuenti monekes, and everech hadde his,
And the Abbotes sige was amidde the queor i-wis.
Seint Brendan echte the Abbot, "Sei me, leove brother,
Hou holde ȝe so wel silence, that non ne speketh mid other?"
"Oure Loverd hit wot," the Abbot seide, "we habbeth her i-beo,
Fourscore ȝer in such lyve as thu miȝte i-seo,
And ther nas nevere among ous alle i-speke in non wise
Er this tyme non other word bote oure Loverdes servise,
Ne we nere never-eft in feblesce, ne in siknesse noȝt on,"
Tho Seint Brendan i-hurde this he wep for joye anon:
"Leove fader," he seide, "for Godes love, mote we bileve here?"

"The wost wel, sir," quath this other, "ȝe ne mowe in none manere.
Nath oure Loverd the schowed wel what thu schalt do?
And come ȝut to Irland aȝe, and thi tuelf bretheren also,
And the thretteoth fram the to the ylle of ankres schal wende,
And the fourteothe to helle al quic, and beo ther withouten ende?"
Tho ther com in a furi arewe at a fenestre anon,
As he fram hevene come, and the tapres tende echon;
Aȝe-ward as he com at a fenestre there,
This tapres brende longe y-nouȝ, ac hi no the lasse nere,
"Loverd Crist," quath Seint Brendan, "ich wondri on mi thoȝt,
Hou this tapres berneth thus, an ne wanyeth noȝt."
"Nastou noȝt," quath this Abbot, "in the olde lawe i-founde,
Hou Moyses i-seȝ a thorn berne fram toppe to the grounde?
The suythere that this thorn brende the grennere the leves were:
Ne wenstou that oure Loverd beo her as miȝti as he was there?"
This monekes were togadere thus forte midewynter was i-do;
Hit was tuelfthe dai er hi departede a-tuo.

ANON to Seint Hillarie's dai Seint Brendan forthe wende,
In the see with his monekes, thur the grace that God hem sende,
Urne up and doun in sorwe y-nouȝ, the see hem caste heȝe.
Fram thulke tyme fur in Leynte ne lond hi ne seȝe,
So that aboute Palmsonede [i] hi bihulde aboute faste,
Hi thoȝte that hi seȝe fur fram hem as a cloude atte laste.
This monekes wondrede moche whar this cloude were:
"Beoth stille," quath Seint Brendan, "er this ȝe habbeth i-beo there;
Ther is oure gode procuratour, that moche god ous haveth i-do,
In the Fowelen Parays and in the Lond of Scheep also.
So that the schip atte laste to-ward this yle drouȝ,
A Scher-thursdai thider hi come, with travayl and sorwe y-nouȝ.

This procuratour com aȝen hem glad, and wolcome hem anon,
And custe Seint Brendanes fet, and the monekes echon,
And sitte hem siththe atte soper, for the dai hit wolde so,
And siththe wosch here alre fet, here mandé to do.
Al here mandé hi hulde ther, and ther hi gonne bileve
A Gode-Fridai aldai forto Ester eve;
An Ester eve here procuratour bad hem here schip take,
And the holi resureccioun upe the fisches rug make,
And after the resureccioun he het hem evene teo
To the Fowelen Parays, ther hi hadde er i-beo.

THIS holi men wende forth, and Godes grace nome,
So that to the grete fisch wel sone siththe hi come;
As a lond that hovede, here caudron hi fonde there,
As hi levede upon his rug in that other ȝere,
Loverd Crist! that such a best scholde beo so stille,
And suffri men ther-uppe go, and do al here wille.

THE monekes upe the fisches rug bilevede alle longe nyȝt,
And songe matyns and eve-song, and siththe, tho his was liȝt,
Anone-ward the fisches rug hi songen here massen echon,
And evere was this mochele best stille so eni ston.

AS this resurexioun with gret honur was i-do,
And this monekes hadde i-songe here massen also,
Aboute underne of the dai here wei to schipe hi nome,
And to the Fowelen Parays thulke dai hi come.

ANON so hi seȝe the monekes come, hi gonne to singe ymone,
Aȝen hem with gret melodie, as hit were for than one;
And thulke that spac with hem er sone toward hem drouȝ.
The soun of him murie was, he wolcome de hem faire y-nouȝ:
"ȝe anȝte," he seide, "Oure Loverd Crist onury with the beste,
He purveide ȝou this four stedes to habben in ȝoure reste,
With ȝoure gode procuratour, ȝoure mandé to do,
And siththe ȝoure resurexioun upe this fisches rug also,
And with ous her this eiȝte wyke for to Witsonedai,

And fram Midewynter to Candelmasse in thille of Abbai;
And in the grete see of occian with gret travayl ȝe schulle wende,
And in pyne al thother tyme, forte sove ȝeres ende:
And the Lond of Biheste God wole that ȝe seo,
And ther-inne in joye y-nouȝ fourti dayes beo;
And to the contrai that ȝe beoth of siththe ȝe schulle wende,
Al eseliche without anuy, and ther ȝoure lyf ende.

THIS holi men bilevede ther forte the Trinité,
Here procuratour com to hem ther hi were in gret plenté;
He brouȝte hem mete and drinke y-nouȝ, as he hadde er i-do,
And chargede here schip therwith and let hem wende so.

THIS holi men hem wende forth as God hem wolde sende,
For Godes grace was with hem the bet hi miȝte wende.
As hi wende upon a tyme in gret tempest y-nouȝ,
A gret fisch hi seȝe and grislich, that after here schip drouȝ;
Berninge from out of his mouth he caste,
The water was heȝere than here schip bifore hem at eche blaste,
With his browen wel faste he schef; this monekes were agaste,
And cride ȝurne on Jhesu Crist, and in Seint Brendan also.
After the schip so faste he schef that almest he com therto:
As he hem hadde almest of-take, and hi ne tolde noȝt of here lyve,
Another fisch out of the west ther com suymminge blyve,
And encountrede this lithere fisch, and smot to him faste,
And for-clef his foule book in threo parties atte laste,
And thane wei as he cam er wel evene aȝe he drouȝ.
This monekes thonkede Jhesu Crist, and were joyful y-nouȝ.
So longe hi wende this holi men in the see aboute so,
That hi were afingred sore, for here mete was al i-do.
Ther com fleo a lute fowel, and brouȝte a gret bouȝ
Ful of grapes suythe rede, and evene to hem drouȝ;
This grapes he tok Seint Brendan, this gode man sumdel louȝ,
Ther-bi hi lyvede fourte nyȝt, and hadde alle mete y-nouȝ.

THO this grapes were all i-do, hi were afingred sore,
Bi that o side hi seȝe an yle, and mete ther-inne more:
The yle was ful of faire treon, and so ful everech bouȝ
Of suche grapes as he seȝ er, that to the ground hit drouȝ.
Seint Brendan wende up of this schip, of this grapes he nom faste,
And bar hem to his schip, that fourti dayes hi laste.
Sone ther-after cam a gryp fleo faste in the see,
And assaillede hem faste, and here schip, and fondede hem to sle.
This monekes cride dulfulliche, and ne told noȝt of here lyve;
Tho com ther flo a lutel fowel toward hem wel blyve,
That in the Fowelen Parays so ofte hem hadde i-rad.
Tho Seint Brendan i-seȝ hem come, he has noȝt a lute glad.
This lutel fowel smot to this grymp, and sette his dunt wel heȝe,
The furste dunt that he him ȝaf he smot out aither eȝe;
This lithere best so he sloȝ that he ful into the see;
Thing that God wole habbe i-wist ne mai nothing sle.
This holi men wende in the sea aboute her and there;
Ac in on of the four stedes in reste evere hi were.

OTYME a Seint Petres dai, grete feste with here tunge
In the see hi makede of Seint Peter, and here servise sunge;
Hi come in o stede of the see, the see so cler hi founde
That hi seȝe on bi eche half clerliche to the grounde.
Hem thoȝte the ground i-heled was with fisches at one hepe,
That hi ne seȝe non other grounde bote as hi leye aslepe.
This monekes hete Seint Brendan that he softe speke,
That hi ne weiȝte noȝt the fisches, leste hi here schip breke.
"What is ȝou ?" quath Seint Brendan "whar-of beo ȝe of-drad?
Upe the maistres rug of alle fisches ȝe habbeth y-maked ȝou glad,
And ano-ward his rug fur y-maked, and doth from ȝere to ȝere."
This holi man makede loudere song, as hit for than one were.

THE fisch sturte upe with here song, as hi awoke of slepe,
And flote al aboute the schip, as hit were at one hepe;

So thikke hi flote aboute bi eche half, that non other water me ne seȝ,
And bisette this schip al aboute, ac hi ne come ther neȝ.
So thikke hi were aboute the schip, and suede hit evere so,
The while this holi man his masse song, forte he hadde i-do;
And tho the masse was i-do, eche wende in his ende.
Moche wonder he mai i-seo, ho so wole aboute wende.
The wynd was strong, and stif y-nouȝ, and drof the schip faste,
As fur as hi wende sove niȝt the clere see i-laste,
So that hi seȝe in the see as clerliche as hi scholde alonde,
Gret wonder hadde the gode men, and thonke de Godes sonde.

THO com ther a southerne wynd, that drof hem forthward faste
Riȝt evene noȝth hi nuste whoder, that eiȝte dawes hit laste;
Tho seȝe hi fur in the north a lond durk y-nouȝ,
Smokie as ther schipes were, thider-ward here schip drouȝ.
Tho hurden hi of bulies gret blowinge there,
And gret beting and noyse y-nouȝ, as ther thundre were;
So that Brendan agaste sore, and him blescede faste.
Ther cam out a grislich wiȝt wel lither atte laste;
Thurf suart and berning al his eȝen upe hem de caste,
And turnde him in anon; this monekes were agaste.
This lither thing maked a cri that me miȝte i-hure wide;
Tho come ther suche schrewen mo wel thicke bi eche side,
With tangen and with hameres berninge meni on,
To the brym hi urne of the see after the schip echon.
Tho hi ne miȝte come ther neȝ, hi gonne to crie faste,
And here oules al brenninge after the monekes caste;
That me ne miȝte nothing bote fur i-seo ne i-hure,
The see as he ful a-doun thoȝte ek al a-fure.
Ech caste upon other his oules al an heȝ,
And aboute the schip in the see, ac nevere ne cam non neȝ.
Atte laste hi turnde hem aȝen, tho hi ne spedde noȝt there,
And al that lond thoȝte hem ek a-fur as theȝ hit were,
And al the see ther-aboute smokede and brende faste
Strong was that stench and that longe i-laste.
Tho the monekes were so fur that hi ne miȝte i-seo no-more,
Here ȝullinge ȝut hi hurde, the schrewen wepe sore.
"Hou thinȝth you," quath Seint Brendon, "was this a murie pas?

We ne wilnyeth come here no more, an ende of helle hit was,
And the develen hopede wel of ous habbe i-had a god cas;
Ac i-hered beo Jhesu Crist, hi caste an ambesas."

THE Southerne wynd i-laste ȝut, and drof hem evere forth,
So that hi seȝe an hulle wel heȝ fur in the north,
Cloudi and berninge smoke, gret stench was there;
The lie of the fur stood an heȝ as hit a was there:
If ther was moche smoke in than other, ȝut was ther wel more.
On of his monkes bigan tho to wepe and ȝulle sore;
For his tyme was to i-come that he ne miȝte no leng abide,
He hipte him amidde the see out of the schip biside,
And orn him faste upon this water to this grisliche fure;
He cride and ȝal so dulfulliche, that ruthe hit was to hure;
"Allas!" he seide, "mi wrecche lyf! for nou ich i-seo myn ende,
Mid ȝou ich habbe in joye i-beo, and y ne mai mid ȝou wende:
Accursed beo heo that me bar, and the tyme that ich was i-bore,
And the fader that me biȝat, for ich am nou for-lore!"

AȝEN him develen come anon, and nome thane wrecche faste,
And defoulede him stronge y-nouȝ, and amidde the fur him caste.
Tho he fonde that Seint Brendan seide tho he out wende,
Him faillede grace, hou so hit was, his lyf to amende.
So stronge brende the mountayne, that nothing hi ne seȝe,
The ȝut hi were fur ther-fram, bote fur and lie.
Tho turnde the wynd into the north; and south-ward hem drof faste,
In thulke side strong y-nouȝ sove nyȝt the wynd i-laste.

SO longe hi wende evene South, that hi seȝe attan ende
A hard rock in the see, and the see ther-over wende;
Ther-over the see caste i-lome and ofte he was bar.
Tho hi come the roche neȝ of other hi were i-war:
Ano-ward the se hi seȝe sitte, wan the see withdrouȝ,
A wrecche gost sitte naked, bar and meseise y-nouȝ;

Above him was a cloth i-teid mid tuei tongen faste,
The nyther ende tilde to his chynne, over al the wynd him
caste,
That the water withdrouȝ, the cloth that heng heȝe
Beot as the wynd bleu the wrecche amidde than eȝe.
The wawes beote him of the see bifore and eke bihynde;
Wrecchedere gost than he was ne mai noman fynde.
Seint Brendan bad him a Godes name telle him what he were,
And what he hadde God mis-do, and whi he sete there.
"Ich am," he seide, "a dulful gost, wrecche Judas,
That for pans oure Loverd solde, and an urthe mid him was;
Nis this noȝt mi riȝte stede, ac oure Loverd me doth grace
To habbe her mi parays, as ȝe seoth, in this place,
For no godnisse that ich habbe i-do, bote of oure Loverdes
milce and ore,
For y ne miȝte habbe so moche pyne that y nere worthe
more;
For in the brenninge hul that ech of ȝou i-say
Mi riȝt is to beo and brenne bothe nyȝt and day.
Ther ich was this other dai tho ȝoure brother thider com,
And was into pyne i-lad, and sone haddie his *dom;*
Therfore helle was the glad y-nouȝ, that he makede the
grettere lye
For joye tho he was i-come that ȝe so fur i-sye.
So he doth whan eni soule furst is thider i-come.
Thurf oure Loverdes suete milce ich am nou thanne y-nome;
For ich am her ech Soneday, and fram the Saterdayes eve
Forte hit beo thane Soneday eve her ich shal bileve,
And at Midewynter ek forte twelfthe day beo i-do,
And fram byginning ek Ester forte Whitsoneday also,
And at oure Lefdi feste ek, for ful of milce heo is;
In al the other tyme of the ȝer in hell ich am i-wis,
With Pilatus, Herodes, Anne, and Kayfas.
Bote ich mai cursi the tyme that ich i-bore was;
And ich bidde ȝou for the love of God that ȝe fondie in alle
wyse,
That ich bileve her al niȝt forte the sonne arise,
And that ȝe wite me fram the develen that cometh sone
after me."

SEINT Brendan seide, "Thurf Godes grace we schulle
schulde the:
Tel me what is the cloth that so heȝe hongeth there.'

"Tho ich was an urthe," quath Judas, "and oure Loverdes pans ber,
This cloth ich ȝaf a mesel, and for myne nas hit noȝt,
Ac hit was mid oure Loverdes pans and mid oure bretherne i-boȝt;
Ac for ich hit ȝaf for Godes love nou hit is me bifore,
For me ne schal nothing for him do that schal beo forlore;
And for hit was other mannes, as myn inwit understod,
Hit me doth theȝ hit hongi her more harm than god,
For hit bet in myn eȝen sore, and doth me harm y-nouȝ."
Her me mai i-seo which hit is to ȝyve other manes with wouȝ,
As woleth meni riche men mid unriȝt al dai take
Of pore men her and thar, and almisse siththe make;
That hi doth for Godes love ne schal hem noȝt beo forȝute,
Ac to pyne hit schal hem turne, as hi mowe thanne wite.
"The tongen also," quath Judas, "that ȝe seoth hongen an heȝ,
Preostes ich ȝaf an urthe, therfore here hi beoth;
For clenliche me schal eche thing fynde that me doth for his love.
The ston upe whan ich sitte, that maketh me sitte above,
Ina wei ich him fond ligge ther no neod nas to ston,
Ich caste him in a dupe dich that me miȝte ther-over gon.
Fewe gode dede ich habbe i-do that iche mowe of telle,
Ac non so lute that y ne fynde her other in helle."

THO hit was eve thane Sonedai, the develen come blaste,
T lede to helle this wrecche gost; hi cride and ȝulle faste,
"Wend hunne," hi seide, "thu Godes man, thu nast noȝt her to done,
Let ous habbe oure felawe and lede to helle sone;
For we ne thore oure maister i-seo er we him habbe i-brouȝt:
Wend from him, for hit is tyme, and ne lette ous nouȝt."
"I lette you noȝt," quath Seint Brendan, "ne ne witie ȝou her,
That doth oure Loverd Jhesu Christ, that is of more poer."

"HOU therstou," quath this develen, "bifore him nemne his name?
Ne bitrayde he him and solde ek te dethe with grete schame?"

Seint Brendan seide, "In his name ich hote ȝou as ich mai,
That ȝe ne tuouche him noȝt to niȝt, er to morwe that hit
beo day."
Grisliche the develen ȝulle, and aȝen gonne fleo.
Judas thonkede pitousliche, that deol hit was to seo.
A-morwe, so sone as hit was dai, the develen gonne blaste,
Grisliche hi cride and ȝulle also, and chidde also faste,
"Awei!" he seide, "thu Godes man, acursed beo the stounde
That thu come her owhar about, and that we there here
founde:
Oure maister ous hath i-turmented so grisliche allonge niȝt,
And stronge y-nouȝ, for we ne brouȝte mid ous this lithere
wiȝt.
Ac we wolleth ous wel awreke, upe him silve hit schal go,
For we schulle this six dayes therfore dubli his wo."
This wrecche gost quakede tho, that reuthe hit was to telle;
The develen him nome wel Grisliche, and bere into helle.
Ac Seint Brendan hem forbed in oure Loverdes name,
That he nadde for thulke niȝt nevere the more schame.
Seint Brendan and his monekes in the see forth wende
Riȝt threo dayes evene south, as oure Loverd hem sende;
The furde dai hi seȝe an yle al bi southe an heȝ,
Seint Brendan siȝte sore tho he this yle i-seȝ,
"Poul," he seide, "the ermite, is in the yle that ich i-seo,
Ther he hath withoute mete this fourti ȝer i-beo."

THO hi come to this yle, yn hi wende echon,
The ermite that was so old aȝen hem com gon;
His her to his fet tilde of berde and of heved,
And helede al about his bodi, nas ther no bar on him bileved;
None other clothes nadde he on, his lymes were all hore,
Seint Brendan him bihulde, and gan to sike sore,
"Allas!" he seide, "ich have so ȝare in stede monek i-beo,
And nou in lyf of an angel a man ich i-seo."

"BEO stille," quath this Ermite, "God doth bet bi
the,
For he schoweth the more than eni other of his priveité:
For o monek lyveth bi the swynk of his owe honde,
And thurf oure Loverdes grace the lyvest, and thurf his
sonde;
Of the Abbey of Seint Patrik monek ich was i-wis,
And of his church ai a wardeyn, ther as purgatorie is:

Adai ther com a man to me, ich eschte what he were,
Ich am, he seide, thyn abbod, of me nave thu no fere.
Non other man than Seint Patrick abbot nis, ich sede.
No ich hit am, quath this other," ne therstou nothing drede
To morwe arys sone days to the see thu must wende,
A schip thu schal fynde ȝare, as oure Loverd the wole sende:
Do the forth in thulke schip in the see wel wide,
And hit wole the lede into the stede ther thu schalt abide.
Sone a morwe ich aros to don his holi bone,
Forth ich wende to the see, a schip ich fond sone,
Mid me ich let the schip i-worthe; wel evene forth hit wende,
Thane sovethe dai into this yle oure Loverd me sende.
So sone ich was out of tho schip, aȝe thane wei hit nom,
As evene as hit miȝte drame riȝt as hit thider com.
Eling ich ȝeode her alone, confort nadde ich non,
So that upe his hynder fet an oter ther com gon,
Mid his forthere fet he brouȝte a fur-ire and a ston,
Forto smyte fur therwith, and of fisch god won.
This oter wende aȝe anon; ich makede me fur wel faste,
And seoth me fisch a Godes name that threo dayes i-laste,
So that evere the thridde dai this oter to me drouȝ,
And brouȝte me mete that ich hadde threo dayes y-nouȝ;
Water of this harde ston, thurf oure Loverdes sonde,
Ther sprong out ech Sonedai to drinke and to wasche myn honde.

THO ich hadde her in thisse lyve thretti ȝer i-beo,
This welle him gan furst to schewe, that thu miȝt her i-seo.
Bi this wille ich have i-lyved fonr and tuenti, er nou non,
And vyfti ȝer ich was old tho ich gan hider gon;
So that of an hondred ȝer and tuenti ther-to
Bi this tyme ich am i-redi oure Loverdes wille to do,
And mi deth ich abide her, whan hyne wole me sende,
Whan God wole that ich come to him and out of this wordle wende.
And nym with the of this water what thu hast neode ther-to,
And wend forth faste in the see, for thi wei nis noȝt i-do;
For thu schalt ȝut in the see fourti dayes fare,
Thanne thu schalt thin Ester holde ther thu hast i-do ȝare,
And thanne thu shalt wende forth to the Lond of Biheste,
And ther thu schalt fourti dayes bileve atte meste,
And to thin owe lond aȝe thu shalt wende so."
This gode men with deol y-nouȝ departede there a-tuo.

THIS gode men hem wende forth in the see faste,
Fourti dayes evene south the while Leynte i-laste;
To here gode procuratour an Ester eve hi come.
With hem he makede joye y-nouȝ, as he dude er i-lome,
He ladde hem to this grete fisch, thider hi come an eve,
This Ester niȝt forte a-morwe ther hi scholde bileve,
Ther hi seide here matyns and here masse also.
This fisch bigan to moevi him tho the mass was i-do,
And bar this monekes forth with him, and swam forth wel faste,
In the grete see wel grislich, this monekes were agaste,
A wonder thing hit was to mete, ho so hit hadde i-seil,
A so gret best abonte wende into al the contreye.
To this Fowelen Parays this monekes he ladde echon,
And sette hem up ther hol and sound. and wende aȝe anon.
Tho this monekes thider come wel joyful hi were;
Forte after the Trinité hi bileved there,
For here procuratour bi thulke tyme brouȝte hem mete y-nouȝ,
As he hadde er ofte i-do, into here schip hit drouȝ,
And wende forth with hem whoder oure Loverd hem sende.
Riȝt evene toward than est fourti dayes hi wende;
Tho this fourti dayes were i-do hit bigan to haweli faste,
A wel durc myst there com also that wel longe i-laste.
"Beoth glad," quath this procuratour, "and makieth grete feste,
For ich hit wot ye beoth nou neȝ the Lond of Biheste."

THO hi come out out of this durke mist, and miȝte aboute i-seo,
Under the faireste lond hi come that evere miȝte beo;
So cler and so liȝt hit was, that joye ther was y-nouȝ,
Treon ther were ful of frut wel thikke on everech bouȝ,
Thikke hit was biset of treon, and the treon thicke bere,
Thapplen were ripe y-nouȝ, riȝt as hit harvest were.
Fourti dayes aboute this lond hi hem gonne wende,
Hi ne miȝte fynde in non half of this lond non ende;
Hit was evere more dai, hi ne fonde nevere nyȝt,
Hi ne wende fynde in no stead so moche cler liȝt.
The eir was evere in o stat, nother hot ne cold,
Bote the joye that hi fonde ne mai never beo i-told.
So that hi come to a fair water, hi ne miȝte noȝt over wende.;
Ac over hi miȝte the lond i-seo fair withouten ende.

THO cam ther to hem a ȝunglich man, swyse fair and hende,
Fairere man ne miȝte beo, that our Loverd hem gan sende.
He wolcome ech bi his name, and custe hem echon,
And honurede faire Seint Brendan, and nom him bi the hond anon.
"Lo," he seide, "her is the lond that ye habbeth i-soȝt wyde,
And the lengere for oure Loverd wolde that ȝe schulde abyde,
For ye scholde in the grete see his priveitez i-seo.
Chargieth ȝoure schip with this frut, for ȝe ne mowe no leng her beo,
For thu most to-ward thin owe lond aȝe-wardes wende,
For thu shalt sone out of the wordle, thi lyf is neȝ than ende.
This water that ȝe her i-seoth deleth this lond a-tuo;
This half ȝou thinȝth fair y-nouȝ, and thother half also;
A ȝund half ne mowe ȝe come noȝt, for hit nis noȝt riȝt.
This frut is evere i-liche ripe, and this lond i-liche liȝt.
And whan oure Loverd ech maner man to him hath i-drawe,
And ech maner men knoweth him, and beoth under his lawe,
This lond wole thanne schewe to-ward the wordles ende,
Hem that beoth him next i-care er hi hunnes wende."
Seint Brendan and his felawes of this frut nome faste,
And of preciouse stones, and into here schip caste,
And faire and wel here leve nome tho this was al i-do,
And mid wop and deol y-nouȝ departede tho a-tuo,
And wende hem ham-ward in the see, as oure Loverd hem sende,
And wel rathere come hem hom than hi out-warde wende.
Here bretheren, tho hi come hom, joyful were y-nouȝ.
This holi man Seint Brendan to-ward dethe drouȝ;
For ever-eft after thulke tyme of the wordle he ne roȝte,
Bote as a man of thother wordle, and as he were in thoȝte.
He deide in Irlande after thulke stounde;
Meni miracle me hath ther siththe for him i-founde;
An abbei ther is arered ther as his bodi was i-do:
Nou God ous bringe to thulke joye that his soule wende to

AMEN.

PROSE LIFE OF ST. BRANDAN.

Here begynneth the Lyfe of Saynt Brandon.

Saynt Brandon, the holy man, was a monke, and borne in Yrlonde, and there he was abbot of an hous wherein were a thousand monkes, and there he ladde a full strayte and holy lyfe, in grete penaunce and abstynence, and he governed his monkes ful vertuously. And than within shorte tyme after, there came to hym an holy abbot that hyght Beryne to vysyte hym, and eche of them was joyfull of other; and than Saynt Brandon began to tell to the abbot Beryne of many wonders that he had seen in dyverse londes. And whan Beryne herde that of Saynt Brandon, he began to sygh, and sore wepte. And Saynt Brandon comforted him the best wyse he coude, sayenge, "Ye come hyther for to be joyfull with me, and therefore for Goddes love leve your mournynge, and tell me what mervayles ye have seen in the grete see occean, that compasseth all the worlde aboute, and all other waters comen out of hym, whiche renneth in all the partyes of the erth." And than Beryne began to tell to Saynt Brandon and to his monkes the mervaylles that he had seen, full sore wepynge, and sayd, "I have a sone, his name is Mernoke, and he was a monke of grete fame, whiche had grete desyre to seke aboute by shyppe in dyverse countrees, to fynde a solytary place wherein he myght dwell secretly out of the besynesse of the worlde, for to serve God quyetly with more devocyon; and I counseyled hym to sayle into an ylonde ferre in the see, besydes the Mountaynes of Stones, whiche is ful well knowen, and than he made hym redy, and sayled thyder with his monkes. And whan he came thyder he lyked that place full well, where he and his monkes served our Lorde full devoutly." And than Beryne sawe in a visyon that this monke Mernoke was sayled ryght ferre eestwarde into the see more than thre dayes saylynge, and sodeynly to his semynge there came a derke cloude and overcovered them, that a grete parte of the daye they sawe no lyght; and as our Lorde wold, the cloude passed awaye, and they sawe a full fayr ylond, and thyderward they drewe.

In that ylonde was joye and myrth ynough, and all the erth of that ylonde shyned as bryght as the sonne, and there were the fayrest trees and herbes that ever ony man sawe, and there were many precyous stones shynynge bryght, and every herbe there was ful of flyures, and every tree ful of fruyte; so that it was a glorious sight, and an hevenly joye to abyde there. And than there came to them a fayre yonge man, and full curtoysly he welcomed them all, and called every monke by his name, and sayd that they were much bounde to prayse the name of our Lorde Jesu, that wold of His grace shewe them that glorious place, where is ever day, and never night, and this place is called Paradyse Terrestre. But by this ylonde is an other ylonde wherein no man may come. And this yonge man sayd to them, "Ye have ben here halfe a yere without meet, drynke, or slepe." And they supposed that they had not ben there the space of half an houre, so merry and joyfull they were there. And the yonge man tolde them that this is the place that Adam and Eve dwelte in fyrst, and ever should have dwelled here, yf that they had not broken the commaundement of God. And than the yonge man brought them to thyr shyppe agayn, and sayd they might no lenger abyde there; and whan they were all shypped, sodeynly this yonge man vanysshed away out of thyr sight. And than within shorte tyme after, by the purveyaunce of our Lorde Jesu, they came to the abbey where Saint Brandon dwelled, and than he with his bretherne receyved them goodly, and demaunded where they had ben so longe; and they sayd, "We have ben in the Londe of Byheest, to-fore the gates of Paradyse, where as is ever day, and never night." And they sayd all that the place is full delectable, for yet all theyr clothes smelled of the swete and joyfull place. And than Saynt Brandon purposed soone after for to seke that place by Goddes helpe, and anone began to purvey for a good shyppe, and a stronge, and vytaylled it for vij. yere: and than he toke his leve of all his bretherne, and toke xij. monkes with him. But or they entred into the shyppe they fasted xl. dayes, and lyved devoutly, and eche of them receyved the Sacrament. And whan Saynt Brandon with his xij. monkes were entered into the shyppe, there came other two of his monkes, and prayed him that they myght sayle with hym. And than he sayd, "Ye may sayle with me, but one of you shall go to hell, or ye come agayn." But not for that they wold go with hym.

And than Saynt Brandon badde the shypmen to wynde up the sayle, and forth they sayled in Goddes name, so that on the morow they were out of syght of ony londe; and xl. dayes and xl. nightes after they sayled playn eest, and than they saw an ylonde ferre fro them, and they sayled thyderwarde as fast as they coude, and they sawe a grete roche of stone appere above all the water, and thre dayes they sayled aboute it or they coude gete into the place. But at the last, by the purveyaunce of God, they founde a lyttell haven, and there went a-londe everychone, and than sodeynly came a fayre hounde, and fell down at the feet of Saynt Brandon, and made hym good chere in his maner. And than he badde his bretherne, "Be of good chere, for our Lorde hath sent to us his messenger, to lede us into some good place." And the hounde brought them into a fayre hall, where they founde the tables spredde redy, set full of good meet and drynke. And than Saynt Brandon sayd graces, and than he and his bretherne sate down, and ete and dranke of suche as they founde; and there were beddes redy for them, wherin they toke theyr rest after theyr longe labour. And on the morowe they returned agayne to theyr shyppe, and sayled a longe tyme in the see after or they coude fynde ony londe, tyll at the last, by the purveyaunce of God, they sawe ferre fro them a full fayre ylonde, ful of grene pasture, wherein were the whytest and gretest shepe that ever they sawe; for every shepe was as grete as an oxe. And soone after came to them a goodly olde man, whiche welcomed them, and made them good chere, and sayd, "This is the Ylonde of Shepe, and here is never cold weder, but ever sommer, and that causeth the shepe to be so grete and whyte; they ete of the best grasse and herbes that is ony where." And than this olde man toke his leve of them, and bad them sayle forth ryght eest, and within shorte tyme, by Goddes grace, they sholde come into a place lyke paradyse, wherein they shold kepe theyr Eestertyde.

And than they sayled forth, and came soone after to that lond; but bycause of lytell depthe in some place, and in some place were grete rockes, but at the last they wente upon an ylonde, wenynge to them they had ben safe, and made thereon a fyre for to dresse theyr dyner, but Saynt Brandon abode styll in the shyppe. And when the fyre was ryght hote, and the meet nygh soden, than this ylonde began to move; whereof the monkes were aferde, and fledde anone to the shyppe, and lefte the fyre and meet behynde them, and mervayled sore of the movyng. And Saynt Brandon comforted them, and sayd that it was a grete fisshe named Jasconye, whiche laboureth nyght and daye to put his tayle in his mouth, but for gretnes he may not. And than anone they sayled west thre dayes and thre nyghtes or they sawe ony londe, wherfore they were ryght hevy. But soone after, as God wold, they sawe a fayre ylonde, full of floures, herbes, and trees, whereof they thanked God of his good grace, and anone they went on londe. And whan they had gone longe in this, they founde a ful fayre well, and thereby stood a fayre tree, full of bowes, and on every bough sate a fayre byrde, and they sate so thycke on the tree that unneth ony lefe of the tree myght be seen, the nombre of them was so grete; and they songe so meryly that it was an hevenly noyse to here. Wherefore Saynt Brandon kneled down on his knees, and wepte for joye, and made his prayers devoutly unto our Lord God to knowe what these byrdes ment. And than anone one of the byrdes fledde fro the tree to Saynt Brandon, and he with flykerynge of his wynges made a full mery noyse lyke a fydle, that hym semed he herde never so joyfull a melodye. And than Saynt Brandon commaunded the byrde to tell hym the cause why they sate so thycke on the tree, and sange so meryly. And than the byrde sayd, "Somtyme we were aungels in heven, but whan our mayster Lucyfer fell down into hell for his hygh pryde, we fell with hym for our offences, some hyther and some lower, after the qualyté of theyr trespace; and bycause our trepace (*sic*) is but lytell, therefore our Lorde hath set us here out of all payne in full grete joye and myrth, after his pleasynge, here to serve hym on this tree in the best manner that we can. The Sonday is a day of rest fro all worldly occupacyon; and, therefore, that daye all we be made as whyte as ony snow, for to prayse our Lorde in the best wyse we may." And than this byrde sayd to Saynt Brandon, "It is xij. monethes past that ye departed fro your abbey, and in the vij. yere hereafter ye shall se the place that ye desyre to come, and all this vij. yere ye shal kepe your Eester here with us every yere, and in the ende of the vij. yere ye shal come into the Londe of Byhest." And this was on Eester daye that the byrde sayd these wordes to Saynt Brandon. And than this fowle flewe agayn to his felawes that sate on the tree. And than all the byrdes began to synge evensonge so meryly, that it was an hevenly noyse to here; and after souper Saynt Brandon and his felawes wente to bedde, and slepte well, and on the morowe they arose betymes; and than those byrdes began matyns, pryme, and houres, and all suche service as Chrysten men use to synge.

And Saynt Brandon with his felawes abode there viij. wekes, tyll Trinité Sunday was past, and they sayled agayne to the Ylonde of Shepe, and there they vytayled them wel, and syth toke theyr leve of that olde man, and returned agayn to shyppe. And than the byrde of the tree came agayn to Saynt Brandon, and said, "I am come to tell you that ye shall sayle fro hens into an ylonde, wherein is an abbey of xxiiij. monkes, whiche is fro this place many a myle, and there ye shall holde your Chrystmasse, and your Eester with us, lyke as I tolde you." And than this byrde flewe to his felawes agayn. And than Saynt Brandon and his felawes sayled forth in the occyan; and soone after fell a grete tempest on them, in whiche they were gretely troubled longe tyme, and sore forelaboured. And after that, they founde by the purveyaunce of God an ylonde whiche was ferre fro them, and than they full mekely prayed to our Lord to sende them thyder in safeté, but it was xl. dayes after or they came thyder, wherefore all the monekes were so wery of that trouble that they set lytel price by theyr lyves, and cryed contynually to our Lord to have mercy on them, and bringe them to that ylonde in safeté. And by the purveyaunce of God, they came at the last into a lytell haven; but it was so strayte that unneth the shyppe might come in. And after they came to an ancre, and anone the monkes went to londe, and whan they had longe walked about, at the last they founde two fayre welles; that one was fayre and clere water, and that other was somewhat troubly and thycke. And than they thanked our Lorde full humbly that had brought them thyder in safeté, and they wolde fayne have droken of that water, but Saynt Brandon charged them that they sholde take none without lycence, "for yf we absteyne us a whyle, our Lord wyll purvey for us in the best wyse." And anone after came to them a fayre old man, with hoor heer, and welcomed them ful mekely, and kyssed Saynt Brandon, and ledde them by many a fayre welle tyll they came to a fayre abbey, where they were receyved with grete honour, and solempne processyon, with xxiiij. monkes all in ryal copes of cloth of golde, and a ryall crosse was before them. And than the abbot welcomed Saynt Brandon and his felawshyp, and kyssed them full mekely, and toke Saynt Brandon by the hande, and ledde hym with his monkes into a fayre hall, and set them downe a-rowe upon the benche; and the abbot of the place wasshed all theyr feet with fayre water of the well that they sawe before, and after ladde them into the fraytour, and there set them amonge his covent. And anone there came one by the purveyaunce of God, which served them well of meet and drynke. For every monke had set before hym a fayre whyte lofe and whyte rotes and herbes, whiche were ryght delycyous, but they wyst not what rotes they were; and they dranke of the water of the fayre clere welle that they sawe before whan they came fyrst a-londe, whiche Saynt Brandon forbadde them. And than the Abbot came and chered Saynt Brandon and his monkes, and prayed them to ete and drynke for charité, "for every day our Lorde sendeth a goodly olde man that covereth this table, and setteth our meet and drynke to-fore us; but we knowe not how it cometh, ne we ordeyre never no meet ne drynke for us, and yet we have ben lxxx. yere here, and ever our Lorde (worshipped mote be he!) fedeth us. We ben xxiiij. monkes in nombre, and every feryall day of the weke he sendeth to us xij. loves, and every Sondaye and feestful day xxiiij loves, and the breed that we leve at dyner we ete at souper. And nowe at your comynge our Lorde hath sente to us xlviij. loves, for to make you and us mery togyder as brethern, and alwaye xij. of us go to dyner, whyles other xij. kepe the quere; and thus have we done this lxxx. yere, for so longe have we dwelled here in this abbey; and we came hyther out of the abbey of Saynt Patrykes in Yrelonde; and thus, as ye se, our Lorde hath purveyed for us; but none of us knoweth how it cometh, but God alone, to whome be gyven honouy and laude worlde without ende. And here in this londe in ever fayre weder, and none of us hath ben syke syth w we came hyther. And whan we go to Masse, or to on other servyce of our Lord in the chirche, anone seve tapers of waxe been set in the quere, and ben lyght at every tyme without mannes hande, and so brenne daye and nyght at every houre of servyce, and never waste ne mynysshe as longe as we have been here, which is lxxx. yere."

And than Saynt Brandon wente to the chirche with the abbot of the place, and there they sayd evensonge togyder full devoutly. And than Saynt Brandon loked up-ward to-warde the Crucifyxe, and sawe our Lorde hangynge on the crosse, which was made of fyne cristal and curyously wrought; and in the quere were xxiiij. setes for xxiiij. monkes, and the vij. tapers brennynge, and the abbottes sete was made in the myddes of the quere. And than Saynt Brandon demanded of the abbot how longe they had kepte that scylence that none of them spake to other," And he sayd, "This xxiiij, yere we spake never one to another." And than Saynt Brandon wepte for joye of theyr holy conversation. And than Saynt Brandon desyred of the abbot that he and his monkes might dwell there styll with hym. To whom the abbot sayd, "Syr, that may ye not do in no wyse, for our Lorde hath shewed to you in what maner ye shall be guyded tyll the vij. yere be fulfylled, and after that terme thou shalte with thy monkes returne into Yrlonde in safeté; but on of the two monkes that came last to you shall dwell in the Ylonde of Ankers, and that other shall go quycke to hell. And as Saynt Brandon kneled in the chirche, he sawe a bryght shynynge aungell come in at the wyndowe, and lyghted all the lyghtes in the chirche, and than he flewe out agayn at the wyndowe unto heven; and than Saynt Brandon mervayled gretly how the lyght brenned so fayre and wasted not. And than the abbot sayd that it is wryten that Moyses sawe a busshe all on a fyre, and yet it brenned not, "and therefore mervayle not thereof, for the myght of our Lorde is now as grete as ever it was."

And whan Saynt Brandon had dwelled there fro Chryst-masse even tyll the xij. daye was passed, than he toke his leve of the abbot and covent, and returned with his monkes to his shyppe, and sayled fro thens with his monkes to-warde the abbey of Saynt Hylaryes, but they had grete tempestes in the see fro that time tyll Palme Sondaye And than they came to the Ylonde of Shepe, and there were receyved of the olde man, whiche brought them to a fayre hall and served them. And on Sher-Thursdaye after souper he wasshed theyr feet, and kyssed them, lyke as our Lorde dyd to his disciples, and there abode tyll Saturdaye, Eester even, and than they departed, and sayled to the place where the grete fysshe laye, and anone they sawe theyr caudron upon the fysshes backe whiche they had left there xij. monethes to-fore, and there they kepte the servyce of the resurreccyon on the fysshes backe ; and after they sayled the same daye by the mornynge to the ylonde where as the tree of byrdes was, and than the sayd byrde welcomed Saynt Brandon and all his felawshyp, and went agayn to the tree, and sang full meryly. And there he and his monkes dwelled fro Eester tyll Trynité Sondaye, as they dyd the yere before, in full grete joye and myrth ; and dayly they herde the mery servyce of the byrdes syttynge on the tree. And than the byrde tolde to Saynt Brandon that he sholde returne agayne at Chrystmasse to the abbey of monkes, and at Eester thyder agayn, and the other dele of the yere labour in the occean in full grete perylles, "and fro yere to yere tyll the vij. yere ben accomplysshed, and than shall ye come to the joyfull place of Paradyse, and dwell there xl. daye in full grete joye and myrth ; and after ye shall returne home into your owne abbey in safeté, and there end your lyf, and come to the blysse of heven, to whiche our Lorde bought you with his precyous blode." And than the aungell of oure Lorde ordeyned all thynge that was nedefull to Saynt Brandon and to his monkes, in vytayles and all other thynges necessary. And than they thanked our Lorde of his grete goodnes that he had showed to them ofte in theyr grete nede, and than sayled forth in the grete see occean abydynge the mercy of our Lord in grete trouble and tempestes, and soone after came to them an horryble fysshe, which folowed the shyppe long tyme, castynge so moche water out of his mouth into the shyppe, that they supposed to have ben drowned. Wherefore they devoutly prayed to God to delyver them of that grete peryll. And anone after came an other fysshe, greter than he, out of the west see, and faught with him, and at the laste clave hym in thre places, and than returner agayne. And than they thanked mekely our Lord of theye delyveraunce fro this grete peryll ; but they were in gretd hevynesse, because theyr vytayles were nygh spente. But, by the ordynaunce of our Lorde, there came a byrde, and brought to them a grete braunche of a vine, full of reed grapes, by whiche they lyved xiiij. dayes ; and than they came to a lytell ylonde, wherein were many vynes full of grapes, and they there londed, and thanked God, and gadred as many grapes as they lyved by xl. dayes after, alwaye saylynge in the see in many a storme and tempest. And as they thus sayled, sodeynly came fleynge towarde them a grete grype, which assayled them, and was lyke to have destroyed them; wherefore they devoutly prayed for helpe and ayde of our Lord Jesu Chryst. And than the byrde of the tree of the ylonde where they had holden theyr Eester to-fore came to the grype, and smote out both his eyen, and after slewe hym; wherof they thanked our Lorde, and than sayled forth contynually tyll Saynt Peters daye, and than songen they solempnely theyr servyce in the honour of the feest. And in that place the water was so clere, that they myght se all the fysshes that were aboute them, whereof they were full sore agast, and the monkes counseyled Saint Brandon to synge no more, for all the fysshes lay than as they had slepte. And than Saynt Brandon sayd, "Drede ye not, for ye have kepte by two Eesters the feest of the resurreccion upon the grete fysshes backe, and therefore dread ye not of these lytel fysshes." And than Saynt Brandon made hym redy, and wente to masse, and badde his monkes to synge the best wyse they coude. And than anone all the fysshes awoke, and came about the shippe so thicke, that unneth they myght se the water for the fysshes. And whan the Masse was done, all the fysshes departed, so that they were no more seen.

And seven dayes they sayled alwaye in that clere water. And than there came a south wynde, and drove the shyppe north-warde, where as they sawe an ylonde full derke and full of stenche and smoke; and there they herde grete blowynge and blastyng of belowes, but they myght se no thynge, but herde grete thondrynge, whereof they were sore aferde and blyssed them ofte. And soone after there came one stertynge out all brennynge in fyre, and stared full gastly on them with grete staryng eyen, of whom the monkes were agast, and at his departyng from them he made the horryblest crye that myght be herde. And soone there came a grete nombre of fends, and assayled them with hokes and brennynge yren malles, whiche ranne on the water, folowyng fast theyr shyppe, in suche wyse that it semed all the see to be on a fyre; but by the wyll of God they had no power to hurte ne to greve them, ne theyr shyppe. Wherfore the fendes began to rore and crye, and threwe theyr hokes and malles at them. And they than were sore aferde, and prayed to God for comforte and helpe;

for they sawe the fendes all about the shyppe, and them semed that all the ylonde and the see to be on a fyre. And with a sorowfull crye all the fendes departed fro them, and returned to the place that they came fro. And than Saynt Brandon tolde to them that this was a parte of hell; and therefore he charged them to be stedfast in the fayth, for they shold yet se many a dredefull place or they came home agayne. And than came the south wynde and drove them ferther into the north, where they sawe an hyll all on fyre, and a foule smoke and stenche comyng from thens, and the fyre stode on eche syde of the hyll, lyke a wall all brennynge. And than one of his monkes began to crye and wepe ful sore, and sayd that his ende was comen, and that he might abyde no lenger in the shyppe, and anone he lepte out of the shyppe into the see, and than he cryed and rored full pyteously, cursynge the tyme that he was borne, and also fader and moder that bygate him, bycause they sawe no better to his correccyon in his yonge age, "for now I must go to perpetual payne." And than the sayenge of Saynt Brandon was veryfyed that he sayd to hym whan he entred into the shyppe. Therfore it is good a man to do penaunce and forsake synne, for the houre of deth is incertayne.

And than anone the wynde turned into the north, and drove the shyppe into the south, whiche sayled vij. dayes contynually; and they came to a grete rock standynge in the see, and theron sate a naked man, in full grete mysery and payne; for the waves of the see had so beten his body that all the flesshe was gone of, and nothynge lefte but synewes and bare bones. And whan the wawes were gone, there was a canvas that henge over his heed whiche bette his body full sore with the blowynge of the wynde; and also there were two oxe tongues, and a grete stone that he sate on, which dyd hym full grete ease. And than Saynt Brandon charged hym to tell hym what he was. And he sayd, "My name is Judas, that solde our Lorde Jesu Chryst for xxx pens, which sytteth here moche wretchedly; how be it I am worthy to be in the gretest payne that is; but our Lorde is so mercyfull that he hath rewarded me better than I have deserved, for of ryght my place is in the brennynge hell; but I am here but certayne tymes of the yere, that is, fro Chrystmasse to twelfth daye, and fro Eester tyll Whytsontyde be past, and every feestful daye of our Lady, and every Saterdaye at noone tyll Sonday that evensonge be done; but all other tymes I lye styll in hell in full brennynge fyre with Pylate, Herode, and Cayphas; therefore accursed be the tyme that ever I knewe them." And than Judas prayed Saynt Brandon to abyde styll there all that nyght, and that he wolde kepe hym there styll that the fendes sholde not fetche hym to hell. And he sayd, "With Goddes helpe thou shalt abyde here all this nyght." And than he asked Judas what cloth that was that henge over his heed. And he sayd it was a cloth that he gave unto a lepre, whiche was bought with the money that he stale fro our Lorde whan he bare his purse "wherefore it dothe to me grete payne now in betyng my face with the blowynge of the wynde; and these two oxe tongues that hange here above me, I gave them somtyme to two preestes to praye for me. I bought them with myne owne money, and therefore they ease me, bycause the fysshes of the sea knawe on them and spare me. And this stone that I syt on laye somtyme in a desolate place where it eased no man; and I toke it thens and layd it in a foule waye, where it dyd muche ease to them that wont by that waye, and therefore it easeth me now; for every good dede shall be rewarded, and every evyll dede shal be punysshed." And the Sondaye agaynst even there came a grete multitude of fendes blastyng and rorynge, and badde Saynt Brandon go thens, that they myght have theyr servaunt Judas, "for we dare not come in the presence of our mayster, but yf we brynge hym to hell with us." And St. Brandon sayd, "I lette not you do your maysters commaundement, but by the power of our Lorde Jesu Chryst I charge you to leave hym this nyght tyll to morow." "How darest thou helpe hym that so sold his mayster for xxx. pens to the Jewes, and caused hym also to dye the moost shamefull deth upon the crosse?" And than Saynt Brandon charged the fendes by his passyon that they sholde not noy hym that nyght. And than the fendes went theyr way rorynge and cryenge towarde hell to theyr mayster, the grete devyll. And than Judas thanked Saynt Brandon so rewfully that it was pitó to se, and on the morowe the fendes came with an horryble noyse, sayenge that they had that nyght suffred grete payne because they brought not Judas, and said that he should suffre double payne the sixe dayes folowynge. And they toke than Judas tremblynge for fere with them to payne.

And after Saynt Brandon sayled south-warde thre dayes and thre nyghtes, and on the Frydaye they sawe an ylonde, and than Saynt Brandon began to sygh and saye, "I se the ylonde wherin Saynt Poule the heremyte dwelleth, and hath dwelled there xl. yere, without meet and drynke ordeyned by mannes hande." And whan they came to the londe, Saynt Poule came and welcomed them humbly. He was olde and for-growen, so that no man myght se his body, of whom Saynt Brandon sayd weepyng, "Now I se a man that lyveth more like an aungell than a man, wherfore we wretches may be ashamed that we lyve not better." Than Saynt Poule sayd to Saynt Brandon, "Thou art better than I; for our Lord hath shewed to the more of his prevytees than he hath done to me, wherfore thou oughtest to be more praysed than I." To whome Saynt Brandon sayd, "We ben monkes, and must labour for our meet, but God hath provyded for the suche meet as thou holdest the pleased, wherfore thou art moche better than I." To whom Saynt Poule sayd, "Sometime I was a monke of Saynt Patrykes abbey in Yrelonde, and was wardeyn of the place where as men entre into Saynt Patrikes purgatory. And on a day there came one to me, and I asked hym what he was, and he sayd I am your abbot Patryke, and charge the that thou departe from hens to morowe erly to the see syde, and there thou shalt fynde a shyppe, into the which thou must entre, whiche God hath ordeyned for the, whose wyll thou must accomplysshe. And so the nexte daye I arose and went forth and founde the shyppe, in whiche I entred, and by the purveyaunce of God I was brought into this ylonde the seventh daye after, and than I lefte the shyppe and went to londe, and there I walked up and downe a good whyle, and than by the purveyaunce of God there came an otter goynge on his hynder feet, and brought me a flynte stone, and an yren to smyte fyre with, in his two fore clawes of his feet; and also he had about his necke grete plenté of fysshes, which he cast down before me and went his waye; and I smote fyre, and made a fyre of styckes, and dyd sethe the fysshe, by which I lyved thre dayes. And than the otter came agayn, and brought me fysshe for other thre dayes; and thus he hath done li. yere, through the grace of God. And there was a great stone, out of whiche our Lord made to sprynge fayre water, clere and swete, wherof I drynke dayly. And thus have I lyved this li. yere; and I was lx. yere olde whan I came hyther, and am now an hondred and xi. yere olde, and abyde tyll it please our Lorde to sende for me; and if it pleased hym, I wolde fayne be discharged of this wretched lyfe." And than he bad Saynt Brandon to take of the water of the welle, and to carry it into his shyppe, "for it is tyme that thou departe, for thou hast a grete journey to do; for thou shalt sayle to an ylonde which is xl. dayes saylyng hens, where thou shalt holde thyn Eester lyke as thou hast done to-fore, wher as the tree of byrdes is. And fro thens thou shalte sayle into the Londe of Byheest, and shalt abyde there xl. dayes, and after returne home into thy countree in safeté." And than these holy men toke leve eche of other, and they wepte bothe full sore, and kyssed eche other.

And than Saynt Brandon entred into his shyppe, and sayled xl. dayes even southe, in full grete tempest. And on Eester even came to theyr procuratour, whiche made to them good chere, as he had before tyme. And from thens they came to the grete fysshe, where they sayd matyns and masse on Eester daye. And whan the masse was done, the fysshe began to meve, and swamme forth fast into the see, whereof the monkes were sore agast which stode upon hym, for it was a grete mervayle to se suche a fysshe as grete as all a countree for to swymme so fast in the water; but by the wyll of our Lorde God this fysshe set all the monkes a-londe in the Paradise of Byrdes all hole and sounde, and than returned to the place that he came fro. And than Saynt Brandon and his monkes thanked our Lorde God of theyr delyveraunce of the grete fysshe, and kepte theyr Eestertyde tyll Trinité Sondaye, lyke as they had done before tyme. And after this they toke theyr shyppe and sayled eest xl. dayes, and at the xl. dayes ende it began to hayle ryght fast, and therwith came a derke myst, whiche lasted longe after, whiche fered Saynt Brandon and his monkes, and prayed to our Lord to kepe and helpe them. And than anone came theyr procuratour, and badde them to be of good chere, for they were come into the Londe of Byheest. And soon after that myst passed awaye, and anone they sawe the fayrest countree eestwarde that ony man myght se, and was so clere and bryght that it was an hevenly syght to beholde; and all the trees were charged with rype fruyte and herbes full of floures; in whiche londe they walked xl. dayes, but they coude se none ende of that londe; and there was alwaye daye and never nyght, and the londe attemperate ne to hote ne to colde. And at the last they came to a ryver, but they durst not go over. And there came to them a fayre yonge man, and welcomed them curtoysly, and called each of them by his name, and dyd grete reverence to Saynt Brandon, and sayd to them, "Be ye now joyfull, for this is the londe that ye have sought; but our Lorde wyll that ye departe hens hastely, and he wyll shewe to you more of his secretes whan ye come agayn into the see; and our Lorde wyll that ye lade your shyppe with the fruyte of this londe, and hye you hens, for you may no lenger abyde here, but thou shalt sayle agayne into thyne owne countree, and soone after thou comest home thou shalt dye. And this water that thou seest here departeth the worlde asondre; for on that other syde of the water may no man come that is in this lyfe. And the fruyte that ye se is alwaye thus rype every tyme of the yere, and alwaye it is here lyght as ye now se; and he that kepeth our Lordes hestes at all tymes shall se this londe, or he passe out of this worlde." And than Saynt Brandon and his monkes toke of that fruyte as much as they wolde, and also toke with them grete plenté of precyous stones; and than toke theyr leve and went to shyppe, wepynge sore bycause they myght no lenger abyde there. And than they toke theyr shyppe, and came home into Yrelonde in safeté, whome theyr bretherne receyved with grete joye, gyvynge thankynges to our Lorde, whiche had kepte them all those seven yere fro many a peryll, and brought them home in safeté, to whome be gyven honour and glory worlde withouten ende. Amen. And soone after, this holy man Saynt Brandon wexed feble and seke, and had but lytell joye of this world, but ever after his joye and mynde was in the joyes of heven. And in shorte tyme after, he, beynge full of vertues, departed out of this lyfe unto everlastyng lyfe, and was worshypfully buryed in a fayre abbey, which he hym selfe founded, where our Lorde sheweth for this holy saynt many fayre myracles. Wherfore let us devoutly praye to this holy saynt that he praye for us unto our Lord, that he have mercy on us, to whom be gyven laude, honour, and empyre, world withouten ende. Amen.

NOTES ON THE METRICAL LIFE.*

Page 1, line 1.—The name is spelt diversely in the different MSS., *Brendan* and *Brandan*. The commencement of our English poem agrees closely with that of the prose English version here printed, but they differ very much from the original Latin, and all the other versions, which give a more exact account of the family of the saint. "Sanctus Brendanus, filius Finlocha, nepotis Alti de genere Eogeni, e stagnile regione Mimensium ortus fuit."

P. 1, l. 4.—*A thousend monekes.*] So the English prose version. The original Latin, and all the other versions, say three thousand.

L. 6.—*Barint.*] The Latin calls him Barintus, nepos Neil regis. In the Prose Life he is corruptly called Beryne.

P. 2, l. 5.—*Mernoc.*] The Trin. Col. MS. reads *Menrok*. The prose version, probably by a mere error of the printer, calls him *Meruoke*.

P. 2, l. 5.—*Mountayne of Stedes.*] MS. Trin. The Latin text has *juxta Montem Lapidis*.

P. 2, l. 23.—*Ane lond.*] The Tr. C. MS. reads *a nywe lond*.

P. 3, l. 6.—*A yung man.*] The original Latin, and the versions made immediately from it, have only *quidam vir*, without saying anything of his youth.

P. 4, l. 4.—The Trin. Col. MS. reads, *agen—ward he wende tho, and that.*

P. 4, l. 13.—*Smyl.*] MS. Tr. C. reads *smelle*.

P. 4, l. 14.—*In thogt he stod*, MS. Tr. C. This MS. adds after this line the following, which is evidently omitted in our text—He thogt fondy ther-of yf hit were Godes wylle.

* The references in those Notes are to the pages in the "Percy Society" edition, from which this has been printed. As the words of the text to which the Notes apply, are here given, the reader can easily find the references in our text.

P. 4, l. 17.—We should probably read *Thuse tuelve*, as the line seems as present imperfect. MS. Tr. C. has *Thes twelve he clyped to consail.* There are also evidently two lines omitted in our text, which should form the commencement of St Brandan's address to his monks, and which stand thus in the Tr. C. MS. :—

"Ich thynche to a privé thyng, ther-of ye mote me rede,
To seche the Lond of Byheste, if oure Lord wole me thuder lede."

The omission has arisen from the number of consecutive rhymes. In the English prose version the preparations for voyage are told more briefly.

P. 5, l. 5.—The Tr. C. MS. reads, *Hu leten make a stronge schip.* The Latin text differs here from our narrative. "Transactis jam quadraginta diebus, et salutatis fratribus accomendatis præposito monasterii Sin, qui fuit postea successor in eodem loco, profectus est contra occidentalem plagam cum quatuordecim fratribus adinsulam cujusdam sancti patris nomine Aende. Ibi demoratus est tribus diebus et tribus noctibus. Post hæe, accepta benedictione sancti patris et omnium monachorum qui cum eo erant, profectus est in ultimam partem regionis suæ, ubi demorabantur parentes ejus. Attamen nobuit illos videre, sed cujusdam summitatem montis extendentis se in oceanum, in loco qui dicitur *Brendani Sedes*, ascendit, ibique fuit tentorium suum, ubi erat et introitus unius navis. Sanctus Brendanus et qui cum eo erant, acceptis ferramentis, fecerunt naviculam levissimam, costatam et columnatam ex vimine, sicut mos est in illis partibus, et cooperuerunt eam coriis bovinis ac rubricatis in cortice roborina, linieruntque foris omnes juncturas navis, et expendia quadraginta dierum et butirum ad pelles præparandas assumpserunt ad cooperimentum navis, et cætera utensilia quae ad usum vitæ humanæ pertinent. Arborem posuerunt in medio navis fixum, et velum, et cætera quæ ad gubernationem navis pertinent."

This is a curious description of a very primitive ship.

P. 6, l. 4.—*An hulle at the laste.*] MS. Tr. C.

P. 6, l. 8.—*Hu wende aboute as moppysche men that nuste wer hu were*, MS. Tr. C.

P. 6, l. 13.—*To an halle.*] The Latin has—"usque ad unum oppidum, intrantes autem viderunt aulam magnam."

In the early French version it is—"It sivirent le chien dusques au chastel. Dont enterent en i. chastel, et virent une grande sale." The English versions omit the incident of one of the two monks who followed St. Brandan voluntarily, who stole a bridle of silver from the hall, and died and was buried in the island.

P. 7, l. 7.—The Island of Sheep, answering closely to this description, is described by some of the Arabian geographers as existing in the Western Ocean.

P. 8, l. 7.—*Eyre.*] MS. Tr. C., which adds after this line, the two following:—

" And here wey to here schyp eche after other nome,
God hym thogt levyste was that sonest thyder come."

P. 8, l. 16.—*Jascom.*] The MS. Tr. C. reads *Jastoyn*; the Latin has *Jasconius*. It has been already observed in the preface, that the incident of the great fish is founded in the Arabian voyages of Sinbad. The existence of this great fish was a very popular legend in the middle ages; it was doubtless the Craken of the north. In the mediæval bestiaries it is sometimes identified with the whale. The story is the subject of an Anglo-Saxon poem in the Exeter MS. Philippe de Phaun gives the same incident in a few lines; adding that the fish, before rising to the surface, throws the sand of the sea on its back, which gives it still more the appearance of land:—

" Cetus ceo est mult grant beste, tut tens en mer converse;
Le Sablun de mer prent, sur son dos l'estent,
Sur mer s'esdrecerat, en pais si esterat.
Li notuners la veit, quide que ille sait,
Iloc vait ariver sun cunrei aprester.
Li balain le fu sent e la nef e la gent;
Lores se plungerat, si il pot, si's neierat."

"Cetus is a very great beast, which lives always in the sea; it takes the sand of the sea, spreads it on its back, raises itself up in the sea, and will lie without motion. The seafarer sees it, thinks that it is an island, lands there to prepare his meal. The whale feels the fire and the ship and the people; then he will plunge, and drown them, if he can."

See also the account of this monster given in the early

English metrical bestiary, printed in the *Reliquiæ Antiquæ*, vol. i., page 220.

P. 9, l. 9.—The Tr. C. MS. reads:—

"Tho fley ther up a litel foule, and toward hym gan te,
As a fythele his wingen ferd tho he bygan to fle."

P. 9, l. 16.—This notion relating to the distribution of the fallen angels, according to the degree in which they had participated in Lucifer's crime, was very general in the middle ages. I have collected together from old writers some extracts on this subject in my essay on "St Patrick's Purgatory" (page 90). In the Latin text of our legend the bird says:—"Nos sumus de magna illa ruina antiqui hostis; sed non peccando aut consentiendo sumus lapsi, sed Dei pietate prædestinati, nam ubi sumus creati, per lapsum istius cum suis satellibus contigit nostra ruina. Deus autem omnipotens, qui justus est et verax, suo judicio misit nos in istum locum. Pœnas non sustinemus. Præsentiam Dei ex parte non videre possumus, tantum alienavit nos consortio illorum qui steterunt. Vagamur per diversas partes hujus sæculi, aeris et firmamenti et terrarum, sicut et alii spiritus qui mittuntur. Sed in sanctis diebus dominicis accipimus corpora talia quæ tu vides, et per Dei dispensationem commoramur hic et laudamus creatorem nostrum."

P. 11, l. 8.—*Abbey.*] Insulam quæ vocatur *Ailbey*. Text. Lat.

P. 12, l. 3.—*Thother wori.*] unus turbidus. Text. Lat.

P. 13, l. 5.—*White mores.*] The Latin text has—Et quibusdam radicibus incredibilis saporis.

P. 14, l. 1.—*Seint Alvey.*] Et Sancti Ailbei. Text. Lat.

P. 14, l. 15.—*Weved.*] An altar. In the next line MS. Tr. C. reads, *weved, chalys, and croeses*. Erant enim attaria de cristallo. Calices et patenæ, urceoli, et cætera vasa quæ pertinebant ad cultum divinum itidem ex cristallo erant. Text. Lat.

P. 15, l. 13.—*Ylle of ankres.*] *I.e.*, the isle of hermits, or anchorites. MS. Tr. C. reads, *Yle of auntres*. De duobus vero qui supersunt, unus peregrinabitur in insula quae vocatur Anachoritalis; porro alter morte pessima condempnabitur apud inferos. Text. Lat.

P. 15, l. 15.—*A furi arewe.*] *Sagitta ignea*. Text. Lat. The prose English version has misread *Angel* for *Arrow*.

P. 16, l. 5.—*Midewynter.*] It is perhaps hardly necessary to observe that this is the Anglo-Saxon name for Christmas.

P. 16, l. 16.—*Fowolen Parays.*] Insula quæ vocatur Paradisus Avium. Text. Lat. A curious incident of the Latin legend, where the monks were made ill by drinking water in another island, is omitted in the English.

P. 15, l. 18.—*Scher-thursdai.*] Shere Thursday, or Maunday Thursday, is the Thursday before Easter, when it was the custom to wash each other's feet in imitation of Christ, which ceremony was called his *mandé* (or commandment), whence is derived one of the names given to the day.

P. 17, l. 25.—*Ymone.*] The Tr. C. MS. reads *echon.*

P. 19, l. 15.—*Afingred.*] *I.e.*, hungry. See the Glossary to *Piers Ploughman.* In the original Latin text the monks are twice exposed to extreme hunger, and on the first occasion relieve themselves by eating of the flesh of the beast which had been killed. Several incidents in this part of the original story are omitted in the English version. It would appear also that in the Latin legend the great beast which had been killed was the same on whose back they had lit the fire, for Brandan says to them when they express their fear of the fishes they saw asleep at the bottom of the sea:—" Cur timetis istas bestias? Nonne omnium bestiarum maxima devorata est? Sedentes vos et psallentes sæpe in dorso ejus fuistis, et silvam scindistis, et ignem accendistis, et carnem ejus coxistis."

P. 22, l. 2.—For a full illustration of the notions relating to hell and paradise contained in the latter part of this legend, I would refer the reader to the materials I have collected in the essay on " St. Patrick's Purgatory."

P. 23, l. 8.—*Ambesas.*] A term in the game of dice, frequently used in mediæval writers, which shows the great prevalence of gambling in the middle ages.

P. 26, l. 7.—*And oure Loverdes pans ber.*] It was a prevalent notion in the middle ages that Judas was the purse-bearer of Christ and His disciples, and that his avarice and dishonesty was partly the cause of his ruin. A curious early fragment on this subject is printed in the *Reliquiæ Antiquæ*, vol. i., page 144. In the *Chester Mysteries* he is made to take offence at the extravagance of the Magdalene in lavishing so much money on a pot of ointment. In the Latin text of the legend of St. Brandan, Judas is represented as having been the Chamberlain of the Saviour: "quando fui camerarius Domini." In the French version it is: "Quand je fui Cambrelens meen Signeur."

P. 30, l. 11.—The Latin text gives his age somewhat differently. "Nonagenarius enim sum in hac insula, et triginta annis in victu piscium, et sexaginta in victu illius fontis, et quinquaginta fui in patria mea; omnes enim anni vitæ meæ sunt centum quinquaginta."

P. 34, l. 11.—*An abbei.*] This abbey was Cluain-fert or Clonfert, in the county of Galway, where it is pretended that St. Brandan was buried in the year 576. (See Archdall, *Monast Hibern*, page 278).

P. 36, l. 11.—*In a visyon.*] The prose version is here rather confused, and the writer appears unintentionally to have overlooked part of the original. It would seem here as though the voyage of *Barintus* was nothing more than a vision, which certainly was not the writer's meaning.

Also published by **Llanerch:**

THE ANNALS OF CLONMACNOISE
facsimile, edited by Denis Murphy.

THE ANNALS OF TIGERNACH
facsimile from *Revue Celtique*
edited by Whitley Stokes.

THE HIGH CROSSES OF IRELAND
facsimile, by J. Romilly Allen.

SANAS CORMAIC - CORMAC'S GLOSSARY
in Irish, edited with English intro. by Kuno Meyer.

LIVES OF THE SAINTS FROM THE
BOOK OF LISMORE
facsimile, edited by Whitley Stokes.

THE BANQUET OF DUN NAN-GEDH
AND THE BATTLE OF MAGH RATH
facsimile, edited by John O'Donovan.

For a complete list of c.200 small-press editions
and facsimile reprints, write to Llanerch Publishers,
Felinfach, Lampeter, Dyfed, Wales, SA48 8PJ.